THE ECCENTRIC TRADITION

Robert A. Hart

THE ECCENTRIC TRADITION

AMERICAN DIPLOMACY
IN THE FAR EAST

CHARLES SCRIBNER'S SONS

New York

Copyright © 1976 Robert A. Hart

Library of Congress Cataloging in Publication Data

Hart, Robert A 1929–
   The eccentric tradition: American diplomacy in the far east
   Includes index.
   1. East (Far East)—Foreign relations—United States.
   2. United States—Foreign relations—East (Far East)
I. Title.
DS518.8.H315   327.73'05   76-13201
ISBN 0-684-14662-2
ISBN 0-684-14645-2 pbk.

THIS BOOK PUBLISHED SIMULTANEOUSLY IN THE
UNITED STATES OF AMERICA AND IN CANADA—
COPYRIGHT UNDER THE BERNE CONVENTION

ALL RIGHTS RESERVED. NO PART OF THIS BOOK
MAY BE REPRODUCED IN ANY FORM WITHOUT THE
PERMISSION OF CHARLES SCRIBNER'S SONS.

Map p. 30 from Meribeth E. Cameron, Thomas H.D. Mahoney
and George E. McReynolds, *China, Japan and the Powers,*
Second Edition, copyright © 1960 The Ronald Press Company, New York (adapted from *Modern Far Eastern International Relations* by MacNair and Lach, copyright 1950 D. Van
Nostrand Company, Inc. Map p. 147 by Harry Scott, copyright © 1963, 1968 by Harcourt Brace Jovanovich, Inc. and
reproduced with their permission from *The National Experience,* second edition, by John M. Blum, et. al. Maps pp. 187
and 210 reproduced with permission from *An Interpretive
History of American Foreign Relations* by Cole (Homewood,
Ill., The Dorsey Press.)

1 3 5 7 9 11 13 15 17 19 V/P 20 18 16 14 12 10 8 6 4 2
1 3 5 7 9 11 13 15 17 19 V/C 20 18 16 14 12 10 8 6 4 2

PRINTED IN THE UNITED STATES OF AMERICA

DS
518.8
.H315

S.7

150214

For Elizabeth

WITHDRAWN
EMORY & HENRY LIBRARY

ACKNOWLEDGMENTS

The writer's gratitude to Robert H. Ferrell, Distinguished Professor of American Diplomatic History at Indiana University—for precious advice and generosities of time—cannot be adequately expressed. The valuable contributions of Elsie Kearns, editor at Scribners, are much appreciated, as are the suggestions of Steven Pelz, Fred Drake, and Richard Minear, who have special interests in Asian history at the University of Massachusetts, and J. K. Holloway, Jr., of the Naval War College. The library staffs of the University of Massachusetts, Amherst College, Harvard University, and the Boston Public Library were also very helpful. The writer, however, is solely responsible for the essay's positions and prejudices, and for any errors that may appear. He hopes that Asia experts will forgive the use of Oriental names in forms most familiar to American readers, and the cursory treatment of their fields in a book intended as a study of United States attitudes. American relations with India and other nations in the region sometimes called South Asia are referred to only when they enter the context of an East Asian subject.

CONTENTS

INTRODUCTION

God grant me the serenity
to accept the things I cannot change,
courage to change the things I can,
and wisdom to know the difference.

Reinhold Niebuhr

AMERICA'S SUCCESSES AT HOME have not always inspired successes abroad. The internal history of the United States is
one of optimism, progress, and fulfillment, of challenges met and
problems solved. In spite of notable flaws, a success story was
written in terms of wealth, power, and the political idea known as
democracy. It was an appealing story, almost as happy as a tale by
Horatio Alger, yet it usually lost something in translation. Its most
disappointing chapters describe the results of great expectations in
foreign affairs. Several years ago there was a popular song concerned with dreaming impossible dreams, righting unrightable
wrongs, and fighting unbeatable foes. Poor advice for diplomats
and generals, perhaps, yet so expressive of American ideals that
the song's true subject, a lovable eccentric in a seventeenth-cen-
tury Spanish novel, could be forgotten.

In the beginning only the idea was powerful, and not much
came of it. During the first half of the nineteenth century Americans developed a habit of viewing their country as democracy's
champion, under special assignment by God, nature, or history to
promote a cause that was good in a world that was essentially evil.
Recognizing the remarkable endurance of this principle, historians
have described Americans as humanitarians, defenders of underdogs, sentimentalists, evangelists, crusaders, romantics, idealists,
or moralists. The righteousness of a mission could not by itself
secure its accomplishment. This lesson was taught, though never
indelibly, during the Manifest Destiny period of the 1840s and

1

1850s when the United States brought democracy to Oregon and the unpopulated half of Mexico but suffered some humiliating rebuffs when its ideals brushed the interests of strong nations outside the Western Hemisphere. It was fortunate that major enterprises were conducted along the country's borders where it possessed enough strength to override the ill effects that normally result from diplomatic overexcitement.

The energies of Manifest Destiny were drained by a long and bloody Civil War, and the postwar generation gave most of its attention to western development, railroads, industry, and other activities that expanded the nation's physical wealth and power—as well as public consciousness of that power. Little of note happened until the end of the century, when a revival of external interests in the 1890s was topped off by an exhibitionist crusade in behalf of Cuban liberty, which led quickly and carelessly to commitments in the Philippines and China. Here was a turning point. As Americans entered the twentieth century, they also entered a new arena of foreign affairs, one that was global rather than hemispheric. The fact of that entry—which would have come sooner or later, in view of the country's growing importance—was less crucial than the manner in which it occurred. Soon it became clear that habits formed throughout the nineteenth century were too firmly ingrained and perhaps too self-flattering to be altered, even though American diplomacy was leaving its safe backyard and moving far afield into complex, unpredictable, and dangerous areas of international relations. In such areas it might be possible to overestimate the influence of old ideals as well as the new power enlisted in their service.

Emotional moods have obscured and often injured the nation's interests throughout the twentieth century. Expectations have been inordinate, leading to impulsive lunges of policy. Geographical and political difficulties have been underestimated and in some cases unstudied and ignored. Complexities have provoked impatience, restlessness, and urges to oversimplify. Too much affection can turn into too much hostility, as in the case of China policies, and it has been possible for unimportant countries such as Vietnam to command a degree of attention that can only be called obsessive. Extravagant involvements have produced extravagant frustrations in the form of petulant isolationism or tantrums of self-loathing. The diplomatic practice of the United States is known more for velocity than sense of direction. Writers have employed numerous metaphors—the ebb and flow of tides, the pendulum, the seesaw, the lively rubber ball, and the student driver zigging against one curb, zagging against the other, accelerating, braking, and moving into reverse with a loud rending of gears—to suggest lines of balance traversed again and again in rushes toward one type of excess or another.

The habit of going to extremes has worried American diplomats. When Alexander Hamilton and George Washington collaborated on the Farewell Address, they were providing a kind of advice that would be repeated by John Adams, John Quincy Adams, Hamilton Fish, Theodore Roosevelt, Franklin D. Roosevelt, George C. Marshall, George F. Kennan, J. William Fulbright, Henry A. Kissinger, and others—advice that Americans ought to calm down, steady themselves, and recognize a need for balance in its several forms:

1. World balances of power may be less than ideal because they preserve stability through fear of war rather than love of peace. Yet throughout two hundred years of history the security of the United States has profited from conditions of equilibrium in Europe and Asia. Therefore, so the advice goes, American diplomats should keep a sharp eye on the scales, doing what they can in the endless task of delicate adjustment in the hope of avoiding a type of precarious tilt that was noticeable in 1941, a tilt requiring violent and costly means of redressment.

2. Balance also relates to time. Professional diplomats have warned against tidal moods of listlessness or hyperactivity, for periods of withdrawal can be as perilous as periods of overcommitment. History moves toward no problem-ending Utopia, nor is it a deterministic force preparing doomsday; it stumbles blindly onward, as it has in the past, and diplomacy's only reasonable goal can be the continuing existence of the civilization it serves, best

3

accomplished through patient, controlled engagement in world affairs—day by day, month by month, year by year, and ideally ad infinitum.

3. Emotional balance is advisable in dealing with specific issues, whether they be England versus France, China versus Japan, Entente versus Central Powers, or Israel versus the Arab states. While "even-handedness" may not be possible or even desirable in all cases, choices should stem from careful studies of the national interest rather than from—as Washington put it in the Farewell Address—"inveterate antipathies against particular nations and passionate attachments for others."

4. Ends and means must be kept in balance. It stands to reason that an invasion of the country or the defense of a valuable ally would call for more vigorous and expensive effort than would some antipodal trouble of small meaning to American security. Interests vary in their importance, and each must be weighed against the costs and difficulties—geographical, political, or military—that might be involved in responding to it. No experienced diplomat would quarrel with Kennan's desire for "options," with Kissinger's need for "choices." Any realistic examination of global variety leads naturally to flexible policies designed to avoid the perils of disproportion. In Aesop there was an elephant that lunged at a gnat, broke a leg, and was eaten by a lion.

So much for advice that has seldom been followed. American diplomatic rationalism was not invented by the "realist school" that emerged in the 1950s; since the era of Benjamin Franklin and Hamilton a realistic tradition has existed, but it could hardly be called a mainstream tradition and it has been represented by a limited number of professionals. Persons of diplomatic education and experience have encountered difficulties in being elected or appointed to high office. Those who have attained decision-making rank have often been forced to shape their policies in accordance with current fads of public opinion. While complaining in their diaries, they have accepted that democratic paradox—to try to

resolve it would be unthinkable—whereby the essential characteristic of the system they defend can encumber that defense. Pressures have been exceptional in a society where the will of the
people—expressed from rostrums and pulpits, by ad hoc committees, by slogan-chanting crowds, by congressmen desperately attuned to sentiment in home districts, by competitive journalism
that must try to reflect the tastes of its customers, and of course in
elections—owns the power to end the career of any official whose
policies fail to measure up to the latest in popular conceptions of
the country's role in world affairs.

Hamilton and the Adamses had their problems with public opinion, and the Age of the Common Man was strongly influencing
diplomacy by the 1840s and 1850s, when Americans liked to think
of their representatives abroad as average citizens in shirtsleeves,
snapping suspenders threateningly as they cussed out highfalutin
European officials. As late as the 1950s congressmen could gain
votes by calling a secretary of state "a sissy in striped pants." According to proverb, the professional is overeducated, an elitist,
somehow alien and not to be trusted with democracy's policies
(best decided by public "common sense"), and it does him no
good to complain that diplomacy is just as important as plumbing,
dentistry, and other fields in which specialized knowledge has
gained widespread acceptance.

The professional who advocates proportion is usually out of step
with one public fancy or another. When Americans are tired or
disillusioned, they want no lectures on patience, courage, and attention to national interest. When they feel fit and confident, they
would rather not be told that some problems cannot be solved and
that some expectations cannot find happy endings. As moods
swerve, a balanced diplomacy is always annoying and may even
appear to be un-American—too soft on adversaries in one decade
and too hard, warlike, or imperialistic in the next. In failing to respect established principles, flexibility smacks of inconsistency
and amorality. The term *national interest* suggests selfishness.
Complexity aggravates headline writers as well as painters of demonstration placards. Balanced views are undramatic; they make
poor slogans and songs. But the professional knows that humdrum

5

diplomacy is successful diplomacy; the society is most secure when its foreign dealings fail to make page one of the papers or bring undercurrents of doom to the voice of a television anchorman. Contrary to belief, diplomats do not develop passionate philosophies of life out of such terms as *realism, flexibility,* and *balance;* they are stuck with these ideas, having learned to reject their alternatives. At any rate, their dull-sounding theories have seldom interfered with the random course of American foreign policy.

Restraint has been best demonstrated, in spite of famous exceptions, in relations with European nations. American understanding of Europe has been relatively high, and that continent has been respected, though often reluctantly, as a power center where intrusions could be dangerous. Policies in Latin America have been less restrained, but circumstances of geography and power have mitigated the hazards of impulse. Policies have been least restrained in the Far East, precisely that region of the world most deserving of careful approaches to perplexities of power, geography, politics, and culture. It is here that the expectations have been greatest and, not surprisingly, the failures most dramatic.

Asia has possessed the ability to offer colorful challenges to American ideals. Its mysteries have appealed to problem-solving. Its backwardness has cried out for progress; its heathen ways, for enlightenment; its ignorance, for instruction; its poverty, for humanitarianism; and its weakness, for benevolent protection. Its vast populations have attracted hopes for trade; its tyrannies, grand and petty, have called for missions in the name of democracy; and its assumed inferiorities have inspired overconfidence.

The "gung ho" idea is as American as chop suey, and precipitate plunges into the swamp of Far Eastern affairs could never hope to succeed. Impulse, excess, oversimplification—such characteristics of American diplomacy have been most damaging in that part of the world known to the point of cliché for its subtlety, complexity, and inscrutability. Youthful pride and self-esteem have encountered ancient beliefs that Westerners are inferior. Energy has confronted inertia. Impatience and haste have ignored delicate and time-consuming customs of Oriental dignity. Grotesque stereotypes, either too admiring or too despising, have substituted for knowledge of Asia. Even diplomats have neglected, all too often, to learn the languages, customs, and histories of nations in which they have been stationed. Shifting moods have propelled the United States too far into Asia and drawn it too far out, and have created periods of intemperate preference for one Eastern nation or another. Americans have overrated their ability to change Oriental history, which a Chinese proverb has likened to "the inexorable flow of the Yellow River, always choosing its own course."

"We must seek fresh insights, better understandings, and find new initiatives"—the standard imperatives have been repeated throughout the twentieth century by presidents, congressmen, diplomats, authors, and practically every journalist back from a trip to China, Japan, or Vietnam. That tradition will not be followed here. There is nothing wrong with understanding, and the nation's diplomacy eventually may profit from patient work by scholars in the difficult field of Asian studies, but urgent and hasty pleas for new insights are best avoided on the ground that all too frequently they have served to renew expectations and launch unsuccessful enterprises. If Americans are intrigued by exotic and curious customs, they can study the history of their own attitudes on diplomacy, finding in that subject an important challenge to problem-solving and one more amenable to change than Asia.

Early Stereotypes

AMERICANS GAINED THEIR first impressions of the Orient from books written by European travelers. Since the age of Marco Polo, China had been described in terms of riches, carvings in jade and marble, bronze vases, delicately styled poetry and painting, a populace of wise philosophers and clever inventors. George Washington assumed that the Chinese were "very smart," though "droll in shape and appearance." Benjamin Franklin hoped that "could we be so fortunate as to introduce the industry of the Chinese, their arts of living . . . America might become in time as populous as China."

The first relations between the United States and a Far Eastern country were provided by the New York trading vessel *Empress of China* in late August of 1784. Expectations were enormous aboard the *Empress*. It was believed that the entire world had been inspired by the American Revolution, concluded in the previous year, and that the freedom-loving multitudes of China would jam the wharves at Canton; amid their hurrahs, backslapping, and general admiration of the Americans the cargo would be sold quickly and at high prices.

There was no welcome, no sign that the *Empress* was more noticed than ships from other countries. It appeared that most Chinese never had heard of the United States, and those who had were not much interested. The officers and crew never saw fabled Canton, China's only port open to foreign trade; they were ordered to drop anchor seventeen miles downriver at the island of Whampoa, where the view was one of opulence, the houses of merchants and customs officials a vista of curved red roofs, ornamental sculptures, shining lacquers, gardens where pavilions and willow clumps formed balanced designs. Galleys with dragon figureheads, propelled by double decks of oarsmen, sometimes visited the American vessel. These were the vehicles of customs inspectors—and now and then a few curious mandarins in cylindrical caps and flowered robes, with mustaches so heavily waxed they resembled tarred ropes. Theatrical in their contempt for "foreign devils," the mandarins sneered unrelentingly, held their noses, and expectorated upon the quarterdeck of the *Empress*. They made clear that the "flowery-flag devils" were to be treated no differently from the British, Dutch, and other barbarians who had come, it was said, to pay tribute to the world's oldest civilization.

More friendly were the Chinese merchants, lifted aboard from richly upholstered sampans. One such visitor, "venerable as Confucius himself, the hairs of his chin long and white, hands hidden within his sleeves," seemed to represent "all of the wisdom and calm philosophy" for which the East was renowned. From his sleeve he drew a firecracker, lighted it, and threw it at some seamen. Their startled expressions so delighted the wise old man that he leaped several times in the air, then made amends by performing a magic trick.

But the old merchant was unimpressed, as were other prospective buyers, by the ship's cargo. The Chinese already possessed cotton and lead, and they did not need fertility drugs—that is, the *Empress*'s cargo of ginseng. Glass beads were beneath contempt, for China was hardly an aboriginal civilization. Only the fur pelts drew interest, and so the Americans exchanged these for small amounts of silk and tea. Six months later, as the *Empress* approached her berth near the Battery, her owners were disappointed to see how high she rode in the water. A full ship would have made a fortune. In the end there was a 25 percent profit due to an unpredictably strong demand for silk and tea.

Boston ships dominated the Whampoa trade for the next half century, and the businessmen of Long Wharf soon discovered what the Chinese wanted most—sandalwood logs, fur pelts, and opium. The latter, the most profitable of commodities, was illegal and could be supplied only at risk of decapitation. Swift galleys bearing customs officers armed with cutlasses could overtake any smuggler's dinghy. Indictment, trial, and execution of sentence followed within minutes after the discovery of a gummy, brick-sized package of "poppy juice." Yankee ingenuity met the challenge. Sad-faced seamen bore coffins ashore; American religious custom, as explained to local officials, required that coffins remain closed as a mark of respect for the dead. The Chinese agreed to expansions of the American cemetery near Whampoa.

Now known as "devils of the plague," Americans reinforced the stereotypes they had formed. Sailors whose view of China had been limited to the wealthy compound of Whampoa brought home stories of a people accustomed to luxuries, proved by the types of products carried back to Boston and New York—intricately carved and enameled boxes, chests, and chairs; flavorful Souchong and Hyson teas; willow-pattern cups and saucers; fine silks; and perfumed body oils. The Chinese were as awesome for their ferocity. They threw stones at American ships, and every school child knew that they had invented gunpowder. And of course there were the customs inspectors, in seamen's yarns portrayed as wild-eyed Genghis Khans, cursing, spitting, and brandishing swords that were four feet long.

Such impressions began to change in the 1840s, after Great Britain's easy victory over China in the Opium War of 1939–42 and the humbling treaties that resulted. The Manchu domain was further "opened" to Britain's lucrative traffic in opium and also to Protestant missionary endeavor; here was an example of good out of evil, an American clergyman commented, God working in mysterious ways. Britain gained the island of Hong Kong, a cash indemnity, and the right to trade in the ports of Amoy, Foochow, Ningpo, and Shanghai, in addition to Canton. Under a most-favored-nation clause Britain automatically would receive all trade advantages accorded other powers in the future. Increased business opportunities would create a sizable English population in China, and therein lay a problem—what would happen to British nationals accused of crimes? Manchu judges were notoriously capricious, ignorant of Blackstone, and punishments often were rendered by the Corps of Imperial Stranglers. Considered necessary was an ancient device called extraterritoriality, which would allow Englishmen to remain under the legal jurisdiction of their own country, their crimes large and small to be tried by British consular officials.

Dismayingly for Britain, its war produced no long-term advantages over trading rivals. The philosophic Chinese, rather than fight interminably, granted similar concessions to any nation asking for them. A special envoy from the United States, Caleb Cushing, applied in July of 1844. His treaty, signed at Wanghsia, included missionary rights, access to the five ports, most-favored-nation status, and even broader extraterritorial privileges than Britain had received. American newspapers could not admit that the success was a gift from the British army. They reported that Cushing, who actually never saw the emperor, brandished a fist near the Manchu ruler's nose and threatened to employ the United States Navy, thus "cowing" China into submission.

A war in 1857–58 proved similar to that of 1839–42 in its effect upon Western activities in China. When Peking officials began to cheat on the "obnoxious treaties" they had signed in the 1840s, Britain undertook to remedy the situation, this time with casual help from France. As in the earlier war, European commanders were careful to fight on their own terms, attacking coastal and river cities vulnerable to their navies. The United States refused an invitation to join the war but participated fully in the division of its spoils at Tientsin in 1858. Extraterritoriality became an umbrella protecting virtually all European and American practices. China was ordered to open additional ports and its interior to salesmen and missionaries and to create a foreign ministry, allow other nations to maintain legations in Peking, and otherwise follow the normal procedures of international relations. No longer would a foreign envoy be forced to enter the Bureau of Tribute, throw himself flat on the floor, and engage in elaborate self-abasement merely to procure an appointment with a Manchu official.

Another round of punishment, chastisement, or spanking—Western newspapers referred to China with increasing

12

condescension—became necessary as Peking officials clung to their own conceptions of superiority among nations. When they refused to ratify the Tientsin treaties, Britain again "administered punishment," aided by the French and a small American naval force under the command of Josiah Tatnall. Acting in defiance of his country's professed neutrality, Tatnall came to the rescue of hard-pressed British troops during a battle on the Pei-ho River near Peking. The Manchu emperor was defeated by 1860, his capital occupied, and his favorite palace burned to the ground. Chinese negotiators, agreeably calling themselves a foreign ministry, now were willing to ratify the Tientsin treaties. Not surprisingly they were confronted by a new document, the Convention of Peking, containing additional concessions. They signed it. "Thrashed Thrice by Our Thrusts"—an attempt by the *Times* of London to treat China in terms of amusement—was typical of Western opinion, for the Manchu dynasty seemed pathetic, humiliated time and again by small European forces.

Nor could the Manchus even control their internal affairs. Among numerous disorders of this era, the Taiping Rebellion was by far the worst, bringing death to perhaps twenty million people before its suppression in the 1860s. It began near Canton, where an American, the Reverend I. J. Roberts, had built a Baptist mission. Roberts's evangelism was thunderously preached, and his favorite hymn, "Onward, Christian Soldiers," could be heard at a distance of three miles when the wind was right. The most energetic of the local converts, a young man named Hung Hsuich'üan, told Roberts of his wish to walk through the countryside distributing Bibles and pamphlets. The two discussed possibilities for an all-Baptist China, but Roberts's gratification turned to concern as the zeal of his pupil passed out of control. Hung revealed himself as Christ's younger brother, with a rank in the Trinity just after the Son but ahead of the Holy Ghost. To the soldier-disciples who flocked to his banner Hung was known as the Heavenly King. His mission to conquer China for the Baptist faith was called Taiping ("Great Peace"). During the 1850s the fanatical Taiping army—looting, killing, building churches—gained control of all China south of the Yangtze River.

The fall of Nanking provided Hung with a Heavenly City and a Heavenly Palace. It was here that the Reverend Mr. Roberts called, hoping to bring Hung back to Baptist church doctrine. A Trinity of four, he insisted, was blasphemous as well as mathematically unsound; nor could he approve of Hung's dozens of voluptuous concubines. This advice enraged Hung, who ordered the Holy Ghost (his prime minister) to expel Roberts from the palace.

Following unsuccessful attempts to take northern China, the Taipings marched east along the Yangtze, besieging Shanghai by the early 1860s. The merchants of this city thereupon subsidized a private force optimistically called the Ever-Victorious Army. Its American commander, Frederick T. Ward, enlisted British deserters, American freebooters, Chinese bandits, and a waterfront assortment who asked for their pay in whiskey rather than money. After an early defeat, blamed on massive drunkenness, the Ever-Victorious won fourteen consecutive engagements in 1862. When Ward was killed, another American, H. A. Burgevine, took command. After assaulting a Shanghai merchant, Burgevine was fired, his place taken by Charles G. Gordon, a British officer on leave from his own army. Years later Gordon would lose his head to religious fanatics in the Sudan, but he easily mastered his present enemies, beating them back to Nanking and forcing his way into the Heavenly Palace. Hung strangled his concubines one by one. Having planned crucifixion for himself, he could find no one to perform the act, so he ended his life by drinking molten gold. Gordon became a hero in England, but the exploits of his American predecessors went unnoticed in a country then concerned with its own civil war.

American impressions, as vaguely focused as ever, had changed radically by the late nineteenth century. The rich and powerful Chinese, inventors of gunpowder, now were objects of contempt, which increased with every news dispatch of easy British victories, humiliating treaties, and inner turmoil both ludicrous and horrifying.

Now able to move freely through city and countryside, travelers wrote of ferment, confusion, faceless crowds, and seething multitudes. Waterfronts always "teemed" with filthy sampans, weak-limbed coolies, children scrambling for garbage, and bleary-eyed degenerates from opium dens. American traders customarily reported that they had to deal with lazy, undynamic, unalert people who were never punctual in their appointments. The Chinese were said to be animals, not men; they pulled each other about in two-wheeled carts. Beyond the cities there was nothing but "disease," "famine," "heaps of excrement," and the "hot sun on baking, treeless hills." Peasants worshipped ancestors, practiced infanticide, and cruelly bound the feet of those girl children allowed to survive.

Missionaries added their criticisms to the unlovely picture. Most were well-meaning and worked diligently building their mission schools and hospitals as well as churches. While they had no wish to repeat the appalling success story of I. J. Roberts, they usually hoped for better results than they were able to achieve. The Protestants had converted only fifty thousand Chinese by 1900, although the Catholics, with several centuries' head start, were able to number some half million adherents to their faith. Disappointments caused missionaries to complain habitually of "thankless tasks" and "difficulties to overcome" in their letters, which often were circularized to congregations throughout the United States. The Chinese were incorrigibly stubborn, the missionaries wrote, in clinging to ancestor worship, their own religions, and other heathen ways. They were inscrutable, congenital liars, sometimes renouncing baptismal vows within hours of the solemn utterance. They were illiterate and unclean; classrooms stank. Concubinage and other lewd customs were prevalent among the rich. Mobs were capable of sadistic barbarism in punishing "secondary devils" (Christian converts), and there were even instances of attacks upon missionaries.

The picture of the Chinese people that fixed itself into the minds of Americans darkened with the appearance in California of a sizable Chinese population. Reciprocal immigration had been established by the Burlingame Treaty of 1868, an agreement prompted in part by the Central Pacific Railroad's need for more cheap labor. At this time the Chinese were laying track eastward from San Francisco while Irish crews of the Union Pacific built west from Omaha. On the day that they met in 1869 the United States possessed a transcontinental railroad, and the Golden Spike was driven amid a Sino-Irish celebration of tentative conviviality. With the railroad completed, the Chinese found themselves competing with the Irish and native Californians in the poor labor market of the depression-ridden 1870s. Orientals got jobs, it was said, through their subhuman ability to exist on wages of a few cents per day. They were beaten and stoned, their pigtails were cut off, and dozens of them were killed in mob violence. "America for Americans," shouted the labor leader Dennis Kearney, recently off the boat from Ireland. "The Chinks must go," his audiences roared. Congress responded by shutting off immigration with its Exclusion Act of 1882. This legislation, designed to be in force for only ten years, would be renewed, and not until 1943, when China was a popular ally in World War II, would exclusion give way to an annual quota of 105 immigrants.

There was no melting pot to absorb the 80,000 Chinese already in America at the time of the Exclusion Act. Some followed Kearney's advice and recrossed the Pacific Ocean. Others, in the manner of European immigrant groups, clustered in big-city ghettos where it was possible to speak their own language and practice their own customs. To native Americans the Chinatowns seemed as remote as China itself. Only the brave dared enter—for bargain prices on laundry or on holidays to hear the firecrackers and see the paper dragons. Chinatown was considered an unwholesome and dangerous place where the *tongs* (gangs) plotted ruthless forays and where an intruder might be robbed or even taken to a dim hideaway to be tortured with "the hundred cuts," "the thousand drops of water," or some other device of cunning ingenuity. Most repugnant were those dens portrayed so often by the artists of the *Police Gazette,* the crime-sex fixture of that male domain called the barbershop. Perverse pleasures were dimly suggested through the haze of opium smoke that dominated the drawings. An accompanying story in the *Gazette* of June 2, 1883, began:

> The general disposition is no longer, as heretofore, to regard the Mongolian as a huge practical joke. The funny side of John China-

1 6

man's character is no longer amusing in the light of the horrid revelations of his iniquities. The committee from the Catholic Young Men's Association has been unearthing frightful practices on the part of the heathen, who are in the habit of luring even little girls into their dens in Mott Street and, after stupefying them with opium candy, debauching the poor creatures.

The literary ancestry of Dr. Fu Manchu and Wu Fang, arch fiends of a later era, dates back to the yellow press of the 1890s. Lurid images were created by *Munsey's, Argosy,* and *Youth's Companion,* as well as by the dozens of nickel and dime pulps. Americans who ventured into Chinatown or China faced incomparably spine-chilling forms of danger. The slant-eyed villain, always "insidious" or "sinister," was second only to the savage of the American West as a standard of adventure fiction.

If Yellow Peril theories provided a more scholarly type of dread—based on population statistics, their projection, and their power potential should China awaken and pull itself together—there was some comfort in "Darwinism." Charles Darwin in 1859 had revealed his natural-selection studies of biological strains, their eternal struggle, and the survival of those that struggled best. Darwinian ideas were later applied to the struggle of men in society and nations in the world. By the 1890s they had become a popular method of explaining international relations, especially in countries whose history books boasted more military victories than defeats. Victories were not won by luck, superior manpower, or even by strategic advantage; they derived from a nation's "fitness," "natural vigor," or "dynamic capacity" for fighting and empire-building. Conversely, a consistent loser was innately inferior. Turkey with its shrinking territories was called the sick man of Europe. Italy lost its "national virility"—according to Prime Minister Francesco Crispi—when it lost a battle to Ethiopia in 1896. Frenchmen feared a degenerative trend when their government backed down in a diplomatic confrontation of 1898. "Are we decaying?" the *Times* wondered after British setbacks early in the Boer War. China with its unenviable record on the battlefield was the world's best target for Darwinian insults—there was not really a Yellow Peril; let them breed like locusts; failing the tests of fitness, they could never prevail.

A variety of attitudes, some of them contradictory (the interesting mixture of fear and disdain), amounted to a generally adverse view of China. The admiration of an earlier era had given way to a different extreme, and here was a pendulum that would never stop.

On the subject of Japan there were no opinions at all, at least until the middle of the nineteenth century. If travelers could have visited the island nation, their reports might have suggested medieval feudalism—an agricultural economy, armored *samurai* (knights), and a vassal system controlled by the Tokugawa shoguns of Edo (Tokyo). The imperial throne, maintained for religious and ceremonial purposes, had long been subservient to the shogunate. For over two hundred years the Tokugawa family had "frozen" Japanese history, fighting any influence that might produce change and thus endanger its rule. Obviously it was necessary to avoid foreigners. With exception of Dutch merchant ships, infrequently allowed to anchor at the small island of Deshima near Nagasaki, there were no visitors, no traders, no diplomatic relations.

Unintended visits occurred. American ships bound for China sometimes lost men overboard, and whaling dinghies were blown ashore. Resenting breaches of their isolation, the Japanese treated castaways with some hostility, the degree of which has become a subject for debate among historians. But by the early 1850s newspaper stories about decapitations and tortures—it was alleged that the island dwellers placed captives in cages and left them for punishment by birds and insects—shaped a first American impression that was understandably critical.

The urge to teach Japan a lesson added incentive to a government program already in the planning stage. It was America's God-given responsibility—indeed Manifest Destiny—to spread the influence of democracy to the four corners of the globe. This belief, popular in mid-century, had inspired war, territorial expansion, instances of diplomatic bravado, and a tendency to boast of a

wide assortment of accomplishments. Sensitive to European criticism, Americans yearned to prove that their democratic system,
despite its "leveling nature," could produce cultural, literary, and
scientific excellence. To help prove the point, the government
sponsored a program of naval explorations, sending officers and
squadrons to the Arctic and Antarctic, the Aleutians and the Dead
Sea, Central and South America, the South Sea islands, Australia,
China. They showed the flag, distributed tokens of democratic civilization, kept an eye out for trade opportunities, and tried to
"make discoveries that [would] astound Europe with our scientific
advancement." The touring scientists, chosen as generalists rather
than specialists, conducted hurried investigations of oceanography,
astronomy, aboriginal linguistics, archaeology, anthropology, bot-
any, and zoology. They brought back great heaps of rocks, skulls,
flora, and *fauna,* often so mixed or damaged as to be of no use to
science.

One of these catch-all missions commanded by Commodore
Matthew C. Perry arrived at Uraga, Japan, in July of 1853. The
squadron comprised four of the navy's newest vessels, powered by
steam as well as by canvas. Smoke from the funnels seemed to
frighten the Japanese more than did cannon muzzles displayed in
open gunports. News of the intrusion reached Tokyo, and refugees
crowded roads to the interior. Perry had asked to see the "Tycoon," but the shogun sent only a Chinese student who stubbornly
rejected all demands concerning trade and treatment of
shipwrecked sailors. A careful diplomat, Perry knew that it would
be unwise to try to force the Japanese to an immedate and humbling decision. He handed over an ultimatum, encased in a golden
box for delivery to the shogun. In seven months, the commodore
warned, the squadron would return for an answer, which if negative might lead to grave consequences. He made smoke for over an
hour before raising anchors.

The Japanese, debating furiously, needed all the time Perry had
given them. Submission would mean the end of isolation, drastic
change in a new and unpredictable era. According to the shogun's
chronicler, most of the feudal barons wanted to resist but found
they were too fat to fit into ancestral armor; they had "neglected

military arts and given themselves up to pleasure and luxury.'' Representatives of a rising commercial class favored trade with foreign nations, as did scholars who pointed to China's self-harming attempts to resist Western demands. The dilemma ''broke all our hearts,'' said the chronicler, who blamed it for the death of the shogun. The latter's son Iyesada then entered the debate, which continued without decision.

Meanwhile Perry prowled the Ryukyus, islands he believed might make useful American bases in the future. They also proved a good hunting ground for geological and anthropological specimens, and Perry grumbled while the civilian scientists loaded his ships with boulders and a goodly number of skulls, which the Smithsonian Institution had requested for purposes of measurement and classification. Inhabitants were incensed when they saw the skulls being packed in crates. ''The black ships are stealing our ancestors.''

The squadron, now seven ships strong, returned to Tokyo Bay in February 1854, anchoring at a point near Yokohama where a throng of barons and shogunate officials had assembled. Most wore swords belted over kimonos and a few were in armor. Impassive expressions gave way to scowls of consternation when the first boatload of Americans reached shore, for the visitors ignored their hosts, running off to inspect rocks, chase insects, and gather *flora*. Again Perry had failed to restrain his dedicated scientists.

But thereafter he controlled the delicate conference with a fine Machiavellian mixture of bluff and flattery. Orders to the engine rooms produced dark clouds of smoke under which three dozen boatloads of marines and armed seamen came ashore. Cannon saluted and a band played ''Hail, Columbia.'' Later Perry gave a dinner that consisted mainly of turkey and whiskey. With an interminable round of toasts he induced joviality, and a *samurai* warrior's bear hug tore off his epaulette. He presented gifts, which he described as symbolic of American democratic culture: lorgnettes, opera glasses, soap, clocks, a toy train, a telescope, Audubon's *Illustrated Birds*, rifles and cannon, a red velvet dress, Webster's *Dictionary*, several crates of whiskey, and a bale of cotton. These gifts, which could be interpreted as a mark of supplication, helped

20

move the Japanese to grant Perry his wishes. It was agreed that shipwrecked sailors would be protected and the ports of Shimoda and Hakodate would be open to American trade. Able diplomacy had arranged a conference from which both nations emerged with pride. The shogun could boast of tribute received, while Americans celebrated the "awesomeness" of the fleet that had forced open the doors of Japan.

Shortly after Perry's departure Japan was visited with an extraordinary number of typhoons and earthquakes, interpreted in some quarters as signs of divine disapproval of the new policy. Another form of inundation threatened when more "outer barbarians" arrived demanding similar concessions for their own countries.

Many individuals in the shogun's court, now regretting the agreements with the United States, were hardly in a mood to welcome the first American consular representative. Townsend Harris had no fleet at his back, no marines at his side; arriving in Tokyo with two carpetbags and a frightened secretary, he was assigned to a ramshackle house infested with roaches and rats. Japanese officials either ignored him, insulted him, or angrily accused him of having instigated the disastrous typhoon of 1856.

Harris remained patient and tactful. Gradually he gained respect, portraying his country as an unselfish friend who wanted only to help Japan resist demands by such greedy foreign powers as Great Britain, France, and Russia. The shogunate agreed in 1858 to concessions more expansive than those won by Perry: additional ports open to American trade on a most-favored-nation basis, an exchange of diplomatic representatives, and extraterritorial privileges (not nearly so broad, as Harris carefully pointed out to the Japanese, as those to which China had submitted).

There followed a considerable change in the forms of Japanese government. European powers, having opened Chinese doors for the United States, now could thank Perry and Harris for similar courtesies. Each month brought news of concessions granted and treaties signed. The tempo of change, along with its immense meaning, frightened many Japanese. Cursing the docility of the shogun, some took matters into their own hands, attacking several of the new consulates, murdering foreigners, and firing on Western commercial vessels in the port of Shimonoseki. American and European naval units retaliated with bombardments of Shimonoseki and Kagoshima. Foreign editors complained that all Orientals were the same; they signed treaties, broke them, had to be punished. It had happened in China again and again. Now, apparently, Western powers faced another series of treaty-enforcement wars. Prospects for war heightened, the commentators said, because of political events within Japan. A growing clique of noblemen loyal to the emperor intended to destroy the long dominion of the Tokugawa shoguns. Revolutionary slogans seemed significant: "Revere the Emperor," "Return to Antiquity," and "Drive Out the Barbarians." In the foreign press the shogun's defeats came under the heading of "ominous tidings," which culminated in an 1868 ceremony restoring imperial government under the youthful Mutsuhito.

Foreigners soon learned that they had misinterpreted the revolution that had resulted in the restoration of the emperor, the displacement of the shogun. Its most important leaders turned out to be businessmen and the more progressive lords. Their enemy had been feudal backwardness, represented by the shogun, and to weaken the latter they had denounced his treaties and employed antiforeign slogans not really meant. True policies could now be revealed. New slogans appeared: "Rich Country," "Strong Arms" and "Progress through Modernization." Four months after the restoration the emperor announced a Charter Oath, which, as it turned out, would be the theme of his forty-four-year Meiji reign: "Knowledge shall be sought for all over the world, and thus shall be strengthened the foundations of the imperial policy." Assuredly all Orientals were not the same. China with its lethargy and unproductive resentments was hardly a model to be copied. Japan chose to emulate those foreigners who had shown off their clanking pistons and smoking funnels. The Japanese did not lack inventive capacities, as many foreigners would come to believe. They were simply in a hurry. Mutsuhito was entirely logical in thinking; why bother to invent the screwdriver, the locomotive, the armored warship when they already had been invented?

Cargoes of books—and not a few crates of eyeglasses—were

unloaded at Japanese docks. The government hired hundreds of Europeans and Americans to serve as naval and military instructors, schoolteachers, agricultural experts, railway and industrial engineers, financial advisers. Western capitalism was much admired, but the government saved time by building and operating the first factories and railroads, which were sold to private individuals and groups as soon as they were judged capable of assuming large responsibilities.

Japanese roamed the world, studying and taking notes on every conceivable subject. Germany was chosen as a constitutional model; there amid republican forms the emperor retained control. The pomp of England's peerage system would mollify those Japanese aristocrats still bitter over the loss of feudal rights. The United States provided patterns for agriculture and banking. Admiring American quantity and British quality, Japan drew on both nations for its educational system. The British navy and the French army served as first models, the latter until its defeat in the Franco-Prussian War, after which the German army became an object of study. British march music was always preferred. Most carefully inspected were industrial centers in all countries. Unlike other tourists, the Japanese avoided Paris, the Riviera, and Rome; they flocked to Essen, Manchester, Clydebank, Lowell, and Pittsburgh.

Americans developed a favorable impression of Japan. To be imitated was flattering. It was good too that Japan seemed so different from China. Instead of fearing for their lives, missionaries could write home of respectful treatment, even adulation, and busy days at baptismal fonts. The Japanese created no immigration difficulties; only 2,039 of them were living in the United States by 1890, and so small a nation could not project a Yellow Peril. Instead of clinging to repulsive Oriental customs, Japan was eager for technological progress. The island empire had "chosen the American way of life," a Chicago editorialist wrote, building a success story similar to that of the United States, though "on a much smaller scale."

On maps Japan was indeed small. Women were tiny even with piled-up hair and stilted footgear, and men bowed eternally. They sat on floors in toylike houses of paper and bamboo or tended

2 3

dwarf trees in miniature gardens. Curious customs were "quaint," never "bizarre" as in China. With energetic confusion these Pooh-Bahs and Nanki Poos bustled about their Titipu. (Gilbert and Sullivan's *The Mikado* was enormously popular in the United States by the late 1880s.)

The policy of imitation, while reasonable to the Japanese, was a further diminishment in the eyes of foreigners, who heard stories of techniques too hastily copied, without full understanding of their operation. It was said that locomotives ran amuck, destroying quaint settings. An Osaka company produced clocks with hands that ran the wrong way; these sold well, with no customer complaints. Cigar smoke and the sound of violent coughing filled business and government offices. A procession including Mutsuhito in his palanquin jounced along to the four-four rhythm of "The British Grenadiers." The wife of a Dutch legation official complained of faces at her bedroom window. "The Japanese are only curious," she was told; "they have so much to learn about Western ways." The fact of rapid progress could be obscured by the sometimes strange means of its attainment.

While not really respected, Japan was regarded with condescending approval. In the manner of a parent rewarding a well-behaved child, the United States in 1894 cancelled its extraterritorial privileges, no longer considered necessary due to the Japanese government's adoption and enforcement of Western-style judicial practices. The same year, 1894, saw the beginning of a series of wars—the Sino-Japanese, the Spanish-American, and the Boxer Rebellion—that would destroy some illusions and create others. These wars would entangle the United States in Asian affairs and sharply alter the course of history.

Stepping Stones
to Asia

TRADE TREATIES, MISSIONARY WORK, a jumble of colorful opinions had created no important involvements for the United States in the Far East. Asia was too distant for inclusion in the vital concerns of foreign policy.

American policies had been attentive to geography ever since President George Washington in his Farewell Address had instructed a young, weak nation to take full advantage of its ocean barriers and stay out of political quagmires on other continents. Whether by intent or instinct, nineteenth-century diplomats followed this advice. The developing Monroe Doctrine insisted that transoceanic forays, European or American, were not in the national interest. Wars were borderland affairs that could turn out well no matter how blindly passionate their origins. Statesmen applied restraints, though often with difficulty, when public opinion exerted itself in behalf of overseas adventures. President Grover Cleveland, who believed in the noninvolvement tradition, was in office when Japan and China went to war in 1894.

It was ironic that no one feared "little Japan," for in later years diplomatic, military, and commercial crises would stem from the very fact of its smallness. The eternal problem—not enough arable land to feed a large population—had forced Tokugawa Japan to rely on infanticide and the play of natural controls; population remained at about thirty million throughout that long period. But Restoration Japan embraced the ideals of Queen Victoria's world. Moral progress and industrial progress had combined to increase the population to nearly forty million by 1890. Every parcel of land was cultivated, and there were instances of locomotives running down peasants who tended gardens between rails and ties.

The problem was not unsolvable, for there existed the shining example of Great Britain, an island group smaller than Japan and yet the most eminently successful of nations. Britain was a giant factory, exporting manufactured goods in order to import food and the raw materials needed to keep the machines in operation. Japan would attain this tense condition by the 1960s, but in the nineteenth century the products of its new factories were too few and too imperfect to compete in the world market and make enough money to pay for necessary imports. If industrialization by itself could not solve the problem, perhaps another British practice could; colonialism appeared able to provide food, raw materials, and living space, so Japan looked west to the nearby Korean peninsula and the continent beyond.

The desire for living space, along with that expansive nationalism strong in all countries in the 1890s, led the Japanese into a war with China. The latter regarded Korea as a vassal state, but as far as Tokyo was concerned, the "Hermit Kingdom" was independent and therefore fair game. Both nations found excuses to send armies to Korea, where clashes were frequent by 1894. On July 25 Japan touched off a war without declaring it. The affair of the *Kowshing,* a Chinese troop ship bound for Korea, was not quite the "surprise attack" described by writers entranced with parallels in history. Six armored cruisers of the Japanese navy stopped the *Kowshing* and demanded its surrender. When the Chinese commander refused, his vessel was shelled until it exploded and sank, drowning over a thousand soldiers. War was declared six days later.

Most nations, wishing to be neutral, simply avoided involvement as best they could, but America's declaration of "strict neutrality" implied a moral responsibility for absolute impartiality and equal treatment. Neutrality should not mean passive indifference, the Cleveland administration believed; it should be active, something to be proud of, worked at, proved. The tidy legal principles of a courtroom—where Judge Walter Q. Gresham had presided before Cleveland named him secretary of state—were applied to the unpredictable conditions of war. Gresham offered his country's good offices to both China and Japan. This practice, undertaken by many governments, usually had been limited to offering means of communication and perhaps mediation. Gresham went further, pledging the United States to protect Chinese in Japan and Japanese in China according to rules of humane behavior.

War is a volatile and unmanageable form of litigation. The loser suffers, grows desperate, breaks rules, and comes to hate a judge as much as an adversary. Chinese nationals in Japan happened to be well treated, and the United States was given no chance to protect them. Subjected to invasion, the Chinese expended their fear and anger on any enemy they could discover. American officials fought off screaming, rock-throwing mobs as they tried, sometimes unsuccessfully, to escort Japanese businessmen and students to the safety of United States consulates. Consul Jacob Child used a "display of rifles" to save a man in Hankow. Consulates were besieged, and protests from the Chinese government, claiming that Americans were harboring Japanese spies, swamped Secretary Gresham.

The secretary tried to be fair. Convinced that two Japanese students who had taken refuge in the Shanghai consulate were really spies, he ordered them handed over to the Chinese, whereupon they were "tortured with horrible ingenuity" and beheaded. Now Japan protested. American newspapers voiced outrage, and Civil Service Commissioner Theodore Roosevelt called for Gresham's impeachment on grounds of cowardice. The latter's friends blamed his death a few months later on controversies that grew out of his audacious neutrality.

Normal conditions were reported by missionaries in Japan, so there was no need to protect them. Those in China were endangered by bandit gangs, deserters from defeated armies, and popular fury based on rumors that among all neutral powers only America was helping the Japanese. The United States government had to send more gunboats and even a few cruisers. These crisscrossed the Gulf of Chihli and churned muddy rivers as they answered distress calls from missionaries and opened fire "only when necessary." China protested all incidents, including the unauthorized landing of a marine contingent at Tientsin. In fur hats and sheepskin coats the troops prepared for a wintry march to save the American legation in Peking. When trouble there proved to have been exaggerated, the marines returned to their ships.

Orientals shopped for munitions in New England factories. Japanese buyers knew exactly what they wanted, but Chinese technological puzzlement resulted in purchases of rifles and cartridges totally unrelated in caliber. John Wilde, a bankrupt inventor in Rhode Island, wanted to sell his "infernal machine," guaranteed to sink entire fleets at the press of a button. The Japanese laughed at Wilde's offering, but China made a large down payment and eagerly awaited delivery.

Unneutral actions, whether intentional or not, were in keeping with the strongly pro-Japanese bias of the American public. On the day before the *Kowshing* attack, the San Francisco *Examiner* called Japan "the most progressive among the oriental nations while China is a lethargic mass of repellant barbarism." Americans always preferred underdogs. In newsprint maps the islands looked minuscule alongside China's mass. How could forty million people defeat four hundred million? Pictures of a brave Mikado in a Western-style army uniform adorned rotogravure supplements in the papers. American lads eager to volunteer stood in lines outside Japanese consulates. Newly formed committees raised money for Japan, collected hunting rifles for shipment, and organized boycotts of Chinese laundries. As reported in the New York *Tribune* of August 5, 1894, the Japanese consul in that city thanked his "Yankee brothers" for "the great moral weight of public opinion . . . which seems to have been thrown almost entirely on the side of Japan."

No help was needed. In a driving rainstorm near Pyongyang, Korea, a Japanese army crushed a much larger enemy force. Even when rifles worked, they were badly aimed by Chinese soldiers encumbered by oiled-paper umbrellas and other unmilitary equipment. Some had carried their own coffins all the way from China. Off the mouth of the Yalu River a sea battle—the world's first large-scale engagement involving modern ships of steel and steam—had similar results. China's navy comprised two German-built battleships and over a dozen cruisers purchased from various European nations. Japan's smaller force of British-built cruisers suffered no losses while severely damaging the battleships and destroying five cruisers. Following an unsuccessful attempt to rent the entire Italian navy, China abandoned operations at sea. Ashore the Japanese crossed the Yalu into Manchuria and forced their way down the Liaotung Peninsula toward Port Arthur.

News from the war surprised and delighted Americans. Editorial writers found Darwinian proofs in the fighting. Disparities of size and population evidently meant nothing when one combatant was dynamic, fit, and progressive and the other sluggish, dissipated, degenerate, and decayed. Japanese biological superiority, "at least in terms of the Orient," had only one flaw and this was being rectified; the Japanese seemed "taller every year." In recalling Japan's emulative policy, the press exaggerated the contributions of the United States. The victors of the Yalu were said to have gained their skills at Annapolis (most Japanese naval officers were British trained), and the strategy of the army, its mastery of modern weapons, and the businesslike manner of operations were all "peculiarly American in character."

It came as a shock when the Yankees of the Orient raped and butchered over two thousand civilians in the streets of Port Arthur. Perhaps the Japanese were "basically barbarians" with only a veneer of civilization. But most papers excused the incident as a brief lapse justified by Chinese atrocities. The Japanese government, regretting the massacre, publicized the perfect behavior of its troops now fighting on China's Shantung Peninsula. Dozens of American and European correspondents were invited to inspect hospital facilities behind the lines. The reporters found a group of bewildered Chinese soldiers lying under crisply clean sheets, their wounds carefully bandaged, being fed candy and nuts by Japanese Red Cross girls. Foreigners forgot Port Arthur.

China's Foreign Ministry, although by now wary of the good offices policy, sought from it one last favor. Minister Charles Denby was asked to advise Chinese officials who must go to Japan and

The Far East at the time of the Open Door notes.

negotiate a peace treaty. It is probable that Peking's bargaining position, affected by military collapse, could not have been improved by the ablest and most dedicated of diplomats—which Denby was not. His interests were mixed. He sympathized with the Chinese but believed their humiliation could have fine results, forcing them to see the need for progress, perhaps to be supplied by American products and services. At any rate, Denby's advice failed to help China avert disaster at Shimonoseki in April 1895. The treaty signed there caused Peking to recognize the independence of Korea, pay a crippling indemnity, and hand over to Japan the Pescadores Islands, Formosa, and the Liaotung Peninsula in southern Manchuria.

30

There followed the triple intervention of European powers. China could forget the disappointing Americans when true friends suddenly appeared on the scene; this was the feeling in Peking when Russia, France, and Germany announced that they could not condone the most important provision of the Shimonoseki treaty. Applying pressure in concert, the three powers forced Japan to return the Liaotung Peninsula to China.

It soon became clear that affection for China had nothing to do with the European intervention. Russia's wish to keep Japan out of Liaotung stemmed from its own Manchurian interests, and France and Germany likewise were attracted by China's newly demonstrated vulnerability. Militarily pathetic, Peking could be threatened; owing a large indemnity to Japan, it could be bribed with loans. Using both techniques, Europeans extorted an assortment of leases, concessions, and spheres of influence from the Manchu government. Russia won the right to build its Trans-Siberian Railway across Manchuria, leased Port Arthur and other areas of southern Liaotung, and began laying tracks connecting Port Arthur with the Trans-Siberian line. The murder of two German missionaries provided Kaiser Wilhelm II with an excuse to extract economic concessions in Shantung and lease its major port, Tsingtao. France, moving up from its Indochinese territory, obtained Kwangchow Bay south of Canton. Although not a partner in the Shimonoseki intervention, Britain could hardly watch while rival colonizers staked out interests. Professing regret, the British made demands—a lease that added to their Kowloon holdings near the colony of Hong Kong, a lease of Wei-hai-wei on the tip of the Shantung Peninsula, and a sphere-of-interest arrangement in the Yangtze valley. Italy, recently defeated by Ethiopia, suffered the humbling distinction of being turned down by the Chinese government.

Under a system sometimes called semicolonialism or informal imperialism, the powers developed naval bases, stationed troops, and controlled almost all aspects of life in the leased ports. In spheres of influence, extending outward from the ports for sometimes hundreds of miles, they owned concessions for the development of industry, mining, and transportation.

Americans could not foresee that the Sino-Japanese War and its lease-taking aftermath would soon affect their own country. When the fighting ended, they lost interest in remote East Asia and turned to exciting occurrences closer to home.

The placidity of the post–Civil War period, in which American diplomacy had practically ignored the existence of foreign nations, was overcorrected by the ebullience of the century's closing years. From 1889 to 1895 there were war scares with Germany, Canada, Italy, Chile, Hawaii, and Britain. Busy neutrality during the Asian struggle of 1894–95 had angered China, but this could not be ranked as a war scare. At the same time troubles between Cuban rebels and Spain drew attention—to an increasing extent that produced a war with the Spaniards in 1898. Cuba was a next-door neighbor; in wanting to fight there, Americans were not abandoning their hemisphere-minded diplomatic tradition, but the war's rush of events led to a first step, in fact a leap, toward a new tradition of overseas commitments.

Historians have tried to explain the powerful urges that created the events of the 1890s. Evidently Americans needed that consciousness of moral superiority derived from belief in democracy as God's chosen system and their own responsibility for its universal promotion. The energies of Manifest Destiny, drained by the Civil War, had returned to an irrepressible extent by the late nineties. Traditional ideals now were mixed with pride in power and the wish to demonstrate new capabilities. Industrial growth had been impressive in recent years; vigorous, dynamic, progressive America obviously possessed those qualities most praised by the philosopher-scientists of natural selection. Too many years had passed since the country had proved its fitness through struggle. This was frustrating. The world was watching. "This country needs a war," Theodore Roosevelt wrote in 1895. His good friend in the navy, Alfred Thayer Mahan, wanted the United States to prove its greatness by building a mighty battle fleet and an overseas empire along British lines. Mahan's writings became almost as popular as "Columbia, the Gem of the Ocean," the best-selling pianola roll of the decade. Audiences sang lyrics adapted from "Rule, Britannia" at every commissioning ceremony that added a new battleship or cruiser to the navy.

In analyzing the temper of the nineties, some writers have remarked that insecurity, needing reassurance, was more fundamental than pride. Real confidence, it is said, could not have produced the outlandish bragging for which the period now is known. Psychologists have described qualities of confusion and loneliness associated with life in a democratic society; people join groups (patriotic organizations multiplied in the 1890s) and crave large-scale causes that can provide the blessings of simplicity and identification. The nineties have been called a time of abnormal unease, even "psychic crisis," when immigration tensions, a depression, labor violence, unrest among farmers, and business monopolies inspired disunity and grave concern over the workability of the democratic system. Such aggravations could have created a yearning—conscious or unconscious—for a national adventure abroad, that time-honored cure for all internal complaints.

Yet another explanation has been presented. Perhaps war could produce new markets for American industry. Some businessmen—though their number and influence remains a subject of debate—apparently thought so. Industrial progress had outdistanced the consumption abilities of the American people, a condition underlined by depression economics early in the decade. Commerce with Europe must increase; Latin American markets needed development; and Denby, the minister in Peking, was not alone in hoping that Asian turmoil might induce change, and with it those spectacular profits long expected of the China trade.

All these impulses and more were combined in the fighting mood of the 1890s, but probably most important was that emotional brew of democratic principles to be reaffirmed and youthful strength to be displayed. In representing both tyranny and weakness, Spain was an attractive target. A "splendid little war" would delight everybody, humanitarians because it would free Cuba, and Darwinists because it would be smashingly one-sided.

Few Americans were thinking of Asia as war approached. Cuba was the focal point of interest. It was here that Spanish treatment of rebels, including "damsels in distress," had been exciting the press since 1895. And on the night of February 15, 1898, the battleship *Maine* had exploded in Havana's harbor; that and other circumstances on the island provided all the excuses for the hostilities that began officially on April 25, 1898. Consequently Americans were surprised to learn, eight days later, that they were fighting a global war complete with a Far Eastern theater of operations.

The Asian mission, today regarded as the war's most important event because of its long-range effects, originated from the interest of a small group of cronies in Washington. Theodore Roosevelt had been appointed assistant secretary of the navy through the influence of his friend Senator Henry Cabot Lodge. Roosevelt and Lodge were close to Captain Mahan, and the three enjoyed talking and corresponding about sea power and colonies as proofs of national fitness. They were vague on which colonies they wanted; imperial greatness was merely an exhilarating topic of conversation, at least until late in 1897 when the probability of war with Spain caused the Roosevelt clique to center its interest on Spanish possessions, mainly the Philippine Islands. Roosevelt began to pester his superiors, Secretary of the Navy John D. Long and President William McKinley, with a plan for an attack on the Philippines once war broke out. The result was frustration. The older men were timid and tradition bound in the view of Roosevelt, who nonetheless managed to arrange that Commodore George B. Dewey be appointed commander of the navy's Asiatic squadron.

Secretary Long trusted neither Spain nor his assistant, for the latter seemed unable to sit still at his desk. Perched on its corner, Roosevelt scribbled memos bound for unknown destinations and made telephone calls which Long could not overhear. His enormous grins were not reassuring. Long was too much the gentleman to make pointed inquiries, but his exasperation showed in brusque remarks about the untidiness of Roosevelt's desk—always littered with files on construction, ordnance, and personnel—and in his petulant refusal to appoint Dewey to the rank of rear admiral.

The destruction of the *Maine* intensified naval preparations, especially Roosevelt's, and Long felt the strain. He decided on Friday, February 25, 1898, to allow his assistant "to look after the routine of the office while I took a quiet day off." He left about noon.

Roosevelt's five-hour command of the navy proved more than routine. Shortly after Long's departure Senator Lodge happened to drop in for a chat. Consultation led to a series of terse messages, sending ships to sea, rearranging fleet components, changing contingency plans. Most important was a cable to Commodore Dewey on the Asian station. Dewey's squadron was to "keep full of coal" and commence "offensive operations in the Philippine Islands" following a declaration of war.

Secretary Long discovered the new strategy when he returned to the office next day (since the *Maine* incident the navy had worked a six-day week). He complained that "the very devil" must have possessed Roosevelt, who had "gone at things like a bull in a china shop." The assistant received a scathing lecture inspired mainly, it would seem, by the impertinence of his methods. For his strategy itself apparently was acceptable; neither Long nor McKinley took steps to countermand it.

Immediately after war was declared, Dewey's squadron steamed out of its anchorage at Mirs Bay in China and set course for Manila Bay. A British naval officer, observing the departure, commented, "A brave set of fellows, but unhappily we shall never see them again."

Eager for naval victories, Americans awaited news from the Caribbean Sea, the expected arena of combat. New York papers carried a shocking report early on the morning of May 3. According to London sources, the United States had suffered a great naval disaster off the coast of China. Stenographers wept as they reported for work. Confused and angry crowds gathered in the streets, awaiting later editions, and a newsboy was knocked down and kicked when he shouted news of the defeat. The first contradictory report appeared about ten o'clock, and for the rest of the day the *Journal, World, Tribune,* and other papers published extra editions that added fresh details to the real story of the battle in Manila Bay. Crowds grew larger, now cheering and singing, and brass bands materialized to lead impromptu parades that continued under torchlight throughout the night.

"Never in history has a battle been more crushingly one-sided," the celebrants were informed in stories that magnified the strength of the losers. In reality the ships that Dewey attacked were smaller than his own, museum pieces that could not be maneuvered due to mechanical failures or tendencies to adhere to the mud when they tried to creep too close to the protection of shore-based guns. From the bridge of his flagship, *Olympia,* Dewey had conducted a target practice, destroying seven vessels and killing or wounding some four hundred Spaniards. Scratches and powder smudges marred the fresh gray paint of the American ships, but no one had been killed. Especially satisfying to newspaper readers were reports of the "British-style behavior" of the officers, who with studied nonchalance had sipped coffee, complained that breakfast was late, and remarked upon the beauty of the hills ashore while the battle raged about them. And they were chivalrous victors. Within hours of the last shell burst the *Olympia*'s band was serenading enemy survivors with the gentle strains of "La Paloma."

Dewey was reluctant to leave the scene of his triumph. He remained at anchor off Manila, wishing that he had enough marines to occupy the city and hoist Old Glory above its central Citadel. He had to settle for the alternative of encouraging the Filipinos to fight Spanish troops. Revolutionaries had been trying for years to end Spain's rule of their islands, but a defeat in 1896 had forced their leader, Emilio Aguinaldo, into exile at Hong Kong. A few weeks after the Manila Bay victory Dewey brought Aguinaldo home from China and placed him ashore outside the capital city. There the rebel commander was joined by thousands of his supporters, who moved into siege positions around Manila. As his dream neared reality, Aguinaldo proclaimed that "the great and powerful North American nation has come to offer disinterested protection for the effort to secure the liberation of this country." Dewey's victory, he said, had been the most significant event in Filipino history.

The battle was significant to others as well. A delighted President McKinley promoted Dewey and ordered the production of suitable medallions and commemorative swords. On a globe in his office he discovered the Philippines. Like many Americans he had been "hardly aware that those islands existed." But everyone was talking about them now. They would make fine bases, naval officers told the president. Letters from businessmen discussed the islands in terms of trade and investment profits. Roosevelt was headed for Cuba with his Rough Riders, but Lodge, Mahan, and converts to their views remained in Washington to exert pressure on McKinley and Secretary of State William R. Day. "We must on no account let the islands go," Lodge insisted. "We hold the other side of the Pacific and the value to this country is almost beyond imagination." The clamor confused both McKinley and Day. Lodge scorned their "effeminate worries," their failure to announce an annexation policy.

The pressure was strong enough to force the administration to take another step—dispatch of an army to occupy Manila. By the first week of August eleven thousand troops under Major General Wesley Merritt had landed near the city. They took over the siege lines, sending the Filipinos to the rear. Against token Spanish resistance Merritt's men moved into Manila, received its surrender, and raised the flag above the Citadel on August 13, one day after the governments of Spain and the United States signed an armistice.

Americans had conquered an overseas colony but would they keep it? A small group of antiimperialists persisted in making known their unpopular opinions. Colonialism would cost too much. Besides, it was immoral, at odds with American principles dating back to 1776 that had always supported freedom, democracy, the rights of all peoples to determine their political destinies. The country would never be the same if it abandoned its ideals and chose to rule over a subject race in the manner of European monarchies. Another form of antiimperialism went almost unnoticed, mentioned from time to time in obscure army and navy publications. At least a few military professionals, it seemed, were questioning the strategic wisdom of owning the Philippines. Had glorious victories over pathetic Spain led to overconfidence? Had naval and military forces—no more than five first-class capital ships and a 90,000-man army—really grown strong enough to rival those of other powers having interests in the Far East? Should

3 7

the United States without careful study and planning discard the ocean barrier policy, which had provided security in the past? Should geographical advantage be exchanged for geographical liability?

A minority of worry warts could be ignored but for the exasperating fact that the president sometimes listened to them. McKinley ruminated, hesitated, postponed a decision. One day he expressed the lackluster view that "if old Dewey had just sailed away when he smashed that Spanish fleet, what a lot of trouble he would have saved us." At other times McKinley could find himself intrigued as much as anybody by some of the imperial themes resounding from pulpits, editorial desks, and head tables at the businessmen's banquets he attended. It was also true that he had never been guilty of stubbornness in the face of public opinion majorities.

Before the war, business leaders had voiced mixed views on the desirability of empire, but Dewey's success so close to the shores of Asia aroused their enthusiasm. In itself the Filipino population was questionable as a market prospect, yet who could deny that the islands seemed an excellent "base," "staging area," or "stepping stone" for increased enterprise in the perennially attractive China market that lay waiting beyond?

Other enthusiasts pointed out that Spain had lost the ability to maintain control of the islands and that, of course, the primitive Filipinos could not care for themselves. If the United States failed to provide this care, some European power would gladly do so. England, the Netherlands, and France had expressed interest, and Germany, far behind in the scramble for colonies, seemed more than interested. A German squadron commanded by Vice Admiral Otto von Diedrichs had entered Manila Bay shortly after the battle there. While other nations had sent ships to observe American activities, only the Germans misbehaved, flouting Dewey's blockade regulations with such frequency that the latter resorted to threats of war. Clearly the Filipinos were going to be somebody's colonials; that being the case, they would fare best under the rule of the United States. The "reasonableness" of this argument impressed McKinley.

So did the theme that imperialism was not immoral when its

motives—unlike those of European nations—were unselfish, based on the wish to help backward peoples rather than exploit them. Filipinos would gain the benefits of American democracy and Protestant Christianity. The Doctrine of Responsibility allowed humanitarianism (the desire to do good) and Darwinism (the desire to prove power) to coexist amicably, often within a single mentality. After all, nature had several means of testing fitness. One was the battlefield and another was imperialism, that heavy responsibility which could only be shouldered by nations of extraordinary strength and stamina. How exciting it was to accept, with the pretense of a weary sigh, Rudyard Kipling's invitation to share "the white man's burden" along with Britain. McKinley could refer to Christian duty and manly duty in the same speech. "Duty determines destiny," he said. The country must pursue "duty for duty's sake," even if "another course may look easier and more attractive. . . . The progress of a nation can alone prevent degeneration. There must be new life and purpose, or there will be weakness and decay." McKinley was comparable to Queen Victoria, stated the New York *Tribune,* for "with the emergence of America as a great power, British leaders now share the awesome burdens of maintaining civilization in the world."

Few Americans could know how real those burdens would be. Upon learning that the United States intended to keep the Philippines, Aguinaldo would declare that his country had been betrayed by those who had promised independence. But in attacking American forces at Manila in February 1899, the Filipinos would "incomprehensibly reward America's good intentions with ingratitude." Glorious battles in the style of Manila Bay would be absent from a three-year war on Luzon, a guerrilla struggle fought with difficulty, frustration, atrocities on both sides, and the loss of seven thousand Americans and undetermined thousands of Filipinos. The United States would rule the Philippines until 1946—a rule so responsible in terms of benefits bestowed that imperial costs would always exceed imperial profits. Far more burdensome would be the diplomatic abrasions and strategic perplexities attending possession of a Far Eastern colony.

But all of this was in the future, unforeseen in 1898 when the language of burden and duty was one of many forms of self-congratulation. The country's shortest war, lasting under four months, was celebrated for over a year, during which some 230 peace pageants and victory pageants were considered important enough for nationwide press description. Small towns rejoiced with bands, bunting, oratory, fireworks. Cities such as Boston, New York, Washington, Atlanta, and Chicago produced extravaganzas lasting four or five days. These were called jubilees in efforts to duplicate Britain's Imperial Jubilee in the summer of 1897, an occurrence envied by the world for its pageantry.

On a jubilee week the Stars and Stripes decorated every shop window. For sale inside were naval toys, usually replicas of the *Olympia;* boxed platoons of soldiers painted blue and khaki; idealized biographies of Dewey and other heroes; hastily written compilations of *History's Greatest Naval Victories,* including Actium, Trafalgar, Navarino, Manila Bay; and premature maps showing American overseas possessions in bright yellow or green (there was some unhappiness that the "best colors"—British pink, French lavender, and German blue—already had been appropriated). Outside in the streets lampposts supported massed flags and bunting festooned for miles along parade routes. Some cities built huge simulations of Europe's arches of triumph. Headlines in the Cincinnati *Enquirer* of September 10, 1899, described a structure in New York City's Madison Square:

DEWEY'S
WHITE TRIUMPHAL ARCH
IS MODELLED AFTER THAT
OF TITUS.
Was A Labor of Love for the
Sculptors.
Best Talent of America Worked
Upon It.
Almost Ready for Our Hero to Ride
Under While New York Goes
Into a Frenzy.

Within two or three years all the wood and plaster arches would crumble, causing traffic jams and casualties, but during the jubilees they looked like genuine marble. Through them passed the bands, cavalry, infantry, and GAR while multitudes on the sidewalks cheered.

Parades over, the crowds converged on reviewing stands. Heads were bowed for invocations, often by the popular John Ireland, Catholic Archbishop of St. Paul, Minnesota: "Verily, this is the year of jubilee. America, the eyes of the world are on thee. . . . Thy greatness and power daze me; thy responsibilities to God and to humanity daze me."

McKinley, who attended eight of the jubilees, usually was the first speaker. "We are obeying a higher moral obligation . . . with the consent of our consciences and with the approval of civilization." Another widely traveled orator, Senator John M. Thurston of Nebraska, told audiences not to be envious of the old boast about the sun never setting on the British Empire. "Well, our flag flies . . . the wide world round, serenely uplifted toward the empyrean blue—kissed by the sun of day, wooed by the stars of night, feared by tyrants, beloved of mankind, it tranquilly floats, the unconquered flag of the greatest nation of the earth."

Most eagerly awaited was a thunderous young Indiana senator, Albert J. Beveridge, who made no fewer than forty appearances. "The American people are . . . the mightiest human force of all time . . . with the brain of organization and the heart of domination. . . . God has made us the lords of civilization that we may administer civilization." Beveridge often referred to "England's imperial renown . . . English energy . . . and English discipline. . . . But we are greater than England . . . a mighty people . . . of masterful blood . . . a virile, man-producing race, a race endowed by God and marked as the people of His peculiar favor."

Following the Chicago Jubilee of November 1898, McKinley cabled Paris, where American peace commissioners had been awaiting instructions. Not surprisingly they were told to demand that Spain cede the Philippines, Guam, and Puerto Rico. The resulting treaty was signed on December 10 and passed its two-thirds Senate test in early February. The United States had annexed Hawaii in the summer of 1898 as "a war measure" and would divide the Samoan Islands with Germany in 1899.

In a more suspicious age the Roosevelt "plot" would be cited as an important reason—rather than the circumstantial beginning of a chain of events—for America's imperial decision. But the aims of Roosevelt and his friends were never kept secret, were not blocked by the administration, and preceded the aims of millions of Americans by only a few months. Commercial pressures were strong but not decisive. Nor was newspaper propaganda, sometimes seen as having manipulated a basically sensible population; journalism in its most competitive era sought only to detect changing moods and give the public what it wanted.

Popular emotions dominated the entirety of 1898—the furious rush to war, news of military triumphs more thrilling than anyone had dared hope, giddy awareness of foreign admiration, and victory celebrations that never seemed to end. The vanity of that incredible year best explains the decision for empire. Annexation came naturally, one of many festive events. Colonies were like medals and commemorative swords, tokens of success according to the era's standards. Along with the war itself they were showcase exhibits of national achievement.

It cannot be argued, of course, that the United States should have limited itself forever to hemispheric concerns; as the country grew stronger and more influential, its decision to play a part in world diplomacy was only a matter of time and place. The time, 1898, may have been a bit early in the light of physical capability, and the place, the Philippines, was not the wisest of choices. But the decision was ominous mainly in the carefree, bedazzled manner of its making. Like an intoxicated chess player, the nation reached far across the board to establish a position unstudied in terms of diplomatic and military strategy.

The Philippines indeed represented a stepping stone—not for lucrative trade with China, as businessmen were expecting, but for further Asian involvements.

A Door
to Commitment

PREOCCUPIED BY CUBA, the American press had given scant attention to the leasing of the China coast, which was East Asia's most important occurrence in the latter nineties despite its complications and lack of color. The State Department still had no Far Eastern division. Legation and consular officials in China viewed their reports as penmanship exercises unread by superiors in Washington. In March of 1898 Sir Julian Pauncefote, the British ambassador, conveyed his government's worry that Western encroachments in China were a threat to free trade there. He suggested some form of Anglo-American statement that would reaffirm what the British called the open door principle, the right of nations to compete for markets in all of China. The McKinley administration quickly dismissed the proposal, and Pauncefote felt that he had committed a faux pas in bothering American leaders with a matter that had nothing to do with Cuba, their only concern.

Then came the war with Spain, the Manila Bay surprise, jubilant annexation of the Philippines, a rejuvenation of interest in the Far East. Standing on their Manila stepping stone. Americans were eager to take that last short stride toward the affairs of mainland Asia. Yet they hesitated, discovering that much had changed in China since last they had looked. The implications of the leases were finally comprehended.

The leaseholders were studying those same implications, pondering dilemmas, considering options. Should they go all the way, establish complete control over their spheres and turn China into another Africa? Or did the immensity of the Chinese population, suggesting the red ink of endless responsibilities, rule out imperialism in its classical form? A more immediate question in 1898 concerned the future of Western commerce in China. The Imperial Maritime Customs Service still operated within the spheres, collecting uniformly low tariffs from traders whose governments participated in the old most-favored-nation treaty system.* The leaseholders of the nineties certainly owned the power to renounce this arrangement, institute restrictive tariffs of their own, and thus set up trade monopolies in the regions they dominated. Yet they were aware of advantages provided by the old treaties. Would exclusive rights in one's own sphere prove more profitable than shared rights in all of China? There were no firm decisions but some movement toward one; Germany was instinctively protectionist, Russian commerce was notably noncompetitive, and France was Russia's ally.

Only the British were known to favor the existing "open door," in keeping with their free trade tradition. More persuasive than tradition was Britain's competitive skill, which had given that country an 80 percent portion of all trade in China. London's preference was clear in early 1898, the time of Pauncefote's poorly timed effort to win American support for the open door. In the following months, however, the British position wavered and became indistinct. London bankers and merchants were talking about their enormous Yangtze valley sphere, its profit-making promise, their belief that it needed "protection." The open door slogan was heard less frequently in Parliament and the Foreign Office. The subject appeared to embarrass the colonial secretary, Joseph Chamberlain, who had instigated the Pauncefote mission, and its mention to Lord Salisbury, the prime minister, drew apathetic shrugs.

---

* The Customs Service, only nominally a bureau of the Manchu government, had been foreign-controlled since its inception by treaty after the Taiping Rebellion. The treaty stipulated Britain's right to appoint the chief inspector of Chinese Customs. Britons and other Westerners working in the service sought to provide China with enough revenue to keep its government stable; at the same time they used customs income to service China's debts to the powers and kept rates uniformly low in accordance with Western demands for broad opportunities and high profits.

While the British changed their minds, moving closer to other Europeans on the issue of turning leases into trade monopolies, the American government debated the "prospect in China." It appeared possible that the United States would lose its existing Chinese markets when most eager for new ones. John Hay, the latest of McKinley's three secretaries of state, considered his options.

The United States could not be frozen out of China if it possessed a lease of its own, an obvious solution advanced by Edwin M. Conger, minister to Peking, in a note to Hay on November 3, 1898. "We ought to . . . own and control at least one good port," Conger wrote, "from which we can potently assert our rights and effectively wield our influence." He wanted nothing less than the province of Chihli, a sphere of influence that would include Peking and thereby the government of China.

Responding to such proposals, the president told Congress there was no need for the United States to become an "actor" in China, a nugget of logic lost in its poorly chosen premises—that the Chinese preferred American products to all others and had the strength to prevent Europeans from building a wall against those products. In any case McKinley was famously persuadable, and his pronouncement had no effect upon cartographical studies in the Departments of State, War, and the Navy.

Chefoo, on Shantung's north coast, looked inviting. But Chihli and Shantung were in the cockpit of German, British, and Russian interests. Promising more troubles than profits, the northern region was rejected. Other considerations were Kiangsu province, the Chusan Islands off the mouth of the Yangtze, and Chekiang province. "The United States might, with becoming modesty, ask for one of the [Chusan] islands," a naval officer wrote in the February 1899 issue of *Forum* magazine. Other powers had ignored the central arc of China's coast, a fact that inspired interest, investigation, and disappointing data on cholera infestations and anchorages too shallow to admit ocean-going ships. The remaining possibility lay in south China—Amoy, the preference of Secretary Hay. The port was close to the Philippines but much closer to the new Japanese colony of Formosa. Hay sounded out the Tokyo government, receiving replies that were none too encouraging. Japanese leaders were thinking of using Formosa and Korea as staging areas for the emulation of Western leasing practices, and at that time Amoy was included in the plan.

The State Department in Washington was hardly less emulative. The failure of its European-style lease hunt led to an alternative policy also European in origin; all participants in the China trade had used the term *open door* as a synonym for the most-favored-nation-status mouthful, and in Britain the phrase had become a cliché throughout fifty years of free trade propaganda.

Not all Englishmen were tired of the open door, at least not those who had found careers in the Imperial Chinese Maritime Customs Service. Collector Arthur Hippisley, for one, saw that the survival of his job, the Customs Service, and perhaps the Manchu dynasty depended upon thwarting a new system of monopolies. He believed the open door must be more than a vague ideal. It needed to be spelled out, endorsed in a way that would demand respect from leaseholders and prevent them from installing customs of their own. Hippisley knew that China could demand nothing. His homeland, traditional advocate of the open door, was losing interest in it. It struck Hippisley that only the United States, influential but a loser in the lease hunt, was qualified to sponsor his project.

When Hippisley was granted furlough in England, he made certain that his itinerary would include Washington. There he planned to seek out an American friend and fellow Sinophile, William W. Rockhill, who had traveled widely in China and the East, immersing himself in language, culture, and history. Acknowledged as a foreign policy specialist, a rarity in that day, Rockhill had been representing his country in the Balkans, about which he knew nothing. Because of the urgent need to formulate a Far Eastern policy, Hay had brought Rockhill back to Washington in April 1899. Hippisley arrived two months later with a notebook full of open door jottings.

The two Asia experts spent a leisurely summer of champagne parties and policy discussions. They sometimes consulted Hay and on one occasion even McKinley. Hay, wishing he had been secretary of state at the time of Pauncefote's overture, believed Anglo-American cooperation might still be possible. Hippisley disagreed, citing current British disinterest. Anyway, the president frowned on a joint effort, explaining that the noble tradition of no entangling alliances prevented even informal agreements. It was his understanding that American policies must always be unilateral in order to be accepted by public opinion. Rockhill wondered how public opinion would respond to an announcement that a Britisher had drawn up a major statement of United States policy. He decided to keep Hippisley's part a secret, and the latter agreed, wanting an open door more than personal credit. A text emerged, written by Hippisley, touched up by Rockhill, seen by McKinley, signed by Hay. In such manner was born a policy later celebrated as uniquely American.

Copies of the document, sent to European capitals as well as Tokyo on September 6, 1899, acknowledged the lease system but asked participants to respect existing treaties, including uniform duties and tariffs, and refrain from imposing restrictions of their own.

Hippisley's concern over Britain's changing mood had been well founded. Salisbury hedged for three months before agreeing to honor the open door in *some* British spheres but only in the unlikely event, as he pointed out, that other powers made similar pledges. Replies from Germany, France, and Japan were masterpieces of equivocation; Italy, leaseless but still hoping, enjoyed a rare opportunity to imply powerful interests veiled in enigma. Each nation said it could not even consider a positive response until convinced that all other leaseholders would do the same—an unpromising situation considering that Russia's reply was close to outright rejection. Thereupon Hay announced that he was well satisfied with these "final and definitive" pledges to maintain the open door. The secretary was not naive. He was bluffing on the grand scale.

Hay's countrymen, unaware of his attempts to gain an American lease, praised the moral stance of a policy that implied opposition to further European aggrandizement. Ironically at a much later date the open door policy would be scorned for the "immorality" of its economic motives. A more sophisticated argument has been limited to diplomatic practicalities. The 1899 note has sometimes been seen as foolish because it could not have prevented other nations from acting in accord with interests. Yet there was a chance that American influence might at least encourage further hesitation in European capitals. Hay, after all, was risking nothing, making no commitments, signing no guarantees. The smallest of gains is a bargain when there is nothing to lose.

If the open door policy of 1899 was a practical, workmanlike piece of diplomacy, the same cannot be said of its enlarged and altered version, which appeared the following year as a result of the Chinese conflict known as the Boxer Rebellion.

Peking's four cities in one were comparable to the nest of boxes, a popular toy exported by China. Within the walls of the Outer City, infested by flies and packs of dogs, lived the multitudes, their houses, dens, and shops reminding one foreign visitor of "piles of packing crates, poorly stacked." A wall forty feet thick separated the Outer City from the Tartar City, a quieter, cleaner compound of imposing residences, expensive shops, Chinese and European banks, the rambling Hôtel de Pékin, which catered to foreigners, and the Hanlin Library, a storehouse of Chinese history and culture. Clustered within the southeast corner of the Tartar Wall were the Imperial Maritime Customs Service, the Foreign Ministry (*tsungli yamen*), and eleven legations. In this small area, no more than eight square blocks, was conducted the day-to-day business of China's decay—palanquin chair trips from legations to Foreign Ministry followed by bluffs and bribes as the ministers attempted to outfox one another and gain new concessions. Competition was fiercest at sunset, when legation flags were lowered and small military bands simultaneously played eleven national anthems.

The business of the day completed, ministers laughed at each other's China jokes over brandy and billiards. Their wives meanwhile had shopped together, exchanged recipes, and applauded the teatime entertainments of Madame Pokotilov, who once had performed at the St. Petersburg Opera. The children of the diplomats congregated at the tennis court or on Sir Robert Hart's verandah.

Hart, who was chief inspector of Chinese Customs, owned a band that could play "Ta-ra-ra-boom-de-ay" and other dance tunes currently popular in England. The magnificent dinners given by Sir Claude MacDonald at the British Legation were envied by all, including Minister Conger, who sometimes complained to his Iowa-born wife that her ice cream socials were less than pinnacles of the formal season. Wanting an American sphere of influence in Peking, Conger had winced when the foreign minister, Prince Ching, spilled melted vanilla down the front of his robe.

Within the Tartar City the walls of the Imperial City enclosed grassy hills, lacquered bridges over streams, and delicate pagodas beside small lakes—an artistically arranged landscape said to include "one thousand perfect perspectives." In one of the lakes was a barge heavily decorated with ivory, jade, rubies, and diamonds, the floating palace of Empress Dowager Tzu-hsi. To equip it she had dipped into funds of the Naval Ministry, frustrating some of her countrymen who had hoped to buy a squadron of cruisers. Also in the park land was the Forbidden City, called the "pink palace" by foreigners, a Throne Hall set in a labyrinth of courtyards and pavilions where dwelled the imperial family, concubines of several generations, and some five thousand courtiers, officials, guards, and servants. All males in the Forbidden City, with the exception of emperors and heirs apparent, were required to be eunuchs.

The dominant personality in the Imperial Court was the empress dowager, who had started out as a favorite concubine in the 1860s and used her beauty, touch for intrigue, and ruthlessness to control the Manchu court for nearly forty years. Sometimes she ruled directly as regent for child emperors; when the latter came to the throne, they did so warily, knowing that Tzu-hsi retained influence over the strongest officials and generals. Her closest advisers, some rumored to be "false eunuchs," were adept in the use of slow-working poisons, smallpox matter, and other means of inducing the appearance of natural death. Her nephew Kuang-hsu occupied the throne during the period of the war with Japan and the granting of the European leases, a time when the "paradox of the devils" most perplexed China.

Throughout all adversities the Chinese talked of their superiority over other nations. They were more beautiful physically, as proved by the rough, blotchy nature of foreign complexions. China was the center of the world, the Middle Kingdom, as proved by any map ever seen. The heritage of an ancient civilization was calm philosophy and subtle logic, in noble contrast to steamships, locomotives, breech-loading guns, and other ugly tokens of barbarian imposition. Most contemptible was Japan, an Oriental nation stooping to copy despised techniques. Yet those very techniques, considered marks of inferiority, had defeated China and threatened its dismemberment. This was the paradox, the hateful dilemma. Most Chinese, especially in the conservative north, were more determined than ever to hold to traditions, but Emperor Kuang-hsu believed otherwise; by 1898 he had convinced himself that China could be saved only through modernization. Tzu-hsi was disgusted, berating her nephew as a dwarf of the East, meaning a Japanese, and blaming herself for having allowed him to play with trains and other Western toys when he was a child.

Kuang-hsu's "hundred days of reform" covered the summer of 1898. Aided by scholars who had studied foreign methods, the emperor issued hastily contrived edicts on education, agriculture, commerce, judiciary, civil service, the military. A large order for artillery was sent to the Krupp works in faraway Germany. Proclamations ordered citizens to think up "excellent ideas" for which they would receive cash rewards. No nation, not even Japan and much less stubborn China, could have achieved modernization in a single summer. The emperor's hurry cost him support, for he was tactless and often destroyed old institutions before inventing others to take their place. The reform program ended when Tzu-hsi ordered the execution of fifty-three eunuchs loyal to the emperor and proclaimed her own return to the throne. She reported a decline in the emperor's health and warned China to prepare for sad news. The British Legation formally protested the illness, whereupon Kuang-hsu rallied and soon was well enough to occupy a palatial prison on the Isle of the Ocean Terrace in a lake just outside the Forbidden City.

Surrounded by eunuchs, singsong actors, and servant girls bearing pots of rouge intended to disguise her sixty-three years of age, Tzu-hsi sat in the Throne Hall awaiting demolishment of the hated foreigners through a means consistent with ancient traditions. One tradition was rebellion. She had learned to fear the rage of the masses, for so often the target had been her own dynasty, but the rebel movement that developed strength throughout 1899 appeared to have different aims. Each month brought news of slaughtered Christian converts and assaults on missionaries and Western businessmen, their families, and properties within leased areas.

Most Chinese were illiterate but well aware of what was happening to their country. The smallest of villages had its scholar, doubling as local official and story teller. The stories might be of dragons, fairies, moon princesses; or history lessons stressing the proofs of China's superiority; or blood-curdling accounts of the foreign devils, their arrogance and cruelty. Chinese who lived within Western spheres needed no scholar to describe the unfairness of extraterritoriality, railroad tracks bisecting peasants' farms, mining enterprises that tore up burial grounds. Lease-burdened north China produced fanatical societies called Plum Blossom Fists, Harmonious Fists, Righteous Fists. Commonly known as the Boxers, they practiced *kung fu,* trained with heavy two-handed swords, and knelt at mystic rites designed to make their bodies invulnerable to bullets. The Boxers were responsible for most missionary and other foreign casualties, and they converged on Peking early in 1900. Their white costumes emblazoned with scarlet ideographs of menacing intent were noticed increasingly by personnel of the legations.

On Queen Victoria's birthday, May 24, 1900, Sir Robert Hart's band played for dancing at the legation. The state dinner that followed was inadequately served, for the Boxers had threatened to kill any Chinese who waited upon foreigners. Peking's trolley cars were destroyed, then the railway station. Wanting to keep foreign troops from reinforcing the legations, Boxers broke into rail stations from the capital to the coast and burned all tickets. This failed to stop 405 marines (Japanese, American, British, Russian, French, Italian, and German) from reaching Peking on the last day of May. A more practical means of cutting off transportation—destruction of the tracks—was then employed by the Chinese.

The reinforcements infuriated the Boxers. In early June in the countryside around Peking they killed thousands of Chinese Christians and scores of missionaries. A Baptist from Missouri, Mrs. Arnold Lovett, worried about her spectacles and was allowed to remove them before she was beheaded. Foreign structures were burned in the country, in the Outer City, and finally in the Tartar City, penetrated by the Boxers in mid-June. Japanese Chancellor Sujimura ventured too far from the legation quarter and met violent death. The Boxers pressed in on the colony of diplomats, forcing most to take refuge in the stoutly constructed buildings of the British Legation. "The trouble is all in our minds," explained Mrs. Conger, who wanted to think well of everybody. Sir Claude told her that this would be no ice cream social. The German minister, the Baron von Ketteler, set out for the Foreign Ministry to demand Chinese government protection for legation personnel. A Manchu soldier killed him. Later the same day, June 20, when it became fully apparent that the siege was on, the bullets that broke the windows of the British Legation were fired by regular troops of the Chinese army.

The defenders, counting women and children, numbered 878 when the siege began. For nearly two months they would hold out against charging Boxers yelling, "Kill, kill, kill," and against the more professional tactics of the Imperial Army, regiments beautifully adorned in black velvet, vermillion silk, rainbow embroidery. With many Chinese soldiers equipped with trumpets, the din was frightening, but more so their rifles, lances, and flaming missiles (bundles of kerosene-soaked rags launched by catapult). Within the compound everyone came to admire the fighting ability of the Japanese marines, and the British and Americans also won praise. Of great help were two American contributions—a Methodist missionary who turned out to be an expert in medieval fortification and a sailor who built an effective cannon out of spare parts. The legation wives sewed bandages and formed bucket brigades to put out fires. During lulls in the fighting they served buffet style and organized international songfests. When one of

Madame Pokotilov's arias drew a fusillade of Chinese bullets, she was told to sing no more. Food supplies dwindled and casualties mounted (in all, 234 Europeans and Americans lost their lives), but the barricades held against attackers generally estimated at around 50,000.

How was the defense possible? A Kipling style of chin-up courage, so easily ridiculed in antiimperialist writings of a later day, deserves much credit. Yet Chinese efforts were something less than the horrifying surge described in American and European newspapers during the summer of 1900. The Boxers were undisciplined rowdies who faded from the scene not long after discovering their vulnerability to bullets. Imperial soldiers were brave enough, but their officers seldom led their assaults. Officers planned great offensives but often postponed them in the belief that the legations eventually would be starved, burned, or scared (by displays of severed heads on poles) into submission.

The empress dowager was not a decisive leader. To be sure, she ordered her own regiments into the battle and personally called for the extermination of every man, woman, and child in the legations; to a badly defeated commander she handed a silken cord, signifying permission to hang himself. Yet she often lost confidence, knowing that the powers would punish China no matter what the outcome of the present battle in Peking. Therefore she called several truces and sent baskets of flowers with her compliments to the British Legation. One hundred new field guns, purchased from Krupp by the deposed Kuang-hsu, stood idle in the park near the pink palace. The antimodernist empress refused to allow her generals to use them.

The end came on August 14, and China had lost again. At the British Legation men cheered and women prepared vats of tea and lemonade as the vanguard of an international army of 19,000 completed its march from the coast and entered the capital. Chinese soldiers fled, as did the empress; disguised as a peasant woman, she led the court and government some seven hundred miles southwest to a refuge in Shensi province. Prince Ching's Foreign Ministry was left behind to accept terms of punishment, expected to be crushing.

The unnecessary destruction of several towns in northeast China was the work of Russian, French, and German detachments in the rescue force; the 2,500 men of the American contingent were restrained, though imperfectly. China's formal punishments were dictated: official apologies, monuments to slain diplomats and missionaries, improved security for foreigners in leaseholds and legations, and indemnities to all nations involved in the siege (the United States later returned a portion of its share to China).

Earlier in the summer, with the Western world fearing that all in the legations would be tortured and killed, discussions of how China would be punished had included its partition into European colonies. For some years governments had been wary of this idea. Salisbury had declared early in 1899, "We are not prepared to undertake the immense responsibility of governing what is practically a third of China." Most historians believe that Western leaders never seriously considered the wholesale dismemberment of Manchu territory, but hindsight was not available to John Hay in June of 1900. Kaiser Wilhelm, enraged by Ketteler's murder, promised to exterminate the Yellow Peril, and news of the siege produced horror in all countries having legations in Peking. Gory eyewitness accounts filled the press, and editorials included "inability for self-government" among China's incorrigibilities. Angry talk in European chancelleries warned of partition and colonial control. It was all bluster, an understandable reaction to shocking occurrences, but Hay and Rockhill took it seriously.

Colonialism was by nature commercially exclusive and would ruin American trade with China. The State Department responded hastily to the assumed threat. Hay and Rockhill worked out a draft, secured McKinley's quick approval, and on July 3 cabled to the capitals of the great powers a document later known as the "second open door note." There was a clause favoring equal and impartial trade in all China, a repetition of the 1899 note. And to discourage colonialism "the policy of the Government of the United States [was] to seek a solution which may bring about permanent safety and peace to China [and] preserve Chinese territorial and administrative entity." In this last phrase was the vague suggestion of commitment but certainly not a binding one.

Vague suggestions can be dangerous in a country where journalism is known for impatience with diplomatic circumlocution and full contexts of documents and speeches. Hay had spoken merely of seeking a solution, but in the days that followed, Americans read that their country aimed to "preserve Chinese territorial and administrative entity." Even this was a bit wordy, at least for editors proud of their seventy-two-point headline type, largest in the world at that time. "U.S. Saves China" contained only twelve letters and would fit nicely.

For Europeans the notes were meaningless. Except for a casual British acknowledgment, governments did not bother to reply. Nor did Rockhill and Hay maintain much interest. Only three days after the notes were sent, Rockhill wrote Hippisley that he was "sick and tired of the whole business" in China and hoped it would be "a long time before the United States gets into another muddle of this description." In November of 1900 Hay renewed another policy—kept secret until 1924—that mocked both of his open door notes. Knowing the Chinese government had been weakened by the Boxer experience, he told Conger to demand a territorial concession near Amoy in Fukien province. As before, Japan could not condone a lease in the shadow of Formosa; in a tongue-in-cheek statement Tokyo cited its deep respect for America's open door policy as the reason for opposition. For the rest of his life Hay disowned the principle he was said to have fathered. He had made no permanent commitment to China; his note of July 3, 1900, had been intended to influence a particular and temporary condition with no lien on future options.

The meaning of the 1900 note lay in the beauty discovered in it by the American public, which already had developed a habit for principle-making. Due to a curiosity of timing, Hay's wish to preserve China's entity—or "territorial integrity," as it was later called—began a progress from policy to principle within a few hours of its announcement. Its first simplified versions appeared in the press on the eve of the Fourth of July. This allowed just enough time for the splicing of a bright new example into run-of-

55

the-mill patriotic oratory. European kings were tormenting China, and the United States—true to those ideals that had confounded George III on another Fourth of July—again stood bravely against monarchy's loathsome designs. Here and there an orator, carried away by annual celebration of political (and moral) polarities, referred to China as a democracy.

It was also an election year. The administration's stand on China was put to good use at the convention that renominated McKinley and in the election campaign that gave him a second term in the White House. To be sure, not many Americans thought the Manchu Empire was a democracy, but China at least qualified as an underdog, enabling McKinley's publicists to extol his knightly consistency. He had saved the Cubans, the Filipinos, and now the Chinese. The open door policy was a popular success more for its own attractions than those of its beneficiary. China offered yet another stage for the international benefactor, an old role but one gaining in practice and enjoyment during the previous two years.

While flattering to Americans, the new principle also prospered from a gradually changing view of China. Any victim of "European tyranny" could become an object of sympathy, and leasing practices had tended to associate the interests of the United States with those of China. Repugnance for China had reached its height at about the time of the Sino-Japanese War of 1894–95, and the opinion pendulum was swinging in another direction by 1900. Stereotypes were changing, one set exchanged for the other. Infanticide was out; strong family ties, proved by veneration of elders, was in. Backwardness and filth became symbols of downtroddenness and human misery. Stubbornness turned into determination, that admirable stoicism derived from serene and ancient philosophies. Slinky cunning became innate intelligence, evidenced in the planning of the Great Wall and invention of gunpowder. Illiteracy could be attractive, crying out for a teacher. Cruelty needed a rehabilitator, and weakness a protector.

Increasingly China would be seen as a ward of the United States, the two nations bound by a special if one-sided affection, a relationship less and less affected by the old hope for commercial profits. The percentage of American trade with China, compared to trade with Japan and other Asian countries, dropped steadily and dramatically in every decade from 1900 to World War II. Losing its original economic meaning, the open door policy changed character and emerged as another proof of American humanitarianism. Frequently called the Monroe Doctrine of the Far East, it established itself in the public mind as a solemn promise to defend China against all invaders. It became a slogan, a standard topic for sermons, congressional speeches, and newspaper editorials. Mere policies can be discarded or altered to fit changing interests. Enshrined as principle, the open door pledge survived as a thing of beauty for public idealism and an embarrassing club foot for professional diplomacy. Enunciated again and again, sometimes by statesmen who admired it but more often because of popular pressure, the open door affected the Asian relations of the United States throughout the first half of the twentieth century.

Protection of China's territory was undeniably a vast undertaking. As the principle began hardening in late 1900 and 1901, caution appeared in those same obscure army and navy publications that two years earlier had warned against overeagerness in the assumption of Filipino responsibilities. How could China's borders be defended when no one knew where they were? The borders of Illinois or even France were demarcated by signposts and clearly drawn maps. Chinese geography was more difficult. Some Manchu officials still claimed Korea and might well ask Americans to defend its integrity. In Manchuria and other leased areas, did integrity refer to nominal or actual sovereignty? Had a borderline been drawn in the northwestern deserts? In the southwest how many Himalayan peaks were Chinese, and could an American army survive in the frozen passes of Namcha Barwa and Minya Konka? Could an army of 90,000 survive any war fought on the world's most densely populated and politically confusing continent? What of the navy? Far from its supply and coaling bases, what combination of rival fleets might it face in the Yellow Sea or Gulf of Chihli? Unnoticed critics pointed out that practical problems should be studied before, not after, the making of commitments. Why leap before looking? Dashing policies were exciting but not always wise.

Despite its implications the open door never produced a military catastrophe. America's defense remained verbal, restated with each violation of Chinese territorial integrity. Damages were limited to such impalpabilities as prestige, credibility, respect.

Open door pronouncements, in character with a national reputation for talking too much, created rounds of American jokes in the capitals of Europe, but three nations were not amused. For decades the object of military attacks and American verbal support, China came to regard the United States principles as *yu ming wu shih* ("having the name without the reality"). As a matter of course, China's main antagonist became the target of open door scoldings. The people of Japan, according to historians in that country, developed a "persecution complex" and came to detest their critics. Such irritations were needless because they were ineffective, and dangerous because they encouraged Japanese contempt for American capabilities. Nor were Americans happy over disparities of talk and action that suggested hypocrisy and even cowardice. For this they often blamed their government for failure to act.

But a foolish promise should not be kept. Embarrassments should be blamed on those who made the promise rather than those who failed to keep it. A long and ludicrous open door experience began in 1900 when a carelessly worded document caught the fancy of a public conditioned to the point of reflex by its principle-building history.

A Period
of Restraint

FOR THE PEACEFUL DOMESTIC scene of the late 1890s—a relief after depression violence earlier in the decade—Republicans thanked slow-moving, even-tempered William McKinley. But foreign policy had missed out on his stabilizing influence. Its course changed radically in terms of Far Eastern commitments.

And if a mole could make a mountain, some Americans asked in 1901, what wonders could be expected from a far more dynamic successor? Theodore Roosevelt had gained fame from intrepid politics in New York, rotogravure pictures of clenched teeth, his charge up Kettle Hill, boxing matches with the heavyweight pugilist James J. Corbett. There was every reason to anticipate an impulsive style of diplomacy. Former Navy Secretary John D. Long, who recalled Roosevelt's five-hour command of the fleet in 1898, expected several world wars. Republican leaders had engineered the young New Yorker's vice presidential nomination of 1900 in hope that a meaningless job would affect the momentum of his political career if not kill it. Senator Marcus Hanna had warned them, "Don't any of you realize that there's only one life between this madman and the White House?" When assassination removed that life on September 14, 1901, Hanna could only plead with the new president to "go slow . . . reserve decisions."

If Roosevelt was impulsive, it was only because he possessed practically every characteristic known to human nature. Americans of his day, accustomed to publicity that followed his wilder antics, could not appreciate his subtlety or know how much his presidency would defy the pigeonholing efforts of historians. He was an athlete, historian, naturalist, adventure novelist, politician, journalist, orator, cowboy, aesthete, policeman, military leader, good typist, humanitarian, autocrat, liar, egotist, world traveler. His acquaintances included college professors, prize fighters, naval officers, Boston Brahmins, labor leaders; he liked most of them, was amused by their obsessions, and mixed them at his dinner table in ways that would provide entertaining confrontations of ideas. Both progressive and conservative motives—historians cannot agree—have been detected in his trust-busting and other reforms.

In foreign affairs he is remembered for a program of naval construction, contempt for "effeminate pacifists," and a Darwinistic fascination for military activity; yet he won the Nobel Peace Prize, supported the Second Hague Peace Conference, and his policies cautiously avoided involvements that could lead to serious conflicts. He could be insufferably moralistic in justifying diplomatic decisions, yet coolly realistic in the making of decisions.

His variety, like Benjamin Franklin's, suggested the Renaissance style more than dilettantism. Owning a sense of humor, a range of interests, and a mind undominated by fixed ideas—traits not commonly associated with twentieth-century Americans—Roosevelt was equipped by nature for the flexible approach to diplomacy, best shown in his understanding of geographical differences and their relationship to power. He knew where to act and where not to act.

His famous strenuosity was discharged mainly within the boundaries of the Caribbean Sea. He "took" Panama for a canal site and, to protect its approaches, resorted to heavy-handed interventions elsewhere in the area. These operations have been criticized in moral terms, but their strategic feasibility has never been an issue. Factors of proximity and power allowed him to do as he pleased in the "American sphere."

Roosevelt was more careful in regions of the world where distance and strong foreign interests could create unpromising odds for exercises of manly vigor. Where Europe was concerned, the president weighed what he called "the risks of isolation" against the "risks of alliance" and pursued a line of useful engagement between the extremes. Through flattery and bluff he kept two alliance systems guessing, giving his country at least a minor role in maintaining the European balance of power that he considered important to American interests. A Far Eastern balance was just as desirable, he believed, if it could be accomplished without risks. He comprehended that America's Oriental interests were not significant enough to justify perilous involvements on the other side of the globe.

Roosevelt declined to share the growing sympathy of his countrymen for China. Abusive language was part of his many-sided nature, and he called the "Chinks" disorganized, listless, and unmanly. They had "no spunk at all." The "Japs" were "plucky little people," "dashing fighters," and "efficient and punctual" (their ambassador, Baron Kogoro Takahira, was "always on time" for his appointments and knew how to work that White House elevator wherein Chinese envoys invariably got stuck and had to call for help). "The Japs interest me and I like them." They had built a "modern, compact, and up-to-date machine." If the British needed an empire to supply food and raw materials, the Japanese deserved one too. As Roosevelt told Takahira in early June 1904, Japan had "a paramount interest in what surrounds the Yellow Sea, just as the United States has a paramount interest in what surrounds the Caribbean."

TR believed that nations pursuing interests far from their own spheres must do so prudently, with an eye to priorities. He had no quarrel with the 1899 version of the open door, a riskless effort to retain markets in China, and he allowed his secretaries of state, John Hay and Elihu Root, to restate it at will. But he despised the 1900 version, with its popular inference that the United States was responsible for defending China. Writing to a British historian on May 15, 1905, Roosevelt complained that "the United States of today is too apt to indulge in representations on behalf of weak peoples which do them no good and irritate the strong . . . peoples to whom the protest is made." He scorned congenital underdogs, finding no virtue in weakness. Yet political instinct warned him not to renounce, at least in public, America's pledge to China. The principle was new, not yet tarnished; people believed in it and

6 1

he was stuck with it. Reluctantly he condoned its reiteration by Hay and Root and throughout his administration won newspaper praise as a square-jawed upholder of principle. In reality—through secret diplomacy, subtle qualifications, and rhetorical sleight-of-hand—he did what he could to undermine a principle he considered silly and dangerous.

During Roosevelt's first few years in office the Sino-Japanese issue was obscured by the heavy presence of Russia in the Far East. Tsar Nicholas II was extending control in Manchuria, threatening to turn it into a colony, and making no secret of similar plans for Korea. A wish to preserve the Far Eastern balance—far more than any desire to preserve China's territorial integrity in Manchuria—prompted several American open door statements from 1901 to 1904. These looked severe in newspapers, but secret diplomacy limited their meaning to what was "practicable" and "expedient." American notes to Russia disassociated the 1899 and 1900 policies, asking that free trade be respected no matter what became of Chinese territorial integrity. Roosevelt told Hay in May 1903 that "we cannot fight to keep Manchuria open. I hate being in a position of seeming to bluster without backing it up. . . . I would like to . . . bring some balance between ends and means in Far Eastern policy." He was hoping that military power—but someone else's—would block Russian expansion.

Japan feared Russian designs on Manchuria and especially Korea, but a decision to fight a Western power, and a huge one at that, could not come easily. Encouragement appeared in the form of an alliance with Britain in 1902, which meant British diplomatic support in any Japanese war against a single nation and British military intervention in case Tokyo's enemy was joined by an additional power. It is possible that further encouragement came from Washington, where Takahira was conferring often with Roosevelt and Hay by late 1903. While Hay told the ambassador that "we could not take part in any use of force in that region, unless our own interests were directly involved," it is likely that Takahira received some prewar hints of the American bank loans and manifestations of diplomatic backing that were to materialize so quickly after the opening hostilities.

The Russian government increased its pressure, wanting Manchuria and Korea and believing that a war might solve its current internal ills. "The country is on the brink of revolution," said Minister of Interior Viacheslav von Plehve, "and the one thing that can stop it is a small, victorious war." Japan broke relations with Russia on February 6, 1904, and two days later a Japanese fleet, striking at night against brightly lighted and unprepared tsarist ships at Port Arthur, inflicted severe losses. "Bully!" Roosevelt shouted when he learned of the surprise attack. Here was an "effective" way to start a war, and he had nothing but contempt for Russian carelessness. In fighting for its own interests, Japan was also the proxy of Roosevelt's power balance policy. "Japan is playing our game," he said.

As in 1894, public sentiment favored the Japanese, whose consulates again were filled with Americans wanting to fight for the Mikado. When Russian ships anchored at San Francisco or New York, their crews were jeered at and stoned. The press ground out familiar praise for the Japanese—progressive and courageous, quaint little people who could fight like white men and were noted for bodily cleanliness. They were underdogs, standing up to the world's largest nation, and their war against a notorious autocracy indicated belief in democratic ideals. They were freedom fighters, sapping the tsar's ability to continue the pogroms and other brutalities that marked his despotic grip on his own people. The timid Nicholas II, who had wielded nothing more wicked than a croquet mallet, was portrayed in cartoons as a fiend with a sword that dripped blood. News out of revolutionary Russia—the slaughter of factory workers in St. Petersburg and Cossack punishment of peasants—helped keep a majority of Americans on Japan's side until the end of the war.

Roosevelt had no love for Russian revolutionaries, and his changing preferences were based upon changing diplomatic realities. He was "dee-lighted" by early Japanese victories, enthusiastically discussing them in the company of the ambassador from Tokyo. The Russian ambassador, Count Arturo Cassini, was seldom invited to the White House, and once when he arrived without an invitation, he was defeated by the elevator, that hostile mechanism regarded by TR as a minor test of fitness. But Japanese victories continued, so many of them that the president began to worry, readjusting his idea of balance, moving away from the mainstream of American opinion. He still hoped Japan would win, "but not overwhelmingly," and wished both combatants would "exhaust themselves as much as possible," though not to the point of a Russian revolutionary success that would alter balances on two continents.

Japanese armies crossed the Yalu, and their series of triumphs on the Liaotung Peninsula threatened Port Arthur, which held out until January 2, 1905. During the siege of Port Arthur other Japanese forces moved north toward Mukden, the capital of Manchuria. The Russians were routed at Fuhsien but fought stubbornly in the trenches of Liaoyang, killing 23,000 of the enemy before falling back on Mukden. American correspondents were appalled by battles that were "bigger and bloodier than anything in our own Civil War." Trains of the Trans-Siberian Railway were bringing Russian reinforcements at the rate of 10,000 men each week.

Roosevelt now hoped for "a Russian victory or two," anything that would keep the front in the Mukden area. He had decided that the best line between Japanese and Russian influence in Manchuria would be one drawn east and west through Mukden. Was he leaning toward Russia? Antitsarist newspapers in the United States were growing suspicious. Roosevelt had openly deplored what he called sensational and inflammatory support for the Russian revolution, and his latest dinner-table favorite was reported to be Ambassador Cassini. "The President does not voice the real sentiments of the people of the United States," charged Robert Baker, a Democratic congressman from New York City.

General Iwao Oyama led 270,000 Japanese against Mukden in February and March 1905. The tsar's troops, 330,000 strong and with an advantage in artillery, fell back, losing Mukden in a struggle that took 89,000 Russian and 71,000 Japanese lives. Roosevelt began to fear that Russia would be driven out of the Far East, losing Siberia as well as Manchuria.

The advisers of Nicholas, in particular his warlike wife, Empress Alexandra, hoped that Russia's Baltic Fleet could reverse the course of the war. Forty-two vessels, including ten battleships, started out from Kronstadt near St. Petersburg in mid-October of 1904. The voyage halfway round the world was plagued by diplomatic troubles, coal shortages, mechanical failures. The fleet lacked trained engineers but carried a full complement of priests who prayed over bent pistons and sprinkled holy water on stripped gears; crew morale was hurt by revolutionary agitation and pessimism over the outcome of the mission. At one port an American Bible salesman boarded two of the Russian vessels and sold his entire inventory of three hundred volumes, even though they were non-Orthodox versions and printed in English. In pathetic condition for battle, the fleet rounded Asia's southeast corner and headed north for Vladivostok. On May 27, 1905, near the island of Tsushima in the narrow strait that separates Korea from Japan, the Russians were sighted by smaller forces under command of Admiral Heihachiro Togo, who outmaneuvered enemy columns and then virtually annihilated them. Only four vessels reached safety at Vladivostok. The battle of Tsushima became the proudest event in Japanese history, an inspiration to confidence in future decades. Togo's flagship, *Mikasa,* would be maintained as a national shrine, and its battle ensign would be flown from an aircraft carrier on the morning of December 7, 1941.

Roosevelt's scale of balance was tipping badly. This was important but not to the degree of any consideration of American military intervention. The best answer lay in peace, signed before the Japanese had a chance to move north of Mukden and perhaps overrun all northeast Asia. In March, following the Mukden battle, Roosevelt had offered himself as a mediator, pressing his ambassador in St. Petersburg, George von L. Meyer, to work toward negotiation. After Tsushima he became a desperate pacifist, shooting off cables to Tokyo and St. Petersburg and urging European governments to support his project.

Surprisingly, Tokyo needed no persuading. TR had not realized that Japan at the time of its greatest triumphs was exhausted in manpower and money, fearing a turn of the tide if the war went on much longer. The Russians could not decide; some advisers, including Alexandra, were determined to continue at least until the conflict could end on a note less humiliating than Tsushima, but others argued for acceptance of Roosevelt's offer on grounds that troops and money being expended in the Far East should be used to crush the revolution before it was too late. Roosevelt also advised Nicholas to turn his attention to internal affairs and used that argument among others in his cables. At last St. Petersburg agreed to send delegates to a peace conference in Washington.

On July 29, a few days before the conference was scheduled to begin, the United States recognized Japan's dominant position in "independent" Korea in return for a Tokyo disavowal of aggressive intent toward the Philippines. Because the Japanese had no interest in the islands at that time, the agreement was important mainly for its Korean concession. In effect Roosevelt was acknowledging a fait accompli before he had to, presenting an inexpensive gift that might prove disarming to Japanese demands at the conference. This move, later called the Taft-Katsura Agreement after the envoys who negotiated it, was kept secret. The American press was given no opportunity for outrage over diplomacy at odds with the open door ideal.

When Washington turned uncomfortably hot, the mediator switched the conference site to a naval base near Portsmouth, New Hampshire. TR did not try to dominate the negotiations that began on August 9, but on his yacht, *Mayflower,* and at his home in Oyster Bay, New York, he played the genial cajoler, frowning bluffer, and subtle persuader in meetings with Jutaro Komura and Serge Witte, the chief delegates of Japan and Russia. One of his aims was to keep proud antagonists talking, for a disruption of the conference, he believed, would mean continued war with unpredictable results. His ultimate aim was a treaty leaving the rivals in a position to check each other in the Far East. He wanted Japanese gains limited to Korea, Manchuria south of the Mukden line, the island of Sakhalin, and a modest indemnity that would save the tsar's government enough money to put down the revolution and maintain itself as a factor in Asian and European diplomacy.

Witte agreed to a Japan-dominated Korea and handed over Russia's leases in south Manchuria. Roosevelt regarded these results as reasonable and in keeping with Japan's legitimate interests. Because Manchuria was part of China, the final and public draft of the treaty had to be adorned with a territorial integrity clause. But TR privately assured Japanese diplomats that their country had won "dominance" and "control" in south Manchuria as well as Korea. The Japanese received only half of Sakhalin and not a ruble from the tsar's treasury. Roosevelt was pleased but surprised, having underestimated Japan's need for peace and the frailty of its bargaining position; not so the Russians, who had threatened to walk out of the conference unless Komura dropped his indemnity demands. The latter gave in, and the Portsmouth Treaty was signed on September 5, 1905.

Roosevelt's mediation tactics had value but were not so decisive as Japanese exhaustion in bringing about a treaty he regarded as "nearly perfect." Yet without a conference there could have been no treaty; in this sense the settlement owed much to the president's fascination for balance, good timing, and persistence in bringing bitter enemies to a conference table and keeping them there. His contribution was recognized throughout the world and won him a Nobel Peace Prize. "The peace is directly and solely due to the President's personal intervention," a British diplomat wrote. "The whole of mankind" was grateful, according to Kaiser Wilhelm, and the tsar thanked Roosevelt for "the great part you have played." Resentments seemed few. Russian revolutionaries blamed TR for a premature ending of the war, for their chances ended when Nicholas was able to transfer his army from Manchuria to the streets of St. Petersburg and Moscow. And thank-you notes from the Japanese government, while polite, were lacking in enthusiasm.

If Japanese-American relations had been remarkably cordial since the Imperial Restoration of 1868, a turning point was 1905. From that time until 1941 relations would follow an uneven but generally deteriorating course.

Japanese national pride had been stimulated by amazing feats of modernization, easy victory over China in 1895, and glorious experiences at Mukden and Tsushima a decade later. The public did not understand the power limitations that had forced the government to moderate its demands at Portsmouth, and so the treaty was unpopular, viewed as an inadequate conclusion to so one-sided a war. To deflect blame from itself, the government exaggerated the American role in blocking the indemnity. Phrases popular during the Perry era—outer barbarian, white devil, round eyes—were resurrected by the press and applied to Roosevelt. Americans were kicked and beaten in several cities, and a rock-throwing mob attacked the embassy in Tokyo.

Signs that American affections were cooling became evident in California. The novelist Jack London, seeking experiences to write about, had traveled in Japan and Manchuria as a war correspondent. Trailed by a Korean valet, he returned to his home state to reveal in print and in speaking engagements the fearsome efficiency of the Japanese war machine, its cruelty to prisoners, its future designs upon the United States. Local publications took up the theme, portraying Japanese plans to invade California amphibiously or by coming up through Mexico. Within the following decade several dozen books would expose the "menace of Japan," often by projecting titanic naval battles, valiant defense of Nob Hill, rape and pillage by occupation forces in San Francisco, Santa Barbara, and San Diego. Most analysts judged that enemy armies would not be able to occupy the entire country; the Rockies would stop them.

The new version of the Yellow Peril stemmed partly from the awesome events of the Russo-Japanese War, but it was abetted by social and economic fears resulting from an upturn in Japanese immigration since the turn of the century. Many Californians were prepared to "teach the same lesson" that Chinese immigrants had been forced to learn in the seventies and eighties. Instances of beatings and stonings made news in Japan, where people were astounded to think that Americans considered them no better than the Chinese. The San Francisco Board of Education in October 1906 ordered that all Orientals be segregated in a special school, a decision based on complaints that Japanese children, ninety-three in all, were crowding whites out of the school system. To be sure, schools were overcrowded after San Francisco's destructive earthquake of April 1906. Money for the city's relief had been contributed by private citizens in many countries; Japanese aid, totaling a quarter of a million dollars, compared favorably with China's $40,000, England's $6,571, Russia's $199, Germany's $50, and Scotland's forty cents. Thus the Japanese had several reasons for unhappiness over the school board's action, their most extreme feelings represented by the newspaper *Mainichi Shimbun* on October 22, 1906:

> Stand up, Japanese nation! Our countrymen have been HUMILIATED on the other side of the Pacific. Our poor boys and girls have been expelled from the public schools by the rascals of the United States, cruel and mercilous like demons. . . . Why do we not insist on sending [naval] ships?

American papers located east of the Rockies tended to deplore the "insane behavior" of Californians. In spite of recent Japanese military feats, it was hard to change a long-standing mood of benevolent condescension—a mood certainly present in New York's Metropolitan Opera House on the evening of February 11, 1907, at the first performance of Giacomo Puccini's *Madama Butterfly*. As a topic of the American stage, Japan had come a long way from the ridicule of *The Mikado,* but *Butterfly* continued the concept of harmless little people drinking tea in paper houses. Its hero, an American naval lieutenant (sung by the famous tenor Enrico Caruso), falls in love with the Japanese girl Butterfly and fathers her child. When he returns a couple of years later, village officials bow low and beg him to restore the woman's honor. The lieutenant is deeply touched, but marriage is out of the question, and so Butterfly kills herself. The audience wept, then hurrahed a production that, along with catchy melodies, was reassuring on such Japanese traits as humility and admiration for Americans. The opera became so popular that it restored Caruso's reputation, recently damaged by his arrest for pinching a woman at the Central Park Zoo.

Roosevelt wanted to deal carefully with the Japanese, whom he believed to be "influenced by two contradictory feelings." (He was a psychologist too.) They were "ferocious and conceited, due to their victory over the mighty empire of Russia," but also sensitive and touchy, "bitterly humiliated" by the school decision. "The infernal fools in California . . . insult the Japanese recklessly." Although the federal government had no jurisdiction in the school case, TR intervened anyway. He invited eight members of the San Francisco Board of Education to Washington, where he bullied, pleaded, and at last persuaded them to agree to a compromise. The board rescinded its segregation order and Japan rejoiced. In return the president, in a quietly negotiated "gentlemen's agreement," secured a Tokyo promise that would limit America-bound emigration to students and upper-class Japanese, thus protecting California's labor market.

Roosevelt's policies continued to erode his nation's position as guardian of Chinese territorial integrity. He still believed that America's interest in Manchuria was small compared to Japan's vital interest there. In 1905 he had allowed Tokyo to know that he respected its dominance and control in south Manchuria, and by 1908 that control was increasing. Japan triple-tracked the main route of the South Manchurian Railway and laid connecting lines throughout the region, projecting new branches of economic development. A watchful American press correctly discerned that Chinese sovereignty became more meaningless with each month. It was high time, some editors demanded, for Japan to become the target of a powerful open door statement. Manchurian changes, abrasive relations in several areas, public pressure in both countries—these were reasons that Tokyo as well as Washington saw need for negotiation. The American capital was the site of lengthy deliberations between Ambassador Takahira and Elihu Root, secretary of state since Hay's death in 1905. The result was approved by Roosevelt, and the Root-Takahira Agreement was announced on November 30, 1908.

The agreement has not been admired by a majority of American historians, who have called it baffling, vague, meaningless. It has frustrated the urge to classify, defeated the wish to define. But this was its intent. Precisely because of its obscure clauses the document was important to the needs of both governments. There was recognition of the "status quo," which Americans could construe as halting further development in Manchuria while the Japanese inferred a continuance of development activities begun before the agreement was signed. The American press hailed a diplomatic triumph suggested by another clause, Japan's pledge to respect the "independence and integrity of China." No one seemed to notice the disappearance of *territorial* from the much repeated statement of principle. *Integrity,* without an adjective, is about as easy to define as *truth, beauty,* and *morality.* The denuded term symbolized Roosevelt's proclivity for disguised escape from responsibilities in China. The signatories agreed to respect each other's possessions, such as Hawaii, the Philippines, Alaska, Formosa, Korea—in a clause dealing with noncritical regions but giving the press in both countries a chance to boast of satisfactory results. Elastic and eye-pleasing phrases prevented Roosevelt's contemporaries from seeing the agreement as a nod if not a bow to Japanese interests in Manchuria.

TR's realism required subtlety. Japan's interests had been recognized through private assurances and secret or ambiguous agreements; at the same time public statements in support of the open door had satisfied the American people and given China no clear opportunity to complain of foul play. But generality must be avoided in dealing with the universal Roosevelt, whose traits included a capacity for blunder. His subtlety had its flaw in a 1907 decision to send the United States Navy on a cruise around the world. Diplomatic language could be pliant, impalpable; sixteen battleships could not. Their physical presence in the Far East would force Roosevelt into a theatrical clarification of his foreign policy.

The president's craving for prestige produced the voyage of the Great White Fleet. TR had worked wonders to build the nation's naval power and said that he wanted to "impress foreign peoples" and "make a gigantic gesture before the eyes of the world." During the months of preparation his exuberant remarks included references to Japan, inspiring West Coast papers to proclaim a warlike purpose for the adventure. He vigorously criticized jingoistic statements. While he felt some need to display the size of his fleet and show Japan that his kindnesses to that nation had nothing to do with fear or weakness, his objective was to "advertise the United States to the world" through a goodwill mission.

It was not a fighting force that departed from Hampton Roads, Virginia, on December 16, 1907. The battleships were on their own, without supporting warships or coaling vessels for most of the journey. The circumnavigation would depend largely upon British coal and supplies, and Britain was Japan's ally. Three of the sixteen battleships had mechanical defects that would have made them liabilities in battle, and another carried an impressive-looking battery of wooden guns. The ships looked beautiful but were highly visible in their gleaming white paint. Armor belts designed to protect waterlines rode several feet below the surface due to heavy cargoes of candy and souvenirs to be passed out, pianos, portable rock gardens, artificial waterfalls, and other decorations for grand balls and banquets. Most of the crew members had never been to sea. Roosevelt had replaced experienced sailors with "apple-cheeked lads from the Midwest" who would be appealing to foreigners. Special presidential orders covered etiquette lessons, dance practice, shower baths, clean fingernails, and elimination of acne and gum chewing.

During the first leg of the cruise its goodwill purpose was almost frustrated by the responses of South American nations. Naval pageantry in Rio de Janeiro, hilariously convivial, prompted the Brazilian government to boast that it had gained American support in its rivalries with Argentina and Peru. Thus when Buenos Aires received a pageant of lesser magnitude, Argentina threatened to break relations with Washington. Uruguay, ignored by the fleet, was enraged. Chile made threats and was partly mollified by a last-minute change of itinerary that allowed a hurried sweep in and out of the harbor at Valparaiso. Peru, at war with Brazil, entertained the American navy for nine days, then protested that Brazilians had received more candy and souvenirs. (The fleet had run out of goodies.) Ecuador protested after having been bypassed. Such experiences made it clear that a fleet visit was regarded as a special honor, a mark of diplomatic support, a subject of envious comparison with festivities in ports of other countries.

Knowing this, Roosevelt accepted invitations from both China and Japan in the last week of March 1908. During the next few months Tokyo's government and press proclaimed that the fleet's visit was intended to be a celebration of Japanese domination in Manchuria. At the same time Peking advertised that the pageant in China would be an anti-Japanese demonstration, signifying America's determination to make good on its territorial integrity promise. Editorials in American papers and speeches by Secretary of War William Howard Taft and others encouraged Chinese hopes. Caught up in the excitement of the random hunt for prestige, Roosevelt had set a trap from which there could be no disguised escape. Now he must make the kind of decision that would amount to a grave insult, public loss of face, to one or the other of the Oriental rivals.

The decision was made. Japan was assured that it would receive maximum-scale pageantry in Tokyo Bay. Meanwhile the American government tried to let the Chinese down easily, minimizing the importance of their pageant in a series of planning changes. The Manchu government spent a half million dollars decorating Shanghai with carved arches, entertainment pavilions, tons of bunting and tinsel. Shanghai was cancelled, Washington announcing that a lesser city, Chefoo, would be the site of the Sino-American celebration. Chefoo was decorated at great cost, yet China could take heart from the city's location, which was much closer than Shanghai to critical Manchuria. This same fact struck Secretary Root, who hoped that "the Chinese government clearly realizes that . . . we favor their legitimate aims, but that we see grave danger in any unduly captious attitude which could give just cause for serious offense in any quarter." So again the site was transferred, this time to Amoy—an out-of-the-way port far to the south—and again the Imperial Decorations Committee commenced its labors. China also learned that it would receive only the leading half of the fleet, eight instead of sixteen vessels. And in a final rearrangement Peking was informed that the trailing half—ships less imposing than those at the head of the line—would visit Amoy.

The four small slaps added up to a diplomatic blow that seriously embarrassed the Chinese government. "Japan has evidently succeeded in causing a change in plans," the Hong Kong *Telegraph* stated on May 8, 1908. Japanese propaganda resounded throughout East Asia, making fun of China's humiliation. As the *Japan Times* said on August 21: "China must be aware of the imbecility of depending on America as support for her hostile attitude against other powers." Peking papers denounced the United States, and anti-American riots broke out in several cities. In an attempt to save face with its own people, the Manchu court announced that a great typhoon had sunk half the touring fleet and this was the reason China would be visited by only eight ships. The explanation was believable due to the recent typhoon that had struck the China coast in the region of Amoy. The work of the Decorations Committee had blown away, and for a fourth time the government appropriated funds for entertainment purposes.

Following celebrations in Hawaii, New Zealand, and three Australian ports, the sixteen battleships had steamed north, weathered the typhoon, and entered Tokyo Bay on October 18, 1908. Roosevelt sent orders denying shore leave to any enlisted men who had accepted intoxicating beverages earlier in the cruise. "There must be no suspicion," he said, "of insolence or rudeness on our part." The Japanese government also had taken precautions, ordering every householder in Tokyo and Yokohama to exhibit paper lanterns imprinted with the Stars and Stripes and posting rules of behavior in public places: Americans must not be "stared at, except when necessary," there must be no "spitting anywhere," and "handkerchiefs shall be used in the clearing of nostrils." In case of trouble Japanese fleets totaling 160 ships cruised on battle alert outside Tokyo Bay.

After some tension the daily celebrations grew convivial. Sailors were entertained at ice cream socials, and a children's chorus, having failed to master "The Star-Spangled Banner," sang "John Brown's Body." The Emperor Mutsuhito gave a luncheon, and the heroic Togo entertained, as did politicians and businessmen at dozens of banquets and balls. American newspapermen were assigned their own paper houses and Butterflies for the duration of the visit, and on its last night thousands of Japanese honored their guests with songs and a torchlight parade. In the wake of the harmonious event American newspapers judged that Japan had been awed by the sixteen battleships and would behave itself in the future; Japanese papers claimed that an obsolescent navy—the era of the dreadnoughts, ships more than twice as powerful as the touring sixteen, had begun in 1906—had paid a tributory call that amounted to an overt American rejection of China. The Japanese had "got what they wanted," reported the British ambassador in Tokyo.

The fleet's better half set course for Manila Bay, where it would await the eight vessels of the rear, making what was now called "a coaling stop" at Amoy. The sailors expected the usual—cheering, flag-waving crowds. Instead the Chinese crowds shook fists and threw rocks. Police whipped troublemakers, "fifteen hundred blows for each," but two days passed before police and troops could clear a safe passage for the Americans to come ashore and begin festivities. The visitors were housed in a cluster of pavilions called Pleasure City, protected by a stockade manned by the Chinese army with its Krupp cannon. Apart from safeguarding lives, the Manchu government wanted nothing to do with the Americans. No important officials made the trip from Peking, and the governor of Fukien province, where Amoy is located, said that he was ordered by "imperial decree" not to attend the pageant. A fire on the night of November 4 burned Pleasure City to the ground, and the fleet left China the next day bound for a rendezvous with its other half and a continuation of the world cruise.

Washington's press releases, less than candid, allowed Americans to marvel over the unbounded enthusiasm of the Amoy welcome, saying that the Chinese idolized their benefactors. "How sweet are the proofs of our popularity and prestige which this week our nation has accepted from the Dragon Empire." Had the news been factual, it would have reported threats of war in Peking papers, destruction of American property throughout the country, and riots in Nanking that forced American missionaries to seek safety aboard British gunboats in the Yangtze. Chinese passions were dampened ten days after the fleet's departure by news that the empress dowager had died only a few hours after the demise of Emperor Kuang-hsu in his lagoon prison.

The voyage of the Great White Fleet provided a final example—though one far too spectacular for the tastes of the normally subtle Roosevelt—of a realistic foreign policy that discounted the open door obligation to China, accepted the fact that Japan considered its mainland interests to be important, and saw nothing in American interests that demanded involvement in the Japanese-Russian-Chinese arena.

V

"Fools Rush in . . ."

THE THREE-HUNDRED POUND DIMENSIONS of William Howard Taft offered plenty of room for anticapitalist cartoonists to draw dollar signs on him, and his presidency in 1909–13 would present historians of economic determinism with their most authentic specimen. For at least in the case of Taft and his secretary of state, Philander C. Knox—a baby-faced corporation lawyer called "Uncle Cupid" by his relatives—American foreign policies were tied to the overseas enterprises of bankers and industrialists. Taft and Knox saw the United States as an enlarged version of the department store owned by their friend John Wanamaker; diplomacy's aim was a high sales volume and a good bottom line that would assure national success. Modern critics err not in discerning such motives, but sometimes they are too impressed by a melodramatic view of businessmen as creatures of cunning calculation. For Taft's deals were not very smart. They showed that the characteristic intensity of American diplomatic practice can ignore realities, in crusades for the dollar as well as for democracy.

Eager to hunt lions in Africa, Roosevelt had planned a vacation from presidential burdens. He perhaps always had intended to return to the White House in 1913 and wanted the controllable Taft to preside until then. With TR's help, Taft won the GOP nomination and the election of 1908. No policy changes were expected, but once the hunter was far away in the wilds of Kenya, Taft proved he had ideas of his own. Or were they the ideas of Secretary Knox or of Willard Straight, the administration's self-confessed expert on Manchuria, or of railroad promoter E. H. Harriman and bankers Jacob Schiff and J. P. Morgan? It has never been perfectly clear. Studying the Taft clique, historians have failed to detect a single dominating influence.

Unlike the flexible Roosevelt, Taft's people did not realize that geographical differences offer variable odds on success. They recognized no limits to their country's power and influence, believing that any desired policy, pressed hard enough, would win in nations large and small, in one corner of the world as well as another.

Their policy, which they referred to as Dollar Diplomacy, could hardly fail in the Caribbean; activities wise or foolish tend to do well in one's own backyard. A process in Dollar Diplomacy might start with the government arranging for private banks to lend money to a foreign state. The loan—profitable in itself through the interest it drew—created an obligation, a special relationship leading toward more trade and more investment in the railroads, mines, and other assets of the debtor nation. Here was the flavor of colonialism without formal political control; it was known that European-style colonialism produced too many responsibilities and was also inconsistent with Progressive Era ideals. Yet, lacking political control, could the United States protect its often unwelcome businessmen and their properties in foreign locations? Roosevelt already had provided the answer. Battleships and marines, which had served his strategic purposes in the Caribbean, were employed by Taft—for example, in Nicaragua—as Dollar Diplomacy's roving police force.

For different reasons both Roosevelt and Taft pushed hard in the Caribbean—but Taft did not stop there. Any dissimilarities he might have noted between Nicaragua and China were uninstructive. As he said of China, "The Government of the United States shall extend all proper support to every legitimate and beneficial American enterprise."

The open door policy, suffering from Roosevelt's disrespect for it, found loving care in the hands of Taft, Knox, and Straight. It was a useful prying tool, a good excuse for getting into China and doing business. Taft mentioned this "practical application" of the policy. But he also said that China's interest, the preservation of its territorial integrity, was the reason for American dealings in that country. How could the United States keep China free without being there? As Knox put it, "Investments will give the voice of the U.S. more authority . . . toward guaranteeing the preservation of . . . China." And Taft confessed to "an intense personal interest in making the use of American capital . . . an instrument for the promotion of the welfare of China." Such statements cannot be dismissed as candy-coated villainy, perhaps not even as conscious rationalizations. Goals of altruism and profit both can be pursued with a fair amount of honesty when they do not seem to be in conflict, a convenience that probably allowed the president to avoid deep rumination on motives. He was furious over accusations that his program had "none but materialistic aims" when actually it "appeals alike to idealistic humanitarian sentiments . . . and to legitimate commercial aims." The open door was not to be "set aside by underhanded methods," as it had been in Roosevelt's time. In the opinion of Willard Straight, TR's disinterest in China had been "moral cowardliness."

Straight spoke romantically of his two loves, China and business enterprise, and of himself as an attractive combination of Rudyard Kipling and Cecil Rhodes. He wished to "reshape the East" as Rhodes had reshaped Africa. For the sake of China and Dollar Diplomacy he yearned to chase the "cocky and hateful" Japanese out of Manchuria, which would become a new American frontier. He was only twenty-six when he gained the consul generalship in Mukden, a post he held from 1906 to 1908. Working for the Roosevelt administration but ignoring its Manchurian policy, he devised such projects as an American-controlled bank that would lend China the money to buy out foreign concessions and purchase by E. H. Harriman, the railroad developer, of Russian and Japanese rail systems (in the event those countries refused to sell, he would force them out of business by helping the puzzled Chinese build competing lines). Straight's tactics succeeded only in helping Japan and Russia to recognize a common interest in protecting their southern and northern spheres of influence. In 1907 the former enemies signed the first in a series of agreements to cooperate in excluding other powers from Manchuria. While Straight's pressures dramatized the need for such an agreement, it stemmed too from British policy. Allied with Japan and preparing an alliance with Russia, Britain wanted to bring the two together.

Straight returned to Washington in 1908 as acting chief of the State Department's new Division of Far Eastern Affairs. Friends assured him that his expert advice was badly needed, but elsewhere the young man gained the impression that Roosevelt considered him an "oaf" and for that reason had recalled him from a sensitive area. At any rate, the acting chief was ignored during the important Far Eastern negotiations of 1908. While he consorted with Chinese envoys and made plans to reshape Asia, Roosevelt and Root talked mainly to Takahira. When Straight learned of the Root-Takahira Agreement, with its deference to Japanese development of Manchuria, he called it "a terrible diplomatic blunder to be laid at the door of T. R." He disliked Roosevelt and waited impatiently for the lame duck to hand over the government to men who could better understand the great work to be done in China.

During his lame duck period Roosevelt retained confidence in Taft but was bothered by the president-elect's friendship with Straight and selection of Knox as secretary of state. On February 8, 1909—surrounded by guns, tents, and the other safari gear he was packing—he took time to write Knox a word of advice on Far Eastern policy. Keep the navy strong, he said, but also bear in mind that "Japan is vitally interested in China. . . . Do everything in [your] power to guard against the possibility of war by preventing the occurrence of conditions which would invite war."

Even in Africa TR would keep an eye on American diplomacy and become deeply disturbed by the time of his return to the United States. Taft would be tutored in a letter of December 22, 1910:

> The vital interest of the Japanese . . . is Manchuria and Korea. It is therefore peculiarly our interest not to take any steps as regards Manchuria which will give the Japanese cause to feel . . . that we are hostile to them, or a menace—in however slight a degree—to their interests. Alliance with China, in view of China's absolute military

helplessness, means of course not an additional strength to us, but an additional obligation which we assume. . . . I do not believe in taking any position anywhere unless we can make good; and as regards Manchuria, if the Japanese choose to follow a course of conduct to which we are adverse, we cannot stop it unless we are prepared to go to war, and a successful war about Manchuria would require a fleet as good as that of England, plus an army as good as that of Germany.

Roosevelt's letter contained some of the soundest ideas ever written about the country's foreign policy, but it would never be famous in the manner of "making the world safe for democracy" and other statements possessing simplicity, moral passion, and enthusiasm for an infinity of American abilities. Certainly the addressee was not impressed; Taft had long since stopped taking orders from a former president. With Knox and Straight as advisers he had sallied forth into terra incognita shortly after assuming the presidency.

Straight enjoyed the Inaugural Ball but accepted only two glasses of champagne and departed well before nine o'clock. At sunrise the next morning he arrived at the State Department, opened his bulging Manchurian file, and sat down to work at projects no longer at odds with government policy.

In following months Manchuria was laid aside, temporarily, due to the appearance of a big opportunity in central China. A British-French-German banking consortium was conferring with Peking on financial arrangements for the building of the Hukuang Railways, planned for the British and French spheres in the Yangtze valley and Kwangtung province. Participating nations would gain profits and increased influence in China, prospects that interested Straight, Taft, Knox, and a banking combine headed by Morgan. In a note to Peking the State Department requested that the Morgan group be admitted to the consortium as a full partner.

The British and French had no desire to see American capital at work in their spheres. The consortium was a restricted club; no one else need apply. They so informed Prince Ch'un, who had ruled China as regent since the death of the empress dowager. When European pressure forced Ch'un to ignore the American request, Knox threatened reversal of an earlier promise to remit Boxer indemnities to China. But the key to the problem, Straight calculated, was in London. There his salesmanship encountered the cold-shoulder treatment or cutting remarks about the American tendency to "intrude where not wanted." Straight's trip was deflating, and he began to doubt the wisdom of the Hukuang deal.

Taft and Knox remained firm, for Hukuang had become more than a business transaction; it was a matter of pride, a challenge to the very basis of their Asian policy. Knox tried the sentimental approach, reminding China that the United States was its best friend, proved by the open door principle. On the same day, July 15, 1909, Taft demanded from Prince Ch'un "equal participation by American capital in the present railway loan," for only in this way could the United States work for the "welfare of China" and the "preservation of her territorial integrity." For two more years, through pleas and demands, the administration invested additional pride, held up construction, disgusted would-be partners in the consortium, and kept the Chinese government in a state of confusion.

The Americans finally were admitted to full partnership in an agreement signed May 20, 1911, a victory won by vanity's needs more than for real economic interests. This became apparent when New York bankers, contracts in hand, suddenly realized that Chinese complexities needed further study. Could their affairs truly prosper in spheres dominated by other powers, in a country where revolution was in progress, through contracts signed with a government that might fall at any time? Prodded by a now embarrassed Taft administration, the bankers put a little over seven million dollars in the Hukuang. There was snickering in London and Paris, for the investment was small considering the trouble it had caused, but by this time American bankers could think only of limiting their future losses.

Long before the Hukuang settlement Straight had given up trying to crash the Franco-British spheres. Manchuria was his real interest. Resigning from the State Department at least in an official capacity, he signed on with the railway promoter Harriman and was back in Mukden by late October 1909. That Straight did not hate all Japanese was evidenced by his locomotive rides on the South Manchuria line. Sometimes he was allowed to work the throttle, at least until the day he lost control; with collision imminent a Japanese switchman in the nick of time turned the speeding engine onto an empty siding. For this and other reasons Straight became known as "the Manchurian Express" among his friends in Mukden.

As Harriman's agent Straight tried to buy the Chinese Eastern Railway (the name for the Manchurian section of Russia's Trans-Siberia line) as well as Japan's South Manchuria line. In this way the United States could "take over" Manchuria and reserve it for China. St. Petersburg and Tokyo hardly bothered to reply to the offers. This setback, or even news of Harriman's death, could not stop the apprentice tycoon, who persuaded a New York banking group to build a railroad parallel to the tracks of the South Manchuria; competition was expected to ruin the Japanese line and force its sale at a bargain price. The bankers spent heavily on engineering studies and supplies before backing down in the face of ever dawning realities—mainly the fact of Russo-Japanese power in the area, demonstrated with increasing cooperation and determination since the 1907 agreement. Straight called the bankers cowardly and "not as rich as they had pretended."

As prospects dimmed for a Sino-American Manchuria, Knox came up with a plan for "some kind of consortium" that would involve the United States and other nations. The consortium would lend money to China for the purpose of buying the two offending railroads or, that failing, building competing lines. Participating banks would operate the railroads (the collateral) until China paid off the loan. With Peking the world's poorest credit risk, foreclosure was a not unwelcome possibility. But Knox reasoned that the Chinese would benefit even if they never gained control of the properties, for Manchuria would be "neutralized," the greedy Russians and Japanese replaced by nations respectful of China's territorial integrity.

The writer Herbert Croly in 1909 had warned of America's "Asia-first orientation" and the Taft administration's tendency to ignore the existence of Europe. Secretary Knox might know all about consortiums, but he understood little of European alliance systems and the way they worked. Britain was his first choice for partnership in a consortium aimed against Britain's own allies. In refusing, Sir Edward Grey explained that he could not conspire against Japan's legitimate interests in Manchuria. With a leaping inference Knox announced British support for a six-nation consortium that would not exclude Japan and Russia but only reduce their influence. This would not suit the Japanese, Grey replied in stating clearly that he wished to drop the matter. Knox persisted, still claiming British support, forcing Grey to consult with his Russian and Japanese allies in the framing of a tripartite note so unmistakably negative that no one could miss its point. The only result of Knox's pressure, much to China's consternation, was a new treaty signed by Russia and Japan on July 4, 1910, exchanging pledges of support for stronger measures of economic and "political" control of their Manchurian spheres. Britain and France applauded; the Entente had never been firmer, for which Grey thanked "the policy adopted by the U.S.A. in China."

Manchuria was Knox's La Mancha. Nursing wounds from the consortium rebuff, he rose to meet the challenge of the Russo-Japanese pact. Wary of railroad deals, he devised a different scheme for throwing the aggressors out of Manchuria. China would receive an American loan and use it to develop mines and industries, thereby establishing economic domination—with the exception of the railroads. After drawing up the mortgage contract with China, Knox encountered a depressing lack of enterprise in American banking circles. Even Straight was wavering, writing from Mukden that he was close to a nervous breakdown. With little American money available, Knox applied in London, Paris, and Berlin for help in arranging a new consortium. The predictable rejection, harmoniously rendered by Britain, France, Russia, and Japan, killed off the idea. The United States was patronizingly reminded of its 1908 agreement to respect the status quo in Manchuria.

Optimism, hard work, pluck, perseverance—Horatio Alger's success formula failed Taft's diplomats, who achieved the reverse of all they had sought. As a brokerage office the government had lost millions of dollars for investors. The open door, restated some seventeen times without result, was hardly restored to glory. China's position in Manchuria was weakened and Japan's strengthened, and in a manner that could only encourage Japanese annoyance and contempt. This manner, presumptuous yet powerless, alienated France and Britain too. Such were the results of assorted noncomprehensions: the mechanics of the Entente and its importance to Britain and other members; the revolutionary condition of China, which made it a poor site for long-range planning; the reluctance of American financiers to gamble against high odds; the value of Manchuria to Japan and Russia and their on-the-spot ability to control events there; and the physical inability of the United States to protect the endeavors of its citizens in a distant and violent region of the world.

While Wall Street was learning to cut its losses, smaller entrepreneurs were exciting themselves over the government's prospectus of Manchuria as a land of opportunity, a new frontier, a place where boom towns would thrive in the midst of American mines, industries, and railway networks. Fortune seekers bought land for speculation and chose promising locations for hotels, stores, and other facilities. Their properties often caught fire, wives and children had "accidents," and "incidents" took many lives. The Russians and Japanese who were in control were capable of using methods other than diplomacy to protect their interests. Taft could do nothing to help those Americans trying to escape Manchuria in 1912 and 1913. In the end he discovered the fundamental flaw in his four-year China policy; he could not use battleships and marines, for the Gulf of Chihli was not the Caribbean. An interested observer, Roosevelt, contributed an I-told-you-so remark: "Unfortunately, after I left office a most mistaken and ill-advised policy was pursued towards Japan, combining irritation with inefficiency."

Provincial disorders and demands for reform had plagued the last years of the empress dowager. The weak Prince Ch'un, who took over as regent for a child emperor in 1908, saw little hope for the crumbling dynasty. Riots continued, reaching revolutionary scope in Szechwan province in 1911, due in part to local resentment over Hukuang railway activities. But unlike the Boxer Rebellion, the new movement was more anti-Manchu than antiforeign. Some army units mutinied, others were massacred by revolutionaries, and city after city declared against the Peking court. By the end of 1911 some fourteen provinces were in support of a provisional republican government set up in Nanking. Its president was said to be Sun Yat-sen, best known among numerous revolutionary leaders.

Americans in the Taft period viewed China fondly if indistinctly. The defeats of Dollar Diplomacy were reported with considerable obscurity in the press, where the big news was the open door, which meant seventeen guarantees to China, a new record. The open door policy suffered some confusion because of the revolution. One of its phrases, after all, supported China's "administrative entity," and this appeared to place the United States on the side of the Manchu government. News reports of revolutionaries eating cats and dogs created some sympathy for the old order, yet most American papers, congressmen, and clergymen seemed to prefer the new republicanism, especially as represented by Sun Yat-sen, whose attainments included Christianity, an M.D. degree, travels in the United States as a fund collector, and a random study of Western ideas. His "Three Principles"—Nationalism, Democracy, and Redistribution of Wealth—were a hash that would enable all future ideologies in China to claim Sun as founding father. American editors saw "some discrepancies" in the doctor's politics but on the whole were gratified that China was "on the way to democracy" and thus "more deserving than ever" of open door benefits.

Through an act of abdication on February 12, 1912, the Manchu dynasty came to a formal end, having ruled since 1644. Shouting praise for Dr. Sun, Congress passed a joint resolution to "congratulate the people of China on their assumption of the powers, duties, and responsibilities of self-government," presuming that under a republic "the happiness of the Chinese people will be secure." Hopes were premature. The president of China, as it turned out, was not to be Sun but the former Manchu official Yuan Shih-kai, the only available statesman who controlled enough military strength to unify the country. China entered an era of constitutional argument (Yuan wanted to found an imperial dynasty in his own name), more revolutions by Sun and others, gradual disintegration of central power, and intense pressure from Japan.

During their last months in office Taft and Knox tried to push American financiers into yet another international consortium, one aimed at subsidizing President Yuan's reorganization of his government. Before plans could be completed, Taft left office, much to the relief of participating bankers.

The administration of the new president, Woodrow Wilson (1913–21), was much occupied with domestic reforms, a Mexican problem, neutrality, world war, and peacemaking, but it did not ignore the Far East. Wilson's dreams were global and there was room in them for China and the open door. In the end China would benefit no more from virtuous promises—Wilson's investment there—than it had from Roosevelt's strategic concepts or Taft's dollars. But Wilson did arrange to end the American involvement in the consortium. He was not fond of international combines seeking profits in China, and he condoned Wall Street's withdrawal from the consortium. He was not averse to building dams and railways for "republican China" but wanted their subsidization limited to American bankers who could be persuaded to discount financial selfishness in favor of humanitarian goals. Such plans failed when prospective investors replied, "No thanks."

The great European war began in the first week of August 1914. With a covetous eye on the holdings of Germany—leases on the Shantung Peninsula of China and islands in the Pacific—Japan proclaimed its obligation to join Germany's enemies. By the end of 1914 Japanese forces had occupied Shantung and key islands in the Mariana, Marshall, and Caroline groups. With the European war preoccupying nations normally active in East Asia, Japan saw its chance for unprecedented gains in China. Tokyo's Twenty-one Demands, presented to Yuan's shaky government early in 1915, included Chinese recognition of the Shantung takeover, more advantages in Manchuria, economic penetration of the Yangtze valley, and vaguely specified "political" functions in all of China. The British, not so preoccupied that they could ignore their Yangtze interests, suggested that the demands be limited to Shantung and Manchuria; otherwise, London might decide to "alter" its alliance with Japan. Valuing the tie with Britain, Tokyo moderated its claims. In return the Entente powers made promises that soon turned into secret treaties pledging postwar support for Japan's Shantung and Pacific ambitions.

In opposing the Twenty-one Demands the American government recited that it could not "recognize any agreement or undertaking . . . impairing . . . the political or territorial integrity of the Republic of China, or the . . . open door policy." At least the nonrecognition phrase was new, or almost new. Wilson had established a precedent, one with unhappy meaning for the future, when in 1913 he had refused to recognize an "evil" government in Mexico. Japan's occupation of Shantung might too be evil; yet, like the Mexican government, it was an existing fact. Officials in Tokyo scratched their heads over the meaning of nonrecognition, surely an ultimate in diplomatic sterility. How could the Americans negotiate to reverse events in Shantung if they refused to acknowledge that those events had taken place? Nonrecognition also implied a sense of moral superiority—suggestive of a shoulder turned or a nose lifted—that had not often been present in open door pronouncements of the past. The American note, which the Japanese foreign minister called outrageous, was a superfluous comment on an issue already decided by other nations. It was consistent with some contemporary observations on the unworldly style of Wilsonian diplomacy. As the *New Republic* editorialized on March 27, 1915:

Ideals, Souls, Spirituality, Unselfishness, Freedom and other aspects of Nobility and Purity languish unless they are nourished by the earth. . . . The thinking of Mr. Wilson is always cleaner, more sterilized, than life itself . . . a style as remote as a Sunday morning. . . . Being too noble is a dangerous business. . . . When you have purged and bleached your morality into a collection of abstract nouns, you have something that is clean and white, but what else have you? Surely nothing comparable to the usefulness of that wisdom which retains the odor of the world, which shrinks from proclaiming superlatives, is sparing in grandiose praise, and rich in tumbled experience.

Wilson's idealized conception of neutrality was one of several conditions that led the United States to war against Germany in April 1917. China made the same decision four months later. Peking had no quarrel with the kaiser, nor were many Chinese leaders stirred by Wilson's appeal for a worldwide crusade of democracy against autocracy. The decision resulted from internal politics and China's natural wish to cancel out any advantages the Japanese might enjoy from the circumstance of their wartime association with the United States.

Japan used that circumstance for all it was worth. Hoping to soften American attitudes toward Japanese moves in China, special ambassador Kikujiro Ishii arrived in Washington for talks with Secretary of State Robert Lansing, a distinguished-looking and usually meticulous international lawyer. The administration, totally dedicated to winning the war it had recently entered, was vulnerable to Ishii's hints that Japan was contemplating a separate peace with Germany. In the view of the Japanese diplomat, Lansing recognized the Shantung conquest merely by talking about it. Furthermore the latter agreed that "territorial propinquity creates special relations" and that Japan had "special interests in China, particularly in the part to which her possessions are contiguous." He added that "the territorial sovereignty of China, nevertheless, remains unimpaired."

Lansing was not happy with a legal document the precise meaning of which he could not explain. All he could do in later months was point to the fact that he had forced Japan to sign an open door pledge—while Ishii was boasting that he had forced the American government to abandon China on the Shantung and Manchuria issues. Because of its ambiguity the Lansing-Ishii Agreement of 1917 has been likened to the Root-Takahira Agreement of 1908. In the latter, however, the sophisticated Roosevelt had sought ambiguity as an end in itself, serving his needs of the moment. A similar result obtained by Lansing and his adviser Wilson was unintended. It pained a president for whom ambivalence was a sign of moral weakness and who believed firmly in the open door. Whatever the agreement had lost for China—and no one knew exactly what—Wilson vowed to retrieve it in the postwar settlement.

Following the Bolshevik revolution and Russia's exit from the war in late 1917, Britain, France, Japan, and finally the United States found a number of reasons for sending troops to occupy strategic points in European Russia and around Vladivostok in the Far East. One of Wilson's reasons for participating at Vladivostok was fear that the Japanese, already there, would use Russia's helplessness to make gains in northern Manchuria, nominally Chinese and therefore guaranteed by the open door. The president won journalistic compliments as "the disciplinarian of Asia" and a leader who was "finally putting some real sinew into our responsibilities" there. If this was his purpose, it had no chance of success. His 9,000-man expeditionary force was too small to influence major events but large enough to create minor ones, such as brawls and shooting incidents with the Japanese. The awkward gesture ended with American evacuation in April 1920, while Japan's 72,000 troops made further Manchurian inroads and were not withdrawn from the Vladivostok region until 1922.

In speeches and press interviews during the war years 1917–18, Wilson was the relentless spokesman for every ideal known to American history. He visualized a new kind of world, one of democracy, self-determination of peoples, Christian brotherhood, international cooperation, eternal peace. In such a world there would be no place for autocracy, militarism, colonialism, secret diplomacy, balance-of-power politics, commercial rivalries. His oratory sounded preachy and impractical to some listeners, but countless millions of people in a world sick of war were grateful for his words and believed them. He made fourteen promises and many more, some dealing generally with peace and justice throughout the world while others were applicable to specific localities of Europe, the Middle East, the Pacific Ocean, and East Asia. Among random pledges were some involving self-determination for German colonial subjects on Pacific islands, the return of

Shantung to China, and "our duty" as spelled out by open door principles.

Presidential exposition on China provided that country with the best news in years. Western-educated leaders such as Sun Yat-sen, Wellington Koo, and C. T. Wang idolized Wilson, whose fame also grew among the general population. American missionaries helped spread the word through pamphlets and sermons and dedicated hymns such as "Lead, Kindly Light" and "Onward, Christian Soldiers" to him. City officials in Foochow and Canton planned statues of Wilson that never were built.

For China was included among the president's failures at the Paris Peace Conference of 1919. Japan kept its Shantung holdings. None of Wilson's pleas for decency or rebukes for the "unclean" diplomacy of power politics could affect certain realities—the existence of those wartime treaties through which Britain and France had guaranteed their ally's Shantung interests and Japanese threats to leave the conference unless they got their way. Nor did Wilson achieve self-determination for colonial populations in the Pacific; another wartime treaty had divided German territories, Japan being assigned islands north of the equator and Britain those to the south. These islands would be ruled as colonies, but Wilson despised that word and arranged for their designation as "mandates" and "trusts" in the text of the Versailles treaty.

These and other Wilsonian failures have been attributed to indifferent preparation of bargaining positions (he knew of the Japanese treaties months before the conference); belief that his "moral suasion" could triumph over power politics, national interests, and other selfish diplomatic practices; and a noncompromising style of negotiation. Perhaps no one—not even Franklin, who had once bargained so cleverly in Paris—could have prevailed against the tangle of interests that dominated the Paris Conference. Wilson's losses might have been quiet ones, of no particular notice amid a shared ineptitude, had they not been introduced by years of promise-making speeches. He had built a towering edifice from which to fall, the resounding effects of which could hardly escape notice. Adulation turned to contempt as the British press singled him out for sneering remarks, Poles sent hate mail, and Italians made obscene gestures at the mention of his name. Parisians who had cheered his arrival soon shouted curses. "What has become of my hero?" asked Daniel Halévy in the December 6, 1919, issue of *L'Opinion:*

> He does not seem to be complete master of the great ideal which was of such service to him in 1917. His words have evoked it; his rhetoric has carried away the people. But he has raised hopes which he cannot fulfill and created situations which he cannot control. Is he, like the magician in the *Thousand and One Nights,* a prisoner and a victim of the forces which he has conjured?

News of the Shantung decision touched off riots in Chinese cities as crowds chanted mixed themes of hatred for Japan and scorn for the source—man and nation—of earlier hopes. American policy was not in a position to balance Chinese losses against gains by the Japanese. The latter, although victorious at Paris, had reasons of their own for not admiring Wilson. Unintentionally he had wounded their racial pride. They recalled his weak response in 1913 to the California Alien Land Law, aimed against Japanese ownership of property, and at Paris he had been maneuvered against his will into opposition to a racial-equality resolution, sponsored by Japan in hope of protecting its nationals against discrimination when they traveled abroad. Nor had Wilson, in his stern if ineffective statements of Asian policy, even hinted that he understood Japan's need to find food and raw materials on the mainland. He wanted the Japanese "to develop perfection and consent to starve in pious peace," Arthur Bullard wrote in *Harper's Monthly* of November 1919. Above all, the president was remembered for long-winded opinions that had adorned every Japanese-American encounter from the Twenty-one Demands to the conference in Paris. Always he had amplified issues in terms of good and evil; there were no shadings. Each time he referred to China's decent, republican, peace-loving people, that country's rival was forced to endure the contrasts. Open door statements, while irritating in the past, had never before been uttered with such lofty disapproval. "Wilson thinks we are an evil country," the Tokyo *Yomiuri* said on April 4, 1919. "He thinks we are low, crawling creatures."

Taft and Wilson had made their contributions to Japanese-American antagonism, but crusades, whether for money or morality, were going out of style. Twenty years of problem-solving—inspired by imperfect conditions in Cuba, the Philippines, China, the Caribbean, and Europe, not to mention the domestic challenges of a Progressive Era—had left Americans tired from their labors and in a mood to relax.

VI

. . . And Out

TWO DECADES OF HYPERACTIVITY gave way to two decades of
lethargy, a tempo that—before it faltered in the 1960s—would
interest graph makers seeking uniform ridges and depressions in
the country's diplomatic mood. An American retreat from responsibility, called isolationism, coincided with a Franco-British retreat
that was known as appeasement by the latter 1930s. In the twenty
years after the World War, Far Eastern nations, in particular
Japan, enjoyed a rare opportunity to conduct their affairs without
much Western interference.

There was a difference between appearance and reality. Imperial
territories had never been larger, thanks to the Versailles treaty.
Occidental compounds in Chinese cities underwent little surface
change. Surrounded by squalor, the clusters of foreign hotels,
commercial houses, and government centers were imposing, clean,
free of unpleasant odors. Croquet lawns and tennis courts were
neatly mowed. Traders, civil servants, and their ladies still sipped
gin and quinine on club terraces, and smartly uniformed bandsmen
still performed on the bunds. But the comfortable era of "ex-
trality" was passing into history. Four years of war had drained
European nations of men, money, the power to dominate, the urge
to colonize. Huge empires were ever more difficult to maintain due
to independence movements and rising costs of providing more
and better services for colonial subjects. Military budgets were cut
to dangerous limits as Europeans, and Americans too, took refuge

in the belief that future wars would be prevented by the League of Nations and other collective security devices of the 1920s that were reassuring at least in their profusion. If commerce continued, the prewar quest for concessions suffered from lack of funds, declining enthusiasm, increasing Chinese nationalism, and finally from Japanese aggression. Westerners relinquished a number of their leases and spheres until the Second World War wrote an end to the old system.

The United States moved from overinvolvement to underinvolvement. Leadership of the Allied cause in the war's last year, followed by Wilson's attempts to reshape the world in his country's image, had represented an unprecedented and unmanageable diplomatic activity. Within months of Wilson's return from Paris the country was rushing backward toward isolation, an equally perilous extreme that would continue during the twenties and reach a critical stage by the late thirties. Editors, congressmen, and professors conveniently rediscovered George Washington's advice about the importance of ocean barriers. Their timing was poor; the Republican twenties had nothing to do with the Federalist nineties. Weakened Europe had better excuses than did America for shying away from international troubles. The United States had emerged from the war as the strongest and potentially the most influential nation in the world. It possessed a large navy, increased industrial capacity, an undecimated population, and a financially enriching creditor relationship with Britain, France, and other wartime borrowers.

Why was this enviable position wasted, allowed no use in the service of national interest and world peace? Cynicism, hurt feelings, and fatigue are often cited as withdrawal symptoms. Cynicism, that juvenile relative of idealism, was the prevalent mood of Americans on campuses, in Greenwich Village, and in Paris south of the Seine. The horrors of war, they said, had convinced them that mankind was incorrigible and all causes meaningless; they wandered rootless, without sustenance from standard prewar beliefs; they were a lost generation and life was a wasteland. Their litany of misery was learned mainly from poems and novels, for few of these privileged Americans had experienced trench warfare, and the liveliness of their bull sessions on cynical subjects attested to the superficiality of their spiritual wounds. There were also the pouters who felt that Europeans, having accepted America's help in the war, had ungratefully spurned its ideals at the Paris Conference. Therefore, they reasoned, the world deserved no more help; let it go its own reprehensible way. (The old theme of self-righteousness has served all kinds of policies, isolationist as well as interventionist.) For others the European rejection of Wilsonism merely offered a welcome excuse to retire from exhausting careers as Galahads and Good Samaritans, these having been popular conceptions of America's foreign and domestic roles during the Progressive Era.

But a dominant American mood can never be described in wholly negative terms. There were far more boosters than knockers in the 1920s. Idealism was irrepressible, flaunted in the notion that the world had at last found enlightenment and entered a Utopia of eternal harmony and peace. The more desperately people placed their faith in the League of Nations and other defective mechanisms of international cooperation, the more they scorned military preparedness, tough-minded diplomacy, attention to power balances, and other "obsolete" practices of foreign relations. Pacifists and internationalists ignored ugly aspects of the real world, took the high road away from the hard work that stability always demands, and thereby made their own contribution to isolationism. "There is a grave danger in unshared idealism," said Senator Lodge, the old Darwinist who knew that most nations were habituated to viewing the world as a fiercely competitive arena.

Isolation was practiced as well as preached. Presidents Harding, Coolidge, and Hoover spent little time and effort on foreign policy. Following Wilson's lead, they refused to recognize Soviet Russia, thus ignoring a historic balancing factor in the Far East as well as in Europe. Shortsighted economic policies—high tariffs and insistence upon war debt repayment—estranged Britain and France, weakened them further, and reduced their usefulness in diplomatic concerns they shared with the United States. There were consistent refusals to allow the country to join the League of Nations or any of its adjunctive bodies.*

Isolation did not mean literal detachment from world affairs. Americans conducted trade, continued to send and accept ambassadors, and, oddly enough, participated in more conferences and signed more international agreements than in any previous decade. But what was the effect of busy negotiations and heaps of documents? Most of the agreements were pudding soft, with operative clauses even less effective than those of the League. In some cases weak pacts replaced strong ones, providing easier escape from responsibilities. The end effect of "paper security" was to formalize the isolationist instinct. Was this also its prior intent? Undoubtedly some statesmen sat down at conference tables for the purpose of creating documentary excuses for reducing military budgets and slipping out of bothersome involvements. Other diplomats honestly believed, along with credulous populations, that the array of clauses would be respected by those who signed them and that security would be guarded by honor and goodwill in welcome contrast to the hard, unlovely devices of the past.

The ideal of peace and a bargain-rate army and navy did not seem contradictory to President Warren G. Harding and Secretary of State Charles Evans Hughes. In July of 1921, four months after assuming office, they sent out invitations to a disarmament conference to be held in Washington the following November. It soon became clear that the invited nations were reluctant to discuss the reduction of their armies or weapons such as artillery, machine guns, tanks, and airplanes, not to mention such naval weapons as cruisers, destroyers, and submarines. Only battleships were seriously on the agenda. This was because they were obsolete,

---

* While symbolic of isolationism, America's snubbing of the League is now—half a century later—seldom viewed as a critical decision, a fateful step toward future tragedy. The League's critical moment had come in 1919, in Paris, with Wilson's invention of a machine without working parts. At that time no one laughed, for the size and beauty of the machine obscured the question of its utility. American membership might even have been harmful, adding to the prestige of an illusion.

skeptics commented, citing a recent test in which Colonel "Billy" Mitchell's rickety airplanes had destroyed an expensive battleship.

"The way to disarm is to disarm," Hughes lectured on November 12, the first working day of the Washington Conference. Relentlessly he drove the delegations toward a plan that would destroy more battleship tonnage, as a British observer said, "than all the admirals of the world have sunk in a cycle of centuries." The battleship was defined as a vessel of 10,000 tons or more and carrying guns larger than eight inches in caliber. (This rule included aircraft carriers even though this new class was not yet regarded as important by many naval experts.) Possession of battleships and carriers was to be limited according to a ratio of 5:5:3:1.67:1.67, applied to the United States, Britain, Japan, France, and Italy. The two favored nations could maintain no more than 525,000 tons of battleships and 135,000 tons of carriers; Japan's figures were 272,000 and 81,000, France's and Italy's 175,000 and 60,000.

During following months naval officers "wept without shame" as they attained assigned limits by breaking up their own fleets. Yet most admiralties managed to preserve their best battleships, reducing tonnage by scrapping those ships that were obsolete or obsolescent; the destruction of some modern ships, nearing completion, helped the United States reach its quota. Meanwhile a new arms race began as shipyards in major nations laid keels for vessels not covered by the treaty—submarines, destroyers, and so-called heavy cruisers, the largest class not limited by the agreement, displacing from eight to ten thousand tons and armed with eight-inch guns. Americans, as Hughes said, were more interested in the spirit of disarmament than its mathematics; for that reason, along with governmental thrift, the United States abstained from the new competition in naval construction.

The Japanese, unhappy over the ratio assigned them, were partly soothed by an additional clause in the five-power disarmament treaty forbidding further fortification and development of bases in the western Pacific. Britain's nondevelopment pledge covered all possessions north and east of Singapore, while the United States promised not to add to the meager defenses of any base west of Hawaii—Midway, Wake, Guam, the Philippines. The economy-minded Harding administration leaped at this chance "to insure the safety of the islands through a firm international agreement." But there were no meaningful limitations on Japan. It promised not to develop certain bases close to the home islands, but everyone knew that these places already were heavily fortified. There was no mention of the Carolines, Marshalls, and Marianas, where Japan would develop strong bases in the 1930s. There were no provisions for inspection and control; any nation wanting to ignore the "firm agreement" could do so. Knowing this, British and American naval officers complained as early as 1922 that the Japanese had been given control of the western Pacific.

Virtual evacuation of Asian seas could hardly be viewed as a reaffirmation of the open door, that theoretical gateway for United States Far Eastern policy. To disown principle, and China too, was unthinkable; yet in an age of withdrawal the State Department longed to be free of its lonely and frequently humiliating commitment. Discovering a solution, the Americans persuaded other nations represented at the Washington Conference to join in a statement of respect for the "territorial and administrative integrity of China." Newspapers hailed the resulting Nine-Power Treaty. Good had triumphed; after two decades of trying to thwart America's single-handed defense of China, other nations now honored that cause by joining it.

In reality the Nine-Power Treaty was an escape from the pointing finger of unilateral responsibility. Multilateral pledges provide a crowd in which to hide; one nation's obligation is divisible by the total number of participants, resulting in a bashful shuffle while waiting for someone else to take a first step toward action. The treaty's only operative clause—to take effect in case China was invaded—required a "full and frank communication between the Contracting Powers concerned." The feeble pact promised China an even less effective defense, if such could be imagined, than that previously accomplished by the United States. But future embarrassments would be multilateral, and that was the main thing.

Also emerging from the Washington potpourri was a four-power treaty through which the United States, Japan, France, and Britain

EMORY & HENRY LIBRARY

agreed to respect one another's possessions in the Pacific region. Any instance of nonrespect would activate a "consultation" among signatories. (In consenting to this agreement, the Senate would insist, somewhat redundantly, that the four-power pact implied "no obligation to join in any defense.") This less than formidable document was designed to replace the Anglo-Japanese Alliance, a security device of real value since its inception in 1902. The British had specified in 1911 that the alliance would be inoperative in event of a Japanese-American war; yet the pact had worried Washington, and its abrogation had long been desired. Postwar Britain, weary of worldwide entanglements, acceded to the American proposal. Rejection by an old friend hurt Japan's pride but encouraged the more ambitious of its military leaders. They recalled that the alliance had been useful in some cases but an irksome restraint in others, as in the Twenty-one Demands crisis of 1915. Now, with the tie severed, Japan would no longer need to display the correct behavior that London expected of an ally.

With a long prayer the Washington Conference was ended on February 6, 1922. It had produced severe cases of writer's cramp, nine thick volumes of treaties, and increased budgets for government printing offices if not for admiralties and defense ministries. Announcing entry into Utopia, newspapers predicted anything from five hundred to a thousand years of peace; the New York *Times,* with customary restraint, placed the figure at a hundred.

Tokyo's estimates were even lower. Journals and mobs denounced the setbacks they believed Japan had suffered at Washington—the "second-rate" battleship ratio, expanded Western support for China, loss of the British alliance. Yet there were those in the army and navy ministries for whom early resentment gave way to the feeling that the conference, with its timid Four-, Five-, and Nine-Power security pacts, had given Japan unprecedented opportunities in mainland Asia and the western Pacific. And it was possible to believe by the mid-twenties that even the conference's most detestable result, the 3:5 disadvantage in capital ships, need not mean permanent inferiority to the American navy. For it was obvious that the sponsor of the Washington Conference—a nation wanting to believe in the disarmament "spirit" and lulled by its 5:3 advantage—was not translating that advantage from paper to steel. The United States was not building the types of ships allowed by the ratio system, while Japan worked at everything permitted by the treaty. The pagoda masts of the *Fuso, Yamashiro, Mutsu, Nagato,* and other dreadnoughts were almost always part of the scene at the Kure or Yokosuka shipyards; if new battleships were forbidden, the old ones allowed by treaty could be modernized on a yearly basis. Construction centered on heavy cruisers of the *Furutaka* class, the envy of admiralties everywhere, and new destroyers and submarines were considered the best in the world. The naval general staff had protested the Washington Conference system in 1922 but was happy enough with it by 1924, when several strong warships were added to the fleet. Without that system and its soporific effects, the Americans would be building too.

Alarmed over the construction of so many foreign cruisers and smaller craft, President Calvin Coolidge in 1927 called for restrictions on all vessels in accordance with the existing battleship ratio. A Geneva Conference in that year failed to agree on the Coolidge proposal, and a worried American government responded with plans to build some twenty-five heavy cruisers. Pacifists were enraged by their country's lapse in setting good examples but grew calmer when it became apparent that Congress, especially after the economic collapse of 1929, intended to appropriate money for very few of the projected cruisers. Concentrating on the depression, the administration of Herbert Hoover (1929–33) practically ignored the navy, a practice of "abysmal ignorance" according to the Navy League, which in turn was ridiculed as a clique of retired admirals and other warmongers.

Japanese military leaders of the 1920s took some advantage of wishful thinking in the United States, and while their "cunning" was not entirely a Hollywood invention of the future, the calculations of a few admirals should not be magnified into that all-too-customary view of an entire nation moving along a plotted course from Port Arthur to Pearl Harbor. Japanese life in the 1920s was anything but monolithic. It was a time of diversity, contrasts, confusion, when circumstance more than calculation directed the country's history.

Japan had graduated from the paternalistic democracy of the Meiji period. The revered and strong-willed Mutsuhito died in 1912, his advisers gradually lost their influence, and the end of the war in 1918 diminished the status of generals and admirals. The prestige of the crown was low during the Taisho reign (1912–26), due in part to an emperor with mental defects so embarrassing to the government that a regency became necessary in 1921. The regent, Crown Prince Hirohito, was admirably intelligent, but a fascination for marine biology left him little time for affairs of state. Liberal reforms flourished in the Taisho period—manhood suffrage, increased civil rights, the appearance of a two-party system, and a strengthened Diet (parliament).

The *Weekly Reader,* distributed in schools throughout the United States, illustrated its articles on Japan with pictures of Fujiyama, trays of silkworms, and maidens in kimonos, holding paper fans or parasols, strolling in temple gardens of exquisite beauty. Unphotographed were the slums and factories pressing in on the gardens. Mountains, while picturesque, so dominated the small country that only a few coastal regions were suitable for the major activities of a population numbering over fifty million and climbing by a million each year. In these enclaves along the east coast agriculture was being driven out by industrial complexes and growing clusters of cities; customs old and new were mixed in a dim and odorous atmosphere not yet called air pollution.

Along with smoke, industrialization meant population growth, rising national power, and also certain *nariken* ("new rich") customs for the executives of Mitsubishi, Mitsui, and other business combines. Wealthy Japanese imported Bentley and Pierce-Arrow motorcars and built ostentatious mansions. Middle-class businessmen sometimes called themselves Babbitts, assumed to be an honorable title denoting success, and developed a Rotary-Kiwanis-Lions network throughout the empire. Evidently a "DAR post" existed in Kobe until its originator discovered what the initials meant. The Taisho democracy was another of those periods of infatuation with Western customs. Crown Prince Hirohito permitted himself to be photographed in knickers and holding a five-iron. Young men wearing raccoon coats took surreptitious drinks from hip flasks, though there was no Prohibition. The Charleston was popular. *Mobo* ("modern boy") held hands in public with *moga* ("modern girl"), with her cloche hat, bobbed hair, and short skirt.

Conservatives felt that too much *"ero, guro, nansensu"* ("eroticism, vulgarity, nonsense") might bring on a display of divine wrath, and a few could not hide their satisfaction—those not living in the Tokyo-Yokohama area—when this center of iniquity was almost totally destroyed by an earthquake. The disaster of September 1, 1923, the worst of its kind in Japanese history, killed over 100,000 people. Dollars, medical supplies, and building materials arrived from the United States in such quantity that the Japanese praised America as the kindest of nations, paying back Japan's generosity after the San Francisco earthquake of 1906.

The impression was reversed only a few months later when the United States Senate, through a vote of seventy-one to four on April 16, 1924, declared all Japanese "ineligible to citizenship," shutting the door tightly to further immigration. Much of the language congressmen used to support the bill—vile beyond anything uttered during California's anti-Japanese legislation of 1906 and 1913—was quoted in the press of the injured country. There were acts of *hara-kiri* during the massive and turbulent protest demonstrations of July 1, 1924, which the Tokyo government had designated as Humiliation Day and Hate America Day. Undoubtedly the immigration act had some effect on the way the Japanese felt about their own democracy, for this political system was famously identified with a nation capable of painful discriminatory actions. But the environmentalist thesis that an insensitive slap ruined a promising experience, turning it toward the ways of delinquency, ignores other causes and suggests that the Japanese had no responsibility in determining their future. Economic changes, emotions both bitter and proud, leaders both strong and weak—a short-rooted democracy would be vulnerable to the play of circumstance in the years that followed.

Hirohito became emperor in 1926, and the first years of his

Showa ("Enlightened Peace") reign saw the appearance of pressures that would bring about an aggressive, militaristic state in the 1930s. Showa began at a time when increasing numbers of Japanese were restless, regarding democracy as chaotic, inefficient, decadent, and disappointing in its accomplishments. Liberal governments seemed confused by economic problems, weak in foreign policy, permissive of *nansensu* with its rowdyism and immorality. The latter twenties saw the appearance of books, newspaper articles, films, and speeches calling for a return to tradition. Buddhism and Christianity lost ground to state Shintoism, specifying the emperor as the divine focal point not only for Japan but for the world. Army prestige was aided when some of its officers rejected modern decadence, associated themselves with the *samurai* codes of *bushido* (the spartan "way of the warrior"), and demanded stronger foreign policies. Fanatical nationalists—many of them members of the Native Land Loving Society, the Blood Sworn, the Black Dragon, the Black Cherry—distributed propaganda and by the early 1930s were resorting to assassination and other means of intimidating government leaders.

Such pressures were stronger than they might have been because of the presence of economic hardship, that time-tested enemy of democracy, which by its nature is unable to solve problems through quick decisions. With agricultural acreage decreasing and the population growing, industrialism had carried the load with its heavy flow of manufactured exports exchanged for imports of food and raw materials. But the tariff walls of the 1920s, around the United States and other nations, were not easily penetrated. An economic downturn, sensed as early as 1927, developed after 1930 into the world's worst depression. It was difficult for other nations to justify imports from Japan when consumer buying was too weak to keep their own factories in operation. The collapse of the American silk market, once that nation's hard times had begun, was the greatest single blow to Japan's economy. Banks failed, industries laid off workers, and some unemployed Japanese preferred suicide to starvation.

With the export-import cycle breaking down, imperialism could be seen as a matter of life or death as well as of national pride. A colony could be forced to provide needed supplies; no tariff negotiations were necessary. Yet the liberal leadership of the 1920s had voluntarily reduced Japan's presence in Shantung, ignored Manchurian development, and pursued a policy of friendship toward China. This "inattention to interests" worried hungry civilians and infuriated certain army officers who were listened to more and more as they called for a dynamic policy on the mainland. Was it too late for such a policy? In the old days Americans and Europeans in their several ways had tried to block the growth of Japanese concessions in southern Manchuria; now, amazingly, China itself was applying pressure—a China boasting new unity, national feeling, and power that might possibly be capable of preventing new concessions and even eliminating those in existence.

While generally unwise, isolationism could offer some rewards; at least the United States was not involved in a more than usually uproarious period of Chinese history—the revolution of the Nationalists and the beginning of their civil war with the Communists.

A kind of republican regime, anemic and ignored by most Chinese, had maintained itself in Peking following the death of Yuan Shih-kai in 1916. Real power was local, in the hands of provincial warlords who either used it responsibly or as a means of banditry. Sun Yat-sen, whose base was Canton, was among the weakest of the regional leaders. Not known as a military expert, he had been pushed out of the presidency in 1912 and since that time had instigated several unsuccessful coups and revolutionary movements. Yet he retained respect as a fountain of ideas. His Three Principles drew Nationalists, Democrats, and Communists to Canton, where they joined a debating society known as the Kuomintang party.

Sun's ideas moved leftward after 1923, when Western powers prevented him seizing control of the Canton Customs; besides, Soviet Russia was the only nation that bothered to send him money and military advisers. Members of the young CCP (Chinese Communist party) joined the Kuomintang; the physical appearance of two of these, Chou En-lai and Mao Tse-tung, would inspire *Time* magazine to call them Laurel and Hardy a few years later. The less dedicated leftist Chiang Kai-shek—to be described by *Time* as strikingly handsome after he clarified his politics—had studied military science in Japan; knowledge of this subject enabled him to rise rapidly in a Kuomintang (Nationalist party) badly in need of it. A journey to Moscow in 1923 left Chiang with a general distaste for communism with the exception of its remarkable discipline.

Using Russian techniques, Chiang improved the Kuomintang army and became its commander not long after the death of Dr. Sun in 1925. Moving out from Canton, Chiang's forces gained control of the southern provinces and then marched north, their general following by train. His railway car was the site of an important political transformation—conferences with the wealthy Charles Soong and his most attractive daughter, forcible ejection of Russian advisers and CCP members from the train, an unfulfilled threat to behead Mao. Considerable slaughter attended the arrival in 1927 of Nationalist troops in Nanking. Some foreigners were among the victims, an experience so discouraging to American missionaries that hundreds of them left China. But labor unions and Communist enclaves in the Yangtze cities were Chiang's main targets; the CCP forces retreated south to rugged country in Hunan and Kiangsi provinces.

For Americans on alert for admirable qualities in China, Chiang was a happy find. He appeared to be strong enough to unify China, and his politics improved with each passing month. The Baltimore *Sun* on January 10, 1927, detected in the Nationalists "a spirit as fine as anything that animated the revolutionary troops of George Washington." The president, Silent Cal Coolidge, said Chiang was "all right," and Secretary of State Frank B. Kellogg called him "apparently a leader of the Moderates." Kellogg stepped up verbal support for the Nationalists as American periodicals increased coverage. A scowling, shaven-headed Chiang made the cover of *Time*. The magazine's young publisher, Henry R. Luce, had been born of missionary parents in Shantung; he loved China, idolized the Nationalists, and for the rest of his life would promote their interests in his powerful publications.

In the light of future events, Chiang's greatest triumph of 1927 occurred in early December in Shanghai's Majestic Hotel before a congregation of 1,300 foreigners and Chinese wearing frocks from Paris and morning coats tailored in London. Seldom in history had a man arranged a more fortunate marriage. Mayling Soong (she preferred the American spelling until 1948) was as beautiful as Pola Negri, a devout Methodist, educated at Wellesley, and a scion, through her father, Charles, and brother, T. V., of one of China's leading business families. The groom, who had been married before, told reporters that he was studying the Bible in preparation for conversion to Methodism. The attractive qualities of the Chiangs were to influence Sino-American relations for half a century.

The warlords north of the Yangtze offered little resistance, and except for the besieged Communist pocket in south-central China the Nationalists attained their goal of unification in 1928. Chiang selected Nanking as his capital and changed the name of Peking ("Northern Capital") to Peiping ("Northern Peace"). Inheriting China's nominal sovereignty over Manchuria, the new government announced a program of "rights recovery" and hoped to force the Japanese and Russians to give up their concessions in that province. For differing reasons the spirit of nationalism was high in both China and Japan, and a Manchurian clash was almost inevitable.

New York papers broke the news in their early evening editions of August 27, 1928. The Pact of Paris, outlawing war for all time to come, had been signed by Japan, China, the United States, and practically every nation in the world.

The Paris (or Kellogg-Briand) Pact was the result of a series of events set in motion the previous year by French Foreign Minister Aristide Briand. Insecure France needed strong allies; the United States would be an ideal partner but of course was uninterested in exchanging bilateral obligations with any country. The next best thing, Briand calculated, would be a treaty pledging the two nations never to attack each other, apparently a meaningless pledge but in fact creating a special relationship out of which France might develop advantages in the future. While proposing the plan to the State Department, Briand cleverly engaged the support of American pacifist organizations, women's groups, college professors, clergymen, and certain businessmen identified with the peace movement. Public excitement swelled. "God-damned pacifists," Secretary of State Kellogg shouted at one persistent enthusiast. He knew that France was seeking subtle advantages, but he could hardly reject a project so appealing to his country's idealism. He admitted that he did not know what to do; then the answer came.

William R. Castle, Jr., an assistant secretary of state, together with other department officials, advised Kellogg to agree to the treaty—but with the proviso that it be enlarged to include the whole world. In this way a worrisome bilateral tie would be replaced by an arrangement so ridiculously multilateral that it would have no meaning at all; at the same time its appeal to the American public would be vastly multiplied. For once the French had been outfoxed, Castle gloated in his diary, and no one knew it better than Briand. Faced with the work of preparing a massive but useless diplomatic event, the foreign minister would have dropped the whole idea had not it aroused such global enthusiasm.

Four Latin American countries refused to promise not to attack each other, and Briand did not bother to send invitations to Liechtenstein, Monaco, Andorra, Morocco, and San Marino. But all other nations signed or later adhered to a treaty pledging them not to engage in offensive war against one another. No one called attention to the rarity of offensive war in the past century, an age in which moral considerations had required nations to arrange maritime or border incidents after which they could conquer their victims in the name of self-defense. Nor was the broadly multilateral nature of the pact considered a weakness. Indeed, it was the "truly grandiose scale of this biggest and best of all treaties" that the press hailed in describing the American public as exhilarated, euphoric, and intoxicated with peace.

The Paris Pact was important only as parody, illustrating in grotesque form the spirit of an age—diplomacy at the mercy of public opinion, isolationism rationalized by idealism, faith in a system of peace guaranteed by nothing more than hundreds of signatures on dozens of documents decorated with yellow wax seals and silk ribbons of many hues. Most Americans believed in paper security for the remainder of 1928 and well into 1929, for the system worked marvelously so long as it was never tested.

In July 1929 the Chinese Nationalists began their rights recovery program by taking over Russia's Chinese Eastern Railway; they occupied stations and imprisoned ticket sellers and local subcommissars of transportation. The Soviet government sent troops into north Manchuria and reappropriated the railroad. While fighting was in progress, some sixty-one nations—signatories of the Paris Pact minus Russia and China—waited for one of their number to step forward and force adherence to pact rules. Edging forward, Henry L. Stimson, who was President Hoover's secretary of state, twice reminded the belligerents that offensive war had been declared illegal. But no policemen were available; besides, Russia explained that it was fighting a defensive war and so did China. The fact that the United States still had not recognized the Soviet Union prompted Maxim Litvinov, deputy commissar for foreign affairs, to joke with newspapermen, how could Stimson say anything to a nation that did not exist?

Other jokes began to circulate at the expense of a paper security that had not even been able to stop "a trifling war over a few Communist railroad stations where ladies and gentlemen have to use the same comfort facilities, if any." The twenties closed on a moment of doubt that could not yet be called disillusionment.

Tilt

Between 1931 and 1939 acts of aggression by Japan, Germany, and Italy were not effectively opposed by Britain, France, and the United States, the chief sponsors of mutual security systems. The British and French ended their appeasement by going to war with Germany in September 1939, but this could not prevent the *blitzkrieg* sweeps of 1940–41—conquests which, as shown on maps in American newspapers, turned important regions of the world from white to black, the latter imprinted with Nazi swastikas and Japanese sunbursts. Through it all, the balance of power tilted, the security of the United States became ever more precarious; and through it all, Americans chose to cling to their isolationism, the character of which changed from the idealism of the 1920s to a paralysis of disillusionment, bitterness, and fear. The persistence of this mood until the country was itself attacked late in 1941 is more difficult to understand than is the fact that it was present in the early thirties, the most severe period of the Great Depression when individuals thought mainly of their own survival and the administrations of Hoover and Franklin D. Roosevelt were preoccupied by the concerns of internal catastrophe.

Paper security, along with popular faith in it, underwent a first major test beginning in 1931. In the summer of that year patriotic young officers of the Kwantung Army, the name Japan gave to its permanent occupation force in the Manchurian concessions, decided to provide their country with a regular colony. The civil government in Tokyo knew little or nothing of the scheme and in any case could do nothing to curb the action that followed; army influence was strong and the nationalist societies had already begun their forceful intimidation of politicians who opposed expansion. On the night of September 18, 1931, an explosion apparently damaged some track of the South Manchuria Railway near Mukden. The Chinese had placed the dynamite as part of their rights recovery program, Japanese officers claimed, but the latter evidently contrived the incident as an inexpensive salute to the Pact of Paris. A "defensive" operation began within hours of the explosion, Japanese soldiers attacking Chinese troops near Mukden and fanning out from the railway zone with the aim of absorbing all of south Manchuria.

As the offensive continued throughout the autumn of 1931, it earned the silent disapproval of President Hoover, Secretary Stimson, and leaders of other nations involved in peace-keeping mechanisms. In private conversation Stimson was wistful, sort of wishing that public opinion would allow American military intervention, wishing the League of Nations would act, hoping some government would invoke the Paris Pact. He was wary of a first step himself, for few nations had followed him into the railway station embarrassment of 1929. But Stimson's patience was known to have limits. With Hoover's help he worked out a statement later called the Stimson Doctrine and proclaimed it to the world on January 7, 1932; the United States would not recognize the aggression because it was illegal.

The Japanese did not halt their Manchurian envelopment, and in late January and February they struck Shanghai with a series of "punitive raids" by land, air, and naval units. Stimson retaliated with an eloquent description of Japan's failure to abide by "principles of fair play, patience, and mutual goodwill." His purpose, the secretary explained, was to compel the sensitive Japanese to bow to the moral force of world public opinion. Privately he admitted that he was an expert on "the oriental mind." Yet the only effect of his psychology was to strengthen Japanese nationalism, resentment of the United States, and the dangerous impression that Americans always talked but never acted. Other governments, knowing they could not act, declined to call attention to their impotence.

Stimson was not really alone in his cause, as he learned on February 24, 1933, about a week before the end of the Hoover administration. After an exhaustive but leisurely study of the crisis, the League recommended—"recommend" was the strongest form of action allowed by its Covenant—that Japan return Manchuria to Chinese sovereignty. The Japanese representative, Yosuke Matsuoka, told the League assembly that as Christ was martyred on the cross, so was Japan being crucified by the international organization. He then led his delegation out of the chamber. Some weeks later, passing through the United States en route back to Tokyo, he said the nations had taught Japan to play poker, but after having won most of the chips they had declared the game immoral and taken up contract bridge.

Having completed their occupation of south Manchuria, the Japanese had renamed it Manchukuo and instituted a regime subservient to their wishes. The new emperor of Manchukuo, who had been the boy emperor of China at the time of the Manchu fall in 1912, was given a throne quite literally made in Japan. At the time of the League's recommendation against Manchukuo the Kwantung Army was already engaged in expanding its borders southwest to within fifty miles of Peking and north into the Russian sphere of Manchuria. The Soviet government, beset with internal woes, meekly relinquished concessions that Russia had held since the 1890s, though Tokyo in 1935 made a token payment for the Chinese Eastern Railway. Pressed back to their own country, the Russians resisted further Japanese expansion in a series of skirmishes and battles fought from 1936 to 1939 along the Manchukuo-Siberia frontier.

Belief in the treaty system, if any remained after the Manchurian affair, could not survive the mid- 1930s. The Japanese had ripped up the Paris Pact and the Nine-Power Pact and were doing the same to the disarmament and island fortification clauses of the Five-Power Pact. The Nazi party leader Adolf Hitler had become Germany's führer in 1933 and by 1936 had ended reparations payments, announced rearmament, and sent his army into the

Rhineland, thus erasing three major clauses of the Versailles treaty. The League suffered another humiliation in 1935 when it failed to deter the Fascist dictator of Italy, Benito Mussolini, from conquering the African nation of Ethiopia. Other documents appeared. The German-Italian Pact of Steel was signed in 1936, as was the Anti-Comintern Alliance between Germany and Japan. These treaties fell short of a binding alliance system, but the amity displayed among the three militaristic nations was regarded as ominous in other countries.

As troubles developed abroad, so did an abundance of isolationist excuses in the United States. Americans ruminated bitterly over the results of their last overseas involvement—its failure to create that better world of which Wilson had dreamed; the treaties it produced now a litter of scraps; the loans to Britain and France no longer being repaid, reason enough not to help them again; the great profits acquired by banks, munitions manufacturers, and other "merchants of death," much resented in the mid-thirties after a Senate committee investigated the last war's causes in a sensational if simplistic manner. Such disappointments reassured an escapist era that all wars were evil in origin, futile in result, and therefore unnecessary. That the experience of 1917–18 must never be repeated was further taught to the millions of Americans who watched celluloid versions of Erich Remarque's *All Quiet on the Western Front* and Ernest Hemingway's *A Farewell to Arms.* (While the latter film was at the height of its popularity, Hemingway was viewing totalitarian power firsthand, changing his mind, and writing that sometimes it was necessary to fight; but *For Whom the Bell Tolls* would not be made into a movie for many years.) Recalling the chain of events that had drawn the country into the last war, Congress passed Neutrality Acts in 1935, 1936, and 1937. These restricted arms sales, loans to countries at war, the presence of American ships in waters where they could be attacked, and other conditions that might possibly lead to a repetition of the 1917 involvement.

A less brooding style of reality avoidance was displayed in the policies of Cordell Hull, named secretary of state when Roosevelt entered the White House in 1933. Hull ignored the disillusionments of the age and maintained a faith in the innate decency of all mankind. After each of their aggressions, German and Japanese leaders received one of Hull's "Sunday School lessons," scolding them for breaking treaties and other misbehaviors. "Principles of right conduct," the secretary said, were "as vital in international relations as the Ten Commandments in personal relations."

Hull was a bore, a reminder of Wilson, in the opinion of President Roosevelt, who was worldly, pragmatic, no firm upholder of commandments either in public or private life. FDR seemed an isolationist too, at least during most of his first two terms. "I hate war," he assured the voting public in 1936. "I have passed unnumbered hours, I shall pass unnumbered hours thinking and planning how war may be kept from this nation." His isolationist statements stemmed neither from idealism nor disillusionment but from practical judgment of priorities. In his opinion the nation's greatest enemy was the depression, which could not be attacked effectively if he estranged Congress and the public by adopting unpopular foreign policies. Events in Asia and Europe concerned him increasingly—he recognized the Soviet Union in 1933 partly because he wanted to be in touch with a nation he considered most likely, because of its geography and ideology, to oppose further Japanese expansion; he toyed with the idea of "doing something" about Mussolini's invasion of Ethiopia in 1935; he signed the Neutrality Acts most reluctantly, and dared to display anger in public when Japan attacked China again in 1937—but his diplomatic practice remained weak, tethered by depression politics and by his own appreciation of American military impotence. On this latter problem he could do a little, very little as it turned out during his first presidential term. He managed to build a few ships for the navy through means that foreshadowed a future relationship with the voting public that was not entirely apart from dissimulation. He might hate war but knew that steel was more useful than philosophy in its prevention.

The relationship between American and Japanese naval planning passed through several stages from 1921 to 1941; through one means or another Japan always gained, gradually closing the gap from 5:3 to 5:5. In writing of militaristic pressures in that country, historians usually have referred to the army, viewing the navy as a force for moderation and restraint. But recent research has shown that the Imperial Japanese Navy—or at least an influential faction of officers in its ministry and general staff—was hardly a model of restraint. Early in the twenty-year period the navy was conscious of rivalry with the American navy, promoted that rivalry, and contributed significantly to the coming of war in 1941.

Several considerations—among them the decline of British interest in the Pacific and the fact that Americans, despite their isolationism, were known for their changeability—influenced the contingency plans of the IJN during the twenties, causing it to designate the United States as the probable opponent in any sea war of the future. This assumption was played out in annual fleet maneuvers. The IJN was traditionally wary of operations ranging far from support bases, but should offensive tactics be necessary the Japanese believed that they could always "determine when the offensive effort has reached its optimum point . . . one step before the line at which the tide of battle turns," a rueful comment by historian Masanori Ito, writing far in the future and looking back on the tragedy of admirals who had broken their own rules. But in the twenties and thirties the general staff believed that impetuosity, in war as well as peace, was the guiding characteristic of Americans. Thus Japan's basic strategy must be defensive, calculating that the United States Navy would race past "points of optimum advantage" in a brave charge toward the home islands, expose a lengthening supply line to submarine attack, then suffer its own Tsushima in a battle fought somewhere within the Mariana-Marshall-Caroline web of strong Japanese bases. It was a very good guess. The United States Navy's contingency Orange Plan of the 1920s and '30s was nearly identical to Japanese expectations, and the Americans were fortunate that unforeseen events in 1940 and 1941 would cause both navies to change strategies.

Japan's defensive strategy was based in part upon its assigned 3:5 inferiority in battleships and carriers. But in terms of overall naval power the Japanese were closing the gap, building vessels not covered by treaty and modernizing those that were, while the Americans worked less diligently at modernization and took little advantage of the permissive document written in Washington. Indeed by 1930 the IJN had grown quite fond of the treaty with its hypnotic effect upon the United States. In that year the general staff estimated the actual power ratio at 4:5 and still climbing in Japan's favor.

But also in 1930 the United States decided to act in its own naval interest, not by building ships but by changing the rules of the treaty. At the London disarmament conference American influence was at last instrumental in extending the ratio system to vessels smaller than 10,000 tons. Heavy cruisers were to be limited at 5:5:3, light cruisers and destroyers at 10:10:7, and Japan received parity in submarines. Yet the Washington treaty's loopholes were now closed, and to the Japanese there seemed no escape from permanent inferiority.

The London Conference of 1930 marked a turning point for Japan. Within months the navy's "fleet faction"—its most determined leader was probably Admiral Kanji Kato of the general staff—was embarked upon a campaign to destroy the Washington and London treaties. While some admirals were sick of disarmament restraints of any kind, others realized that an abrupt end to the treaty system might shock the industrial giant across the Pacific into an enormous shipbuilding program, an unlimited arms race that Japan could never win. Therefore it was considered best to work toward abrogation of the present treaties and to replace them with one granting the IJN full parity. The abrogation campaign prospered through speeches, patriotic songs that emulated "Rule, Britannia," books recounting Togo's deeds at Tsushima, support from Tokyo's four leading papers, and finally through sobering news from Washington.

Pressure from Roosevelt brought about naval acts in 1933 and 1934 that projected construction of the more than one hundred ships needed to bring the navy up to limits allowed by the two treaties. Congress might talk about ships but soon proved unwilling to fund them; in a depression, it was said, money was needed for other things. Roosevelt agreed but had a trick in mind. One of his antidepression devices, the Public Works Administration, had been set up to build dams, highways, post offices, and other projects aimed at reducing unemployment. FDR managed to include a couple of aircraft carriers and half a dozen cruisers in PWA-funded programs. The impecunious Navy Department was allowed a consultive role in projects that, as the president convinced Congress, were exactly like dams and post offices, designed to make work, not war. Naval strength increased—the ships would be completed in 1937 and 1938—but still remained far below levels permitted by the treaties.

Taking the acts of 1933–34 at face value, the Japanese feared they had lost their best chance for naval equality; the Americans seemed to have awakened and would soon turn 5:3 into physical actuality. Why wait for this to happen? Civilians in the cabinet, along with Premier Keisuke Okada, submitted to the navy's Kato faction, and the government formally renounced the Washington and London treaties on December 30, 1934. Another conference at London in 1935 addressed itself to the task of writing a new disarmament treaty. The effort failed when the United States and Britain turned down the expected Japanese demand for full parity. Delegates of the Imperial Japanese Navy walked out of the conference on January 15, 1936, as newspapers announced the death of disarmament and predicted a frantic race in naval development.

The Japanese navy had not expected to succeed in the conference of 1935–36 and understood the meaning of its destruction of the disarmament system. It was a gamble against odds, a chance to win an unlimited arms race only if stronger nations failed to take the challenge seriously. Japan had improved the odds by jumping the starter's gun. Among new ships designed in the early thirties and begun well before the end of the 1935 conference was the 72,000-ton superbattleship *Yamato*. Sister ships *Musashi* and *Shinano* (later converted to a carrier) would follow amid a mighty array of vessels of all types as Japan's rate of naval building increased by over 500 percent between 1936 and 1940. British, German, and Italian shipyards were working three shifts by 1937. Only America obliged Japan, lagging in the race until Congress authorized two 35,000-ton battleships of the *Washington* class in 1937. The following year saw the beginning of impressive authorizations of 45,000-tonners and multitudes of cruisers, carriers, destroyers, and subs; yet for two more years the isolationists who dominated Congress withheld construction funds. By 1940 Japan reached quantitative parity with the United States Navy, and the newer ships of the IJN meant qualitative superiority. In that year the Americans began a serious building program, one promising to regain superiority, whereupon Japanese admirals had to start thinking about an "optimum time" for war. Repugnance for military weapons in the United States, both during the treaty period and after it ended, created an invitation to war.

A spirit of adventure, mixed with tense self-consciousness, dominated Tokyo in 1936; the feeling was similar, old-timers said, to that which had prevailed before the war with Russia in 1904. It was no small thing to have ended the disarmament system and challenged the British and American navies, historically awesome in the eyes of Japanese even if recent statistics indicated otherwise. People spoke of taking a big step, breaking the course of modern history, entering an unknown future. All one could do was work hard, sacrifice, and hope. Along with the surge of naval construction in 1936, the economy was placed under controls, strategic raw materials stockpiled, and heavy industry expanded to increase production of munitions, aircraft, and other weapons. Large appropriations for the army would allow it to grow from twenty divisions in 1936 to over fifty in 1941. Speech making and programs of national music drew enthusiastic crowds as propaganda conditioned the country to anticipate news of conquests. Until 1941 prime ministers would be proexpansionist civilians or frightened men who remembered the words of Premier Okada: "I am going to behave myself from now on." Okada's comment followed his narrow escape from assassination on the night of February 25, 1936, when seven public figures—considered symbols of democratic inefficiency—were shot and stabbed to death by a clique of army officers. Although the murderers were executed, they were hailed as martyrs in an aftermath that enhanced the prestige of the army's extremist faction.

After extending the border of Manchukuo southwest to the Peking vicinity in 1933, the Japanese had never felt constrained by that border. In the next four years businessmen, settlers, and army units filtered into northern Chinese provinces that surrounded Peking. Some Japanese expected to absorb north China without a fight, pretty much as they had Manchuria.

Chiang Kai-shek's nationalist program of rights recovery had been unimpressive. Instead of ejecting foreigners from Manchuria, he had lost the entire province, having been preoccupied at the time, pressing a victorious war against his favorite enemy, the CCP, in south-central China. In 1933 the regiments of Mao Tsetung began their Long March, a wandering retreat that took them far to the west, almost to Tibet, then north to a permanent haven in the Yenan region of Shensi province.

The Communists had suffered mightily during the Long March—Mao's wife, reportedly with fourteen wounds, was one of its few female survivors—but the caves of Shensi offered a defensible position. Mao rested, studied Marx and military tactics, pondered the double problem of Chiang and Japan, and fell in love with the Blue Apple (Chiang Ching), a Shanghai movie actress who had come to entertain the troops. The two were married after Mao dispatched his wife to a Moscow hospital to have her wounds looked after. Meanwhile the other Chiang had followed the trail, bringing the civil war to Shensi. Near the town of Sian in December 1936, he himself was captured by troops friendly to the Communists. Under some duress he listened to lectures from Chou Enlai and others about the advisability of the Nationalists and Communists standing together against the Japanese, for Mao's people had begun to worry about Tokyo's threats to eradicate their movement. Chiang agreed to call off the civil war and was released; back in Nanking he reluctantly kept his word, taking the first steps toward a united front with Mao. So began his great dilemma. He knew that he might be losing his last chance to defeat the still weak CCP, but by 1937 the "dwarfs from the East" could no longer be ignored. He shifted Nationalist troops out of Shensi and sent some of them to the Japanese-infested Peking region.

Shots were exchanged between Chinese and Japanese units at the Marco Polo Bridge near Peking on the night of July 7, 1937. Fighting spread as the Japanese brought in troops and weapons, including aircraft. The invaders were surprised by resistance much stronger than in Manchuria several years earlier; without having intended to fight a major conflict in China, they were becoming involved in one. Hoping to end the war quickly, they expanded it in mid-August with crushing land, sea, and air attacks in the Yangtze valley, the power center of the Nationalist government. The struggle for Shanghai, Soochow, and Nanking drew the world's attention.

Secretary Hull reminded Tokyo, as if it could forget, of America's attitude on Chinese territorial integrity. While the theme never changed, there had been stylistic variations since 1900; Hull's was a shade Tennessee Bible Belt, less seraphic than Wilson's, sermons hurled rather than delivered. He had difficulty remembering, as had Stimson, that China was no longer a solely American burden. Since 1922 it had been the duty of Nine-Power Treaty members to "communicate" whenever China was invaded, an obligation fulfilled at Brussels in late 1937 in a conference that had no result.

At least Roosevelt was prepared to act, or so it appeared when he spoke in Chicago on October 5, 1937, and called for an international quarantine of aggressor nations. He soon seemed to lose interest, probably because his speech drew furious editorials and a mountain of protest mail, and within a week he was shrugging off requests to explain his idea. There was some favorable response to the speech. A few companies quarantined the Japanese by promising not to use their products, and at rallies on college campuses coeds threw their silk stockings and panties into bonfires. Joseph C. Grew, the American ambassador in Tokyo, was dismayed by what he described as Hull's moral thunderbolts and Roosevelt's equally futile quarantine plea. He wrote that the Japanese in their current temper respected power and power alone; empty threats were taken as signs of weakness and only encouraged hostile policies. Grew believed that Washington must make a decision: act against Japan or stop scolding it.

Although Japan was well on the way to totalitarianism, it continued to suffer from the individualistic diplomacy of its patriotic military officers. On December 12, 1937, aviators spotted the gunboat U.S.S. *Panay* in the Yangtze and sank it with the loss of two

American lives. Roosevelt and his advisers discussed economic quarantines—even of a sort imposed by a naval blockade of Japan—but before any decision was reached, Tokyo apologized for the incident and offered reparation.

The more cautious of Japanese leaders worried as the war gained momentum, getting out of hand in several ways. The army took Shanghai, Soochow, Nanking, and was extending itself westward along the Yangtze by the end of 1937. Each new victory stimulated the frenzy of celebrating throngs in Japanese cities; they chanted *banzai* and awaited more battle reports. The intoxicating mood affected the army in a way that horrified the world. Orgies of beatings, rapes, and bayonetings took place in Shanghai and Nanking as between 200,000 and 300,000 civilians were killed. The conquerors took all of China's major ports and moved inland along the main rivers and railways. In 1938 the advance was halted, not by Chinese soldiers but by the limited size of the invading army, which was hard put to occupy the vast territories already taken.

Chiang had set up a new capital in the shabby western city of Chungking, almost five hundred miles from the enemy's farthest point of advance along the Yangtze. The fighting slackened; the Japanese army had more of China than it wanted, and the Chinese army after performing well in earlier battles had little taste for more. Chiang's strategists turned to publicity campaigns, concocting news flashes of titanic struggles to keep the great prize Chungking from falling to the Japanese. These and other informational activities—certainly justified by Chiang's interests—were aimed mainly at the United States but achieved little more than some small loans, private China-relief collection drives, and formation of an American Volunteer Group of aviators (the Flying Tigers) who would not reach China until late in 1941.

Affection for China, which had influenced American public feeling and diplomacy since the beginning of the century, entered a passionate stage with the Japanese onslaught of 1937. Chinese checkers became the rage, and children collected bubble-gum cards showing the slaughter in Shanghai and other scenes enclosed in each penny pack of "War Gum." Hull's voice trembled when he spoke of China's troubles on the radio and for newsreel cameras, and his opinions were seconded and more by ministers, home-coming missionaries, congressmen, and journalists. A poll by the American Institute of Public Opinion released on June 18, 1939, showed 74 percent of Americans in favor of China, 2 percent for Japan, and the rest undecided. Henry Luce's *Life* magazine specialized in atrocity photographs taken in Shanghai and Nanking, and his *Time* described China's battles, real and imaginary, as a series of Verduns. Generalissimo and Madame Chiang were *Time*'s "Man and Wife of the Year" for 1937, and their pictures again made the cover. China's peasants were heroes too. Pearl Buck's best-known novel, *The Good Earth,* sold more than two million copies after publication in 1931; its movie version, seen by an estimated twenty-three million Americans, was released during the Shanghai attack in 1937 and provided faces for the "faceless masses" whose sufferings were described in the papers. Under conditions of severe adversity, Mrs. Buck's Chinese were hard working, freedom loving, kind to children, respectful of elders. Her later novels and movies further endowed the Chinese with American traits as they endured the brutalities of Japanese invasion. In lighter vein were the dozens of Chinese detective movies; the wisdom of East and West blended nicely as Charlie Chan, quoting Confucius, solved cases with the help of his Number One Son, a master of American college slang in his letter sweater and saddle shoes. China's united front allowed the Communists a share of the praise; they were fighting as bravely as Chiang's troops, were said to have dropped out of the Comintern, and were "not really Communists at all" but rather extreme liberals and agrarian reformers. Edgar Snow's best-seller *Red Star Over China* typified the theme.

In a culmination of thirty years of declining regard, Japan after 1937 became an object of resentment for its policies and revulsion for the atrocities of its soldiers in China. The words of Hull and others reduced an entire nation to a condition of hardened criminality. Diminutive size was no longer a mark of quaintness as hordes of Japs, Nips, and Monkey Men with protruding teeth and horn-rimmed glasses joined other standard villains in the comics, pulps, and adventure movies. Hollywood's ugliest, most sinister-looking Orientals entered a period of full employment that would last until 1945.

The Japanese were seen as loathsome but seldom frightening; it was difficult to think of them as a threat to Americans. Newsreels showing people in kimonos shaking tiny paper flags and shouting *banzai* were less ominous than those depicting the giant swastika banners and roars of *Sieg Heil!* and *Duce!* in Europe. The American impression of Meiji Japan, of people bowing low and producing inferior copies of Western machines, was strangely persistent. Hadn't the Japanese bowed and said "so solly" after bombing the *Panay?* Wasn't the label "Made in Japan" a sure sign of poor quality, associated with toy counters in dime stores? No wonder Japan had been able to build so many ships in recent years; they were probably made of tin and would break when wound too tightly. Japanese planes were made of bamboo, and the small tanks, seen in newsreels of the war in China, had been found in Cracker Jack boxes. Cartoonists pushed the idea with drawings of a superman Uncle Sam frowning down at slant-eyed lilliputians, saying, "Any morning before breakfast" or other words to the effect that Japan could be licked easily and quickly. By the start of the 1940s both nations were displaying that tendency, acquired over many years from different sources, for underestimating each other.

Any worries about the Japanese stemmed from their association with other warlike peoples. There was nothing to laugh about in perceptions of Germany, Italy, and Japan as a combined force. The Anti-Comintern Pact between Germany and Japan existed from 1936 to August 1939, when it was voided by the Nazi-Soviet Nonaggression Pact. Japan was then without formal allies until September 27, 1940, when it joined in a Tripartite Pact with Germany and Italy (the Rome-Berlin-Tokyo Axis). This alliance was to produce little cooperation between Berlin and Tokyo in the five years that followed, but in 1940 there was every reason to assume that its members would act in concert—as indeed they would have done had the random play of circumstances and shifting interests so dictated.

For all the feelings it aroused, the war in China seemed remote and lacked the frightening quality of concurrent events in Europe. Britain and France practiced appeasement, a word suggesting cowardice to Americans (isolationism meant something different, more like a spirit of independence). Germany and Italy participated openly in the Spanish Civil War, and Germany took Austria, the Sudetenland, then Czechoslovakia. Hitler's Nonaggression Pact with Stalin was a blow, but Americans felt better when Britain and France in September 1939 at last showed some spine in declaring war on Germany after the latter's invasion of Poland. Even so, the situation darkened throughout 1940 and 1941.

Each evening at six o'clock people in the New York area could tune their radios to the dance music of Glenn Miller, originating from the Glen Island Casino, while listeners in Chicagoland could pick up Ralph Ginzberg's string ensemble as it played for early dinner in the Victorian Room of the Palmer House—soothing preludes to the anguish beginning at 6:30, reported through static by William L. Shirer in Berlin, Eric Severeid in Paris, Edward R. Murrow in London, and summed up in the unchanging comment of broadcaster Gabriel Heatter, "Oh, there's bad news tonight." In the spring of 1940 Hitler's Panzer divisions overran Denmark, Norway, Holland, Belgium, and France with an ease that stunned Americans and confused the theme that this war had no more meaning than the last. The Luftwaffe began its assault on Britain, and the Rome-Berlin-Tokyo Axis was announced with great fanfare.

The shadowed portions of newsprint maps expanded in 1941 as Japan moved from China into French Indochina and made no secret of an intent to add the Dutch East Indies, at the very least, to its Greater East Asia Co-Prosperity Sphere. Germany took Yugoslavia and Greece, then ended the Nonaggression Pact with an attack that slashed into Russia and reached the suburbs of Leningrad and Moscow by December 1941. Continental Europe was gone and East Asia was going; Nazi successes in North Africa projected a thrust into the Middle East and, according to a dejected Gabriel Heatter, a future linkup with the Japanese; French West

Africa, the so-called stepping stone to the Western Hemisphere, was available to Hitler whenever he wanted it.

Some historians have suggested, without full certainty, that the Axis war machine eventually would have slowed and stopped without reference to any American action. Perhaps so, perhaps not. But in 1940–41, in view of the Nazi dictator's amazing accomplishments, it was exceptionally difficult to predict the limits of his ability. The scope and pace of change seemed unbelievable, the balance of power had altered crazily, and even those Americans who could not entertain the thought that their country might one day be attacked—"it can't happen here"—had to wonder what diplomacy, trade, travel, and life itself might be like in a world dominated by a dynamic and hostile ideology.

While approving some of Roosevelt's efforts to send supplies to Britain, a majority of Americans remained "steadfastly opposed," in the words of the Chicago *Tribune,* to military intervention. Antiisolationists were astonished, again and again, by public opinion polls. "I guess people are either blind or scared stiff," Wendell L. Willkie could say openly not long after his defeat by Roosevelt in the presidential election of 1940. His comment was inspired by a glance at a newly published poll, one showing a three-to-one preference for staying out of the war, a proportion that would not change significantly until war came the hard way.

Hard Lines

‘ ‘ T HE PEOPLE ARE ALWAYS RIGHT’’ is an adage that cele-
brates horse sense, democratic instinct, and the assumed
fulfillment of Thomas Jefferson's hope for a public education system of exceptional quality. But history has often withheld endorse-
ment, and certainly FDR was a nonbeliever in 1940 and 1941. He
had lost respect for the innate wisdom of public opinion, though he
was much aware of its power. He maintained the isolationist line
in those radio performances he called fireside chats while engaging
the Axis nations with increasing tenacity. He stepped up the pressure until he was practicing some of the toughest policies known to
American history, a diplomacy that contributed to involvement in
World War II. In the light of conditions both domestic and global,
was he justified in his daring diplomacy?

Roosevelt's ‘‘hard line’’ later became the subject of bitter arguments. As historians and journalists of the late 1940s and early
1950s looked back on his behavior in 1940–41, critics described a
conspiracy through which he hoodwinked the public in schemes to
aid the British, even using naval vessels to create incidents that
could involve the United States in a war with Germany; at the
same time, they said, he was trying to enter the war through the
‘‘back door,’’ tormenting Hitler's Asian ally to incite an attack
that would jolt supine America into a fighting mood. He knew in
advance of the attack on Pearl Harbor, the most extreme of his
critics charged, and declined to warn that base on the theory that

only a great catastrophe could destroy isolationism. The accusations seemed so outrageous that Roosevelt's most ardent defenders made the mistake of denying them all, creating one of those moral issues in which one excess begets another. Sadly for Roosevelt's reputation, at least during that early stage of the argument, he appeared to have been either a monster or else a bystander of unforgivable innocence.

After the shouting died, historians still differed over the point at which truth existed between the extremes. Most are now certain that there was no Pearl Harbor plot but equally certain that Roosevelt sometimes worked deceptively and in opposition to the wishes of the popular majority. There were jaunty days—FDR's advisers often judged his state of mind by the angle of his cigarette holder and the speed at which he drove his wheelchair—when he probably hoped that his diplomatic pressures would bring on the war he feared would ultimately be necessary. On other days his confidence was nil, his depression a source of worry to the advisers; he talked of Axis power, the unreadiness of American armed forces, or his inability to lead public opinion and make it comprehend the scope of the crisis. Lacking evidence to the contrary, most recent historians have concluded that FDR preferred to keep the United States at peace while he did all he could to subsidize Britain against Germany and built a diplomatic barrier against further Japanese moves. He did not look forward to war but was certainly willing to risk it with *blitzpolitik* against both Germany and Japan.

The undeniable fact of his hard line remained a topic of debate long after the extreme arguments had been discounted. The United States should not have opposed the Axis, so one theory goes, because Germany and Japan might have wiped out communism in Russia and China and thus eliminated a great concern of the future. Perhaps so, but in 1940–41 the totalitarian right looked far more menacing than the totalitarian left; indeed, FDR's strongest measures against Axis nations came at a time when Russian strength seemed nearly nonexistent, in the summer and autumn of 1941 when the Red Army was fleeing in panic from Hitler's Panzer columns. He made a lesser-of-the-evils decision, one required by his own era just as future diplomats would have to confront the changed concerns of their times.

Nor are the realities of 1940–41 appreciated by critics who look backward from those years and say that Roosevelt should have been kinder to Japan in view of his own country's contributions to the crisis—decades of opposition to Japanese interests, insulting immigration acts, endless nagging and patronizing remarks upon proper behavior that had ignored sensitivities, inducing a sense of persecution and justified anger. Such blunders and harmful attitudes deserve full treatment in any account of Japanese-American relations, but of course they were not wholly responsible for the intense national pride so much a part of Japanese life since early Meiji times, the army and navy ambitions, the jingoistic atmosphere in which militarism thrived, the crazed behavior of soldiers in China, and the swelling concept of vital interests, the latter not unreasonably focused on Manchuria in 1931 but encompassing all East Asia by 1941. At some point during the 1930s Japan crossed a line, entered a phase of its history no longer excusable by past resentments, and assumed a sizable share of responsibility for all that happened later. Even if Japanese aggression had been entirely the creature of a hostile environment—which it was not—Roosevelt's policy could not have been different from what it was; remorse would have been a preposterous response to the demands of national interest in 1940–41.

Roosevelt's aim was to prevent Japan from adding to its power through acquisition of Far Eastern regions rich in natural resources. Neither country sought war, but each underestimated the other and pursued its own hard policy; each kept lines of negotiation open until the very end, believing the other would submit to diplomatic pressure, and each was surprised when the other did not give in.

With the war in China a stalemate by 1939 Japanese leaders faced two questions. The first—whether to continue a war policy—was not seriously argued in the strong military factions of the government. Peace would frustrate the great army and navy being developed, giving these forces and their commanders no chance to prove boasts of recent years, and the Japanese people, thrilled by victories in China, were impatient for others. Nationalism had created a momentum dangerous to try to stop even if the government's current decision makers had wanted to do so.

The second question—the direction of a new advance—took longer to decide. To continue west into China's hinterland would mean expanded occupation duties in largely worthless territory. A northern thrust into Siberia had been the favorite plan of the army, which had so easily taken Manchuria in the early 1930s. Battles along the border of Manchukuo and Russian territories had been fought from 1936 to 1939, and in the latest clash at Nomonhan the Soviets inflicted a surprising defeat on the Kwantung Army, a result kept secret from the Japanese people. The Russo-German Nonaggression Pact of August 1939 occurred at about the time Japanese lines were breaking at Nomonhan. The double blow, political and military, discouraged proponents of the northern advance.

Another plan, a strike toward the Dutch East Indies, had been the preference of the Imperial Japanese Navy. The bad news of August 1939 added some army support to the southern plan, attractive mainly because the Dutch islands of Borneo, Java, and Sumatra were the most important sources of oil in the Far East. Japan imported 80 percent of its petroleum from the United States and naturally wished to be self-sufficient in the useful commodity. The great disadvantage of the southern plan was not that the Dutch would be formidable defenders but that their islands lay in the midst of British, French, and American colonies. Even if the Western powers did not initially oppose the operation, their bases in Singapore, French Indochina, and the Philippines would always present a threat to the long supply lines between the Indies and the home islands. Japanese leaders weighed the pros and cons, gradually developing a decision that was affected by events elsewhere in the world.

Hitler's easy victories in western Europe in the late spring of 1940 interested the Japanese in several ways, inspiring envy and the urge to emulate, an admiration for Germany that enhanced the appeal of the Tripartite Pact to be signed in September, and new hopes for the southern adventure. The Netherlands and France had been conquered and their Asian colonies were up for grabs, not only the Indies but Indochina too. And the British, fighting for survival at home, obviously had little time to think about Singapore. Hitler encouraged the southern interests of Tokyo, where military officers now discussed the attractions not only of the Indies but of Indochina, Malaya and Singapore, and Burma, areas wealthy in oil, tin, bauxite, and rubber. Only the United States seemed capable of resisting, and so far the Japanese were undismayed by the manner of that resistance, notes from Hull on the sanctity of the Four-Power Pact with its insistence upon mutual respect for French, British, American, and Japanese holdings.

Yet Washington was beginning to stiffen its attitude, and news from that capital also affected Japanese planning. The most worrisome reports concerned embargoes on strategic materials that the United States normally exported to Japan and congressional appropriations for the American navy.

Congress gave Roosevelt the power to control exports of vital commodities, and on July 31, 1940, it was announced that Japan would receive no more shipments of aviation gasoline, the stuff that had fueled the bombing attacks on Chinese cities since 1937. In late September 1940 Japan occupied bases in northern French Indochina, seen by Roosevelt as a first step in the feared advance to the south. He responded with an embargo on scrap metal. This was strong policy, shutting off supplies to a nation badly in need of them and warning that other export bans might follow; yet paradoxically it goaded the kind of action it was intended to prevent. Nervous Japanese admirals and generals took inventories of stockpiles and storage tanks. Reserves were limited, and the Americans might at any time decide to shut off trade in all oil products. Now the military talked of the southern plan as a necessity more than a desirability, and because the fuel situation would go from bad to worse, time was a vital factor in gaining the southern resources.

Japanese admirals watched the calendar for two reasons—the implication of the embargoes and also a new naval policy in the

United States. Congress opposed war, but the fall of France and other adversities had convinced lawmakers that a program of national defense would be desirable; among numerous "preparedness" measures were appropriations for much of the naval expansion that had been planned in 1938—250 warships of all classes, work to begin immediately but with prospects dim that many of the vessels could be completed before early 1943. In Tokyo the navy ministry was impressed by the mathematics and graph projections of Admiral Nobutake Kondo of the general staff. Slowly, over two decades, parity had been achieved, and Japan would reach the peak of its naval strength vis-à-vis the United States in late 1941 and keep the advantage for at least part of 1942. After that—for the first time since the Washington Conference—the Americans would begin to gain, their rate of launchings quickening, their enormous building capacity at last used by the appropriations of 1940. If there was to be a war, Kondo concluded, its decisive battles must be fought before the United States Navy received the new ships. The ministry agreed, drawing up a mobilization schedule to be completed in November 1941, and the army began training divisions for war in the tropics.

Ideally, diplomacy would win the southern goals. Ideally, the Americans were talking bravely but did not intend to fight; yet the latter possibility had to be considered as the Imperial Japanese Navy reviewed its contingency plans for war. Since the 1920s strategy sessions and annual maneuvers had been based upon the assumption of a reckless American charge into the western Pacific, to be met and defeated somewhere in the Marshall-Mariana-Caroline network, the advantage being Japan's because of the proximity of support bases. This strategy had to be discarded, for the new southern plan could force the IJN to do battle near Java and Sumatra, much closer to the bases of potential enemies than to its own nearest installation some 2,500 miles away in the Carolines. Losing one advantage, Japan needed another, and most general staff members were content to rely upon the overall naval superiority that the IJN would retain at least through 1942. An additional advantage could be created, in the opinion of Isoroku Yamamoto, the commander-in-chief of the Combined Fleet, comprising the navy's operational forces. He suggested a surprise attack that would destroy as much as possible of the American navy at the outset of war; thus there could be little or no opposition until 1943, when the enemy's new fleets would be available, and by that time Japan would have taken the Indies and developed another defensive network around a ready supply of oil.

During his studies at Harvard and Annapolis, Yamamoto had learned to like Americans and respect their potentialities more than most Japanese leaders. War against the United States would be suicidal, he had often said, making no secret of a lack of enthusiasm that was considered treasonous by nationalist societies. For a time his life was in danger and also that of the geisha Kikuji, his close companion. But Yamamoto was logical. If he could not prevent war, he could at least plan a kind of war that would give Japan its maximum chance for success. In January 1941 he began to work out details for an attack on the main American naval base at Pearl Harbor, all the while hoping it would remain only a contingency plan and that diplomats would be able to solve the American problem.

In the spring of 1941, following passage of his Lend-Lease Act, Roosevelt increased aid to Britain and China. He had compiled a list of exports needed by Japan and was hinting at further embargoes. At the same time Hull spoke to Japanese Ambassador Kichisaburo Nomura about ''respect for the territorial integrity and sovereignty of each and all nations,'' thus resurrecting the question of Japan's invasion of China. Nomura was friendly, agreeing that international morality was a fine thing but stressing his country's economic requirements. The United States should end its embargoes, he said, and exert diplomatic pressure to help Japan secure further quantities of oil, rubber, and tin from Southeast Asia. In such case Tokyo might reconsider its own plans in regard to Southeast Asia and might even agree to peace in China on its own terms. Even if Nomura's proposals had been less vague—he knew that the Foreign Ministry for which he worked had little influence upon decisions in Tokyo—the American government was not inclined to grant economic concessions that could only increase Japan's ability to make war. The unpromising talks continued for months.

The Japanese on July 24, 1941, occupied bases in southern Indochina, a strategic position that increased the threat to the Indies and British Malaya, not to mention the Philippines. Roosevelt countered immediately, freezing Japanese credits in the United States. This meant the end of trade between the two countries, with crude oil the most significant of the products now lost to Japan.

The Imperial Japanese Navy announced that its oil reserves would last only a year and a half under wartime conditions, and there remained the matter of an optimum time for war based on projection of American naval construction. Whatever was to be done must be done quickly. The army stepped up training for war on beaches and in jungles while the navy continued mobilization and prepared for supporting action in the Malaya-Indies-Philippines region. But the naval general staff consistently rejected Yamamoto's idea for an attack on Pearl Harbor, which was considered a wild gamble, risking valuable aircraft carriers for uncertain results. Yamamoto continued to argue and kept up the practice sessions at Kagoshima Bay, in which his carrier pilots were rehearsing dive bombing and torpedo runs under conditions simulating those of Pearl Harbor. Personnel in some of the dive bomber squadrons called themselves "Hell-divers," after the title of a Clark Gable movie that they had enjoyed.

Preparing for war, the Tokyo government clung to the belief that it would not be necessary, even though diplomacy had reached an impasse by August. As the price of resuming shipments of oil and other materials, Washington was now asking Japan to break with the Axis and withdraw its troops from Indochina and China. The appearance of China in substantive American diplomacy delighted Hull, who liked to think that for the first time the open door principle was being enforced by real demands. Roosevelt's mind was on the south, but he did not mind using China to up the ante in his diplomatic poker, stacking the pot so high that a Japanese cave-in would end the game by amounting to a spectacular rejection of aggressive policies. He wanted to force a decision rather than wait while Japan moved step by step toward enrichment in the Indies.

"After all the sacrifices we have made in China," said the minister of war, General Hideki Tojo, "the army won't agree to any withdrawals. Army morale would not survive it." Neither would public opinion accept so face-losing a settlement. The Japanese position, defined during a conference with the emperor on August 6, demanded that the United States stop meddling in China, stop sending aid to Chiang Kai-shek, and agree to resume exports of oil and other materials. In return Tokyo would promise not to use Indochina as a base for a southward advance, but troops would remain there until the conclusion of the war in China, after which Japan would retain an undefined "special position" in Indochina. These proposals hardly ended the threat to the south and were unacceptable to Washington. Each nation was establishing a position it knew the other could not accept in honor or in accordance with interests. Yet in the continuing collision-course diplomacy, each expected the other to turn aside before the moment of impact.

Premier Fumimaro Konoye's hope for a diplomatic solution was stated at the imperial conference of August 6. Hirohito seemed to agree, though could not say so directly (according to tradition an emperor might endanger his divine status by stooping to participate in politics, diplomacy, and other worldly matters). Normally he revealed his opinions through implicit nods or grunts, but in this case he read a poem of obscure meaning that could be interpreted as favoring further negotiations. War Minister Tojo, nervous about time passing while oil supplies dwindled, gave Konoye six weeks in which to gain Japan's demands through diplomatic means.

Konoye immediately proposed a "leaders' conference" between Roosevelt and himself. Eleven days went by before Washington replied that a conference would be possible only if the Japanese agreed in advance to discuss issues that the latter had already proclaimed to be not open to negotiation. Konoye persevered, telling Ambassador Nomura to keep pressing Hull for a settlement. In reporting his failure, Nomura said that China had become very important to the secretary of state, who would not budge on that issue. When after six weeks Konoye told the cabinet of his own failure, General Tojo forced him to resign. On October 18 Tojo himself became premier, the last step in a long process of influence, then dominance, then formal control of the government by the military.

At about the same time the navy general staff agreed to Yamamoto's Pearl Harbor plan. He had argued for months, trying to assure other officers that an attack on Hawaii was not foolish, did not mean an attempt to invade the United States, but was necessary to the agreed-upon thrust to the south. In mid-October, after the admiral had threatened to resign, the general staff weighed his value to the service and decided to let him have his way. Yamamoto then conferred with Tojo and the army general staff, most of whom had wanted to begin the southern attack on the first day of December. Yamamoto asked for an extra week of preparations and a date was specified: December 7 at about 8:00 A.M. Hawaiian time. From his experience in America, the admiral explained that the United States Navy usually worked a five-day week and that most ships would be at their berths over the weekend; besides, most personnel would have hangovers on a Sunday morning.

All units of the special task force had assembled at Tankan Bay in the snowy Kurile Islands by November 22. Vice Admiral Chuichi Nagumo commanded a fleet that included the navy's six largest carriers, two battleships, three cruisers, nine destroyers. On November 26 the fleet pulled anchors and headed southeast at a speed that would bring it within striking distance of Hawaii on the night of December 6–7. Heavy seas, cloaking mist, and rain prevailed, just as Yamamoto had hoped in choosing an approach from the north at that time of year. The assault was to take place according to plan unless the flagship *Akagi*'s wireless received a certain message from Tokyo. Nagumo's sailing orders of November 25 had included the statement: "Should negotiations with the United States prove successful, the task force shall hold itself in readiness forthwith to return and reassemble."

After having blown the whistle on Konoye's diplomacy, Tojo had decided to try some of his own. With the war schedule arranged, further negotiations would lose no time and there was always the chance they might succeed. Saburo Kurusu was sent to Washington as a special envoy to assist Ambassador Nomura. Both negotiated in good faith, not knowing of the military timetable already in operation. Tojo urged them to hurry. "Absolutely no delays can be permitted. Please bear this in mind and do your best."

From November 5–20 the Japanese repeated demands formulated earlier while Hull stuck to the position that the embargos might be dropped only if Japan evacuated Indochina and China. Nomura and Kurusu delivered their government's "absolutely final proposal" on November 20; the United States must give Japan a free hand in China, stop aiding China, send Japan required quantities of oil and help it gain other oil and resources from the Indies, and stop demanding that Japanese troops be withdrawn from Indochina before completion of the war in China. Nothing had changed except that Nomura and Kurusu had been empowered to make one concession; Japan was willing to shift its forces from southern to northern Indochina, an implication that the drive to the south would be called off if all other demands were met.

For the first time since issues had hardened, Hull did not immediately reject a Japanese proposal. For a few days it appeared as if pressures had finally succeeded in causing one of the adversaries—the United States—to lose its nerve and buckle. Nomura and Kurusu heard that the American government was considering a modus vivendi, a group of concessions aimed at avoiding war at least for the present. In Tokyo there were mixed feelings among the military, poised and waiting for the December 7 signal; the more cautious among them were elated, thinking Japan had won without having to resort to war. Yamamoto, not obsessed by the master plan that could make him a hero, looked forward to sending the radio message that would cancel the Pearl Harbor attack.

Meanwhile Hull deliberated with American chiefs of staff and key subordinates. No one had been taken in by Japan's concession on placement of troops in Indochina, for these could shift from south to north and back again whenever Tokyo wished; besides, Indochina was not the only site from which the Japanese could strike toward the Indies. Yet any "final proposal" had to be seriously weighed. The military chiefs, unprepared to fight and wanting to buy peace for at least a few more months, suggested a concession on oil exports. Hull too was worried, yet to agree to ship oil without sticking to the China and Indochina demands would be "virtually a surrender." Cables arrived from Chiang Kai-shek and the British prime minister, Winston Churchill, stating hopes that the United States would not back down. Roosevelt made the decision, telling Hull to reject the "final proposal." The crestfallen Nomura and Kurusu were informed on November 26 that Japan must evacuate China and Indochina and until then there would be no oil.

Throughout the autumn of 1941 the Japanese public had grown restless with unproductive diplomacy, and the press had demanded positive action. By early November, Ambassador Grew was warning of the "explosive atmosphere" in Tokyo and of current Japanese emotions that he called insane by American standards and capable of producing an "all-out, do-or-die attempt, actually risking national *hara-kiri*. Action by Japan . . . may come with dangerous and dramatic suddenness."

The cabinet in Tokyo decided that Nomura and Kurusu should continue negotiations even if no one expected a last-minute capitulation by the United States. It was feared that a sudden break in the talks might warn the Americans that war was imminent. The two ambassadors, still knowing nothing of the coming attack, saw Hull several times during the first week of December but to no avail. Nor was Roosevelt successful in a cable to the emperor on December 6; his message, a plea for peace but uncompromising on issues, would have changed nothing even if Hirohito had received it prior to the outbreak of war.

How much did the American government know of Japanese plans for war? Ambassador Grew, along with embassy and consular officials at several posts, sent a mixture of facts and rumors to Washington throughout the autumn of 1941. British intelligence helped a little. Russia's agent in Tokyo, Richard Sorge, picked up information that might have warned Washington about the Pearl Harbor plan, but the results of his espionage were not forwarded from Moscow to the American government. American intelligence was better at gathering than analyzing. A great vacuum cleaner called MAGIC drew in thousands of scraps of information during the three months prior to war. A colonel in army intelligence had organized a group of experts who broke Japan's Purple Cipher through which diplomatic and military communications were sent by radio, and MAGIC was the code name given the army-navy cryptography teams that intercepted, decoded, and passed on messages for scrutiny by higher authorities.

Knowing that Japan might attack was not much of a problem. No intelligence experts were needed to understand Japan's oil crisis and deduce that action would probably follow American rejection of the final proposal. MAGIC usefully reported the quickening tempo of Japanese military activity after November 26. Washington alerted army and navy commanders in the Pacific and elsewhere. A message to all bases on November 24 warned of "a surprise aggressive movement in any direction." At Roosevelt's order a "final alert" was sent on November 27, and this was underlined the same day by yet another dispatch "to be considered a war warning . . . an aggressive move by Japan is expected within the next few days."

Other warnings followed—of an attack that seemed imminent but without specifying where it was likely to take place. What was the matter with MAGIC? Hadn't it gathered any information concerning the direction in which the Japanese would strike? The answer is yes. Numerous messages had been intercepted—diplomatic traffic and radio reports to Tokyo from Japanese spies in Hawaii— providing clues that Pearl Harbor would be the target. But MAGIC was indiscriminate, gathering other clues from which could be inferred coming attacks on Vladivostok, Sitka, Malibu Beach, Panama, Samoa, the Philippines, Guam, Singapore, the Dutch Indies, Hong Kong. MAGIC could not analyze the significance of all it collected. As Charlie Chan had said in 1939, "My brain grows numb; a thousand clues are same as no clues at all."

Washington's urgent alerts, while general and sent to bases everywhere, should have been taken more seriously by army and navy commanders in Hawaii. Why so many bleary eyes on the morning of December 7? Why no air patrols, no guns manned, inexperienced personnel at radar posts? With MAGIC babbling incoherently, the decision-making process had reverted to guesswork aided only by long-standing assumptions. The Japanese wanted the Dutch East Indies; therefore they would attack in that direction. The lowly Japanese were afraid to fight the United States, much less risk action at its most powerful base; therefore Pearl Harbor was safe.

A Honolulu businessman who enjoyed Sunday flying circled his small plane over central Oahu. It was almost eight o'clock and the morning was sunny, with only a few banks of cumulus. Emerging from one of these, he found himself in the midst of a formation of military aircraft marked with scarlet circles. The pilot was so startled that he almost crashed, even though the squadrons ignored him. A few minutes later the Japanese were over Pearl Harbor. As Yamamoto had promised, the scene below was one of serenity. No smoke arose from the funnels of battleships moored two-by-two close beside Ford Island. There was no antiaircraft fire, no climbing pursuit craft. Like the battleships, the planes on Hickam Field were tightly clustered, a protection against sabotage, which was the only type of Japanese activity expected in Hawaii. Yamamoto's aviators accomplished their tasks according to the torpedo and bombing tactics they had practiced for almost a year. Out of 353 participating aircraft, all but 29 returned to their carriers. Shortly after noon, still undetected, the IJN task force retired to the northwest.

Behind at Pearl Harbor the battleship anchorage was burning wreckage. The *Arizona* had blown up, and the capsized *Oklahoma* was also a total loss. The *California* and the *West Virginia,* having sunk in shallow water, were later raised, repaired, and returned to action, as were four other damaged battleships. The raid had removed eight capital ships from service, damaged ten other vessels, destroyed or badly damaged 230 aircraft, killed more than 2,400 Americans, and wounded 1,300. There were two consolations. Japanese bombs had missed a critical target, tanks containing over four million barrels of oil; also, through no fault of Yamamoto's fliers and much to his own sorrow, the aircraft carriers *Lexington* and *Enterprise* were at sea at the time of the attack.

Japanese historians have debated the wisdom of Yamamoto's strategy. As intended, it removed the United States Navy as a serious opponent in the march to the Indies early in 1942; yet that navy was showing signs of good health long before 1943, the year of its predicted resurrection. The failure of the attack to destroy or even reduce the American carrier force—a matter of circumstance or imperfect planning?—would prove disastrous to Yamamoto's Combined Fleet only a half year after the start of the war. The Pearl Harbor strategy also destroyed American isolationism, that sturdy ally of Japan's forward policy. What if the December attack had been limited to the Dutch empire, which was its main goal? Could Roosevelt have persuaded Congress and the public that Java and Sumatra were worth military defense at a time when no such defense had been afforded France, Britain, and China? Had Japanese leaders not given in to Yamamoto, they could have told Washington, we are staying in China, we are taking the Indies, and what do you propose to do about it? The long-anticipated diplomatic surrender might well have occurred at that point, forced on Roosevelt by an isolationist Congress, press, and public.

Millions of radios reported the news from Hawaii during the afternoon and evening of December 7, and in those hours public opinion broke sharply from the course it had pursued for two decades. Congress needed no persuading next day when it voted for war. British officials were ready to declare war on Japan even before they heard that their own Asian colonies had suffered air raids; they hoped for a quick American declaration against Germany and Italy. If there remained congressional doubts on the latter issue, a decision became unnecessary when Germany and Italy on December 11 declared war on the United States. The Tripartite Pact was a defensive alliance, and the circumstances of December 7 did not require Hitler to aid Japan against the Americans. He acted in the spirit of the Axis alliance and hoped—forlornly as it turned out—that the Japanese would reciprocate that feeling and join his war against Russia.

"My God, they've dragged us into it again," moaned an isolationist congressman when he heard the Pearl Harbor news while leaving a New York Giants football game. Indeed, America seemed blameless to the furious millions listening to radio tabulations of casualties and descriptions of smoking ruins. It was not a time for historical reflection. That would come much later in arguments over the necessity of Roosevelt's tough policies and, much more importantly, in musings over the interplay of diplomatic extremes, in this case the consequences of twenty years of underinvolvement in world affairs.

Violent
Redressment

ACCORDING TO EUROPEAN DIPLOMATS of the eighteenth and nineteenth centuries, theirs was the job of "redressing the balance of power," tirelessly adjusting and manipulating to prevent shifts of weight that might endanger peace and/or the security of their own societies. If there was a better way of running the world, they hadn't discovered it. With few exceptions they did their work well, maintaining peace or employing miniature wars that in themselves were intended to be tools of adjustment. They would have been appalled by the shoddy craftsmanship of twentieth-century diplomacy whose amateurs and absentees had brought about the necessity for an expensive, unpredictable, and immensely violent form of redressment.

But World War II was not all that bad, at least not for Americans on the home front. The bitterness and fear of the thirties was replaced by the simplicity of total war—absence of internal wrangling and confusion, paychecks with time-and-a-half for overtime, and a sense of unity and participation even if one did no more than squash tin cans for scrap drives or buy war bonds. For better or for worse, the spirit of the early 1940s would never be repeated, and millions of Americans, not excluding ex-servicemen, would remember "the big one" with nostalgia.

It was too big, too serious, to be called fun; yet the struggle against the Axis was a deeply satisfying experience, the playing out of drama in which the forces of darkness seemed invincible and disaster loomed before the tide turned and democracy's cause celebrated in triumph. Unlike the previous war with its trench stalemate, this one swept from continent to continent and over thousands of miles of islands. Despite their tardy entry Americans soon had reason to believe that they were leading the way, their industrial might, superior weapons, and millions of soldiers and sailors the decisive factors in the rescue of civilization. The war would end on a note of ebullient confidence that could lead to hopes far different from isolationism.

For roughly a year after the United States entered the war, Hitler's mobile forces retained the offensive, pushing to the Volga in Russia and almost to the Nile in North Africa. Americans remembered Pearl Harbor but considered Germany their most important enemy. Much to the disappointment of Chiang Kai-shek, Roosevelt and his military chiefs agreed with Churchill that Europe was the first priority of Anglo-American efforts. Plagued by submarine wolf packs that sank ships in record numbers in 1942, convoys carried American troops and equipment to Britain. In November 1942 Allied units landed in Algeria and pushed into Tunisia, where six months later, in conjunction with the British Eighth Army driving from the east, they trapped and destroyed the Nazi presence in Africa. Sicily was then taken and Italy invaded in the summer of 1943. The Americans and British knocked Mussolini's government out of the war before they were slowed by German defenses, which took advantage of the mountains and narrow width of the Italian peninsula. Public attention shifted to more colorful campaigns. After winning at Stalingrad on the Volga, Russian armies began moving toward central Europe, eventually attaining a rate of advance that worried their Anglo-American allies. The latter landed in Nazi-occupied France in June 1944, fought on the beaches, broke into Normandy, took Paris, and raced eastward in a *Blitzkrieg* that by early 1945 had entered a beaten Germany.

But during the half year after Pearl Harbor—before the victories began and when the war's outcome was uncertain at best—news was consistently bad, and most of it came from the Far East. This was the period of Japan's lightning war, an advance so rapid and magnificently coordinated that it stunned Americans, who were in the habit of underestimating the Japanese. In Washington there was regret over having agreed to Churchill's Germany-first strategy.

Within hours of the Pearl Harbor assault, Japanese bombers attacked Wake, Guam, Hong Kong, Singapore, and air and naval bases near Manila, where the commander in the Philippines, General Douglas MacArthur, was no better prepared for battle than were his colleagues in Hawaii. Tojo's army invaded Thailand and landed on the Malay Peninsula. Britain's two most powerful capital ships in the Far East, the *Prince of Wales* and the *Repulse,* cruised north to bombard the Malaya beachhead. Attacked by Japanese planes, both dreadnoughts rolled over and sank; unlike the American battleships at Pearl Harbor, the British vessels had been at sea, ready for action, and their demise provided another lesson in the old argument between advocates of air power and those of surface fleets. Aviation would dominate the naval war in the Pacific, giving battleship fleets little chance to confront one another.

In December the Japanese took Guam, Wake, Hong Kong, and landed on Luzon near Manila. MacArthur abandoned the capital of the Philippines and led his American-Filipino army to the Bataan Peninsula. Proclaiming "I shall return," the general escaped in early March and made his way to Australia, where he was named Allied commander in the Southwest Pacific. Bataan held out until April 9, 1942, and the island fortress of Corregidor in Manila Bay until May 6. Across the South China Sea the Malaya campaign had ended on February 15 when the British surrendered Singapore.

Newspapers in the United States and Britain, explaining the disasters, said that troops on Bataan and Singapore had fought gallantly against overwhelming numbers of Japanese soldiers; skilled Allied fliers, facing great odds, had downed five or ten Japanese crates for every loss of their own, and scores of enemy ships had been destroyed. A popular song described how the American pilot Colin Kelly had sunk the battleship *Haruna* with a single bomb down her funnel. Much later it became known that the *Haruna* had not even been damaged and, moreover, that fast Zero fighters had swept Allied planes from the skies with ease and that the defenders of Bataan and Singapore had outnumbered the invaders but had been unable to match Japanese training and morale.

With the Philippines and Singapore eliminated as flanking threats to the southern advance, the Japanese could fulfill the goal that had inspired their war. In March they conquered Java, areas of Borneo and Sumatra, and other East Indian repositories of oil and other resources. At the same time another objective was being accomplished—occupation of Burma and cutting of the Burma Road, the route by which China had been receiving supplies.

At this point the Japanese army and navy had won every goal mentioned at even the most optimistic of prewar meetings of the cabinet and general staffs. But unhappily for Japan strategic planning was giving way to emotion as a director of operations. Army and navy officers boasted "as if drunk with wine," sharing the exhilaration of the Japanese people over a series of victories so one-sided that they had humiliated the nations of the West and atoned for seventy years of patronizing and insult. Early 1942 was the proudest period of Japanese history, more satisfying than the days of Tsushima when only Russia had been taught the lesson. "We thought we were invincible," a Japanese woman recalled years later on the BBC television series "The World at War." The Americans and British "seemed weak and inferior and we thought that we could win everywhere." While the men were overseas, women gladly became farm workers, rail hands, locomotive and trolley drivers, laborers in factories and mines. Recordings of "Umi Yakuba" and other songs played over loudspeakers in stores and factories urged further women's sacrifices in support of troops fighting in the distant tropics.

> *Across the sea, corpses in the water;*
> *Across the mountains, corpses in the field.*
> *I shall die only for the emperor,*
> *I shall never look back.*

Theaters showed newsreels of laughing soldiers hoisting the Rising Sun over former American and British strongholds and long lines of enemy prisoners, uniforms in shreds and heads bowed as if in shame. Radio stations interspersed victory reports with the national anthem, never boring though heard two or three times an hour on especially glorious days.

1 4 5

Under such conditions Japanese leaders made no effort to halt the offensive. Some talked of taking Australia as convoys of troop transports moved beyond Java and Borneo to the comparatively worthless islands of the Celebes, New Guinea, New Britain, and the Solomons off Australia's northeast coast. In the battle of the Coral Sea, fought near the Solomons in the first week of May 1942, the American navy sank the small carrier *Shoho* while losing the heavy carrier *Lexington.* Japan celebrated another victory, but the Americans had fought with a tenacity that worried Admiral Yamamoto. He was convinced that his country was overextending itself.

Shortly after the battle of the Coral Sea the naval analyst Masanori Ito began a series of articles in the *Chubu Nihon* of Nagoya, warning against a "victory disease" that might carry Japan past "the optimum point of offensive effort" and place it in the same kind of trap that its strategists of the 1920s and 1930s had prepared for the United States Navy. Military forces were dangerously scattered and supply lines long and vulnerable, for some of the recently captured islands were nearly 4,000 miles from home. Ito's articles were unpopular, and an army officer advised him to write no more of them.

Yamamoto's concern was the naval defensive perimeter, now running south from Burma to the islands just north of Australia, east to the Solomons, then north through the Pacific between Wake and Midway islands. How could he defend a line 11,000 miles long? The Americans could choose one of dozens of targets and attack while Japanese squadrons were at other points along the perimeter. The line would be safe, the admiral believed, only after the enemy's carriers and other units that had survived Pearl Harbor could be lured into a battle that would mean their destruction. He decided to attack Midway, the American outpost halfway between Wake and Hawaii; while Yamamoto had no plan to invade Hawaii, he guessed that his enemy would fear such a move and thus commit its remaining ships to a "decisive battle."

The battle near Midway, June 3 to 6, indeed was decisive. Yamamoto had seven battleships, including the 72,000-ton *Yamato,* and some seventy cruisers and smaller ships. Few of these ves-

The Second World War
in the Pacific

⟦▷⟧ Japanese advances
◀━ Allied advances
◀--- Allied air operations

sels saw action in an engagement involving the opposing carrier
fleets—four of the six large carriers that had launched the Pearl
Harbor raid and on the American side the *Yorktown, Enterprise,*
and *Hornet.* The defenses of the Japanese ships seemed impreg-
nable, Zeros and antiaircraft fire knocking down entire squadrons
of attackers. With another victory in sight the Japanese grew careless, more leisurely than usual as they refueled and rearmed planes

during a lull in the fighting. Racks of bombs and torpedoes and gasoline lorries were exposed on carrier decks when a small group of American dive bombers put in an inconvenient appearance. In the devastation that followed, the *Akagi, Kaga,* and *Soryu* were destroyed in a matter of minutes, and the *Hiryu* was attacked and sunk several hours later. Along with the four carriers Japan lost 332 planes and about as many veteran pilots; this meant, as Yamamoto realized, the loss of air superiority in the Pacific. The Americans lost the *Yorktown* and 147 planes in a battle that turned the course of the war in their favor.

Returning to home ports after Japan's first naval defeat in modern history, Yamamoto's crews were interned for several months to guard against any news of the disaster reaching the press or public. The government announced a great victory at Midway, and the customary celebrations commenced throughout the country.

Meanwhile the frightening success of the Japanese during the first months of the war had forced Washington to modify the Germany-first strategy. While most of the American effort remained concentrated on Europe, more men, equipment, and ships were sent to the Pacific than plans had called for. The first counterattack began on August 7, 1942, when American marines came ashore on Guadalcanal in the Solomons. Tokyo decided to fight for this far-flung outpost, reinforcing its garrison by some 30,000 men. New troops and supplies had to be delivered at night, Japan having lost control of the air. Fleet surface actions were illuminated by flares, searchlights, and burning ships. One night the Allies lost four heavy cruisers—three American and one Australian—while scoring nil against enemy ships. Other battles ended the existence of the carriers *Wasp* and *Hornet,* but the Japanese carrier *Ryujo* was sunk and also the battleships *Hiei* and *Kirishima.* On Guadalcanal the jungle fighting was fierce, with bayonet skills as necessary as rifles and machine guns, and the island was not secured until February 1943 when the Japanese evacuated their 13,000 survivors.

By this time the Americans were arguing offensive strategies. Admiral Chester W. Nimitz, navy commander-in-chief in the Pacific, preferred to approach Japan from the southeast, bypassing some islands but capturing others for use as air bases from which

Japanese cities eventually could be bombed. The Nimitz plan turned out to be the most important, ultimately, in ending the war. But MacArthur, the proud Southwest Pacific commander, insisted upon his own idea, a route through the larger land masses of the Solomons, New Guinea, and the Philippines. His clashes with Nimitz were notorious until late in 1943 when Roosevelt confirmed that both strategies would be acceptable.

While MacArthur's forces were moving slowly through the harrowing terrain of the Solomons and New Guinea, in April 1943 Americans took revenge on the enemy they hated most, the man they knew had planned the Pearl Harbor attack. During the entire war they enjoyed the advantage of being able to read Japanese codes and from one intercepted message learned the time when Yamamoto was expected to arrive for an inspection visit to a base in the northern Solomons. P-38 fighters met the admiral's plane and shot it down.

Nimitz's campaign was underway by November 1943 when the Americans lost nearly a thousand men killed and another 2,000 wounded in an invasion of Tarawa, a tiny island in the Gilberts. In the following year the admiral carried out his system of bypassing some enemy islands and attacking others, taking Kwajalein and Eniwetok in the Marshalls and Saipan and Guam in the Marianas. The Japanese navy steamed out to defend Saipan but was handicapped by the inexperience of its carrier pilots, many of whom crashed while taking off from or landing on flight decks. In what Americans called the "great Marianas turkey shoot" Japanese naval forces were diminished by over 400 planes and three carriers, one of them the Pearl Harbor veteran *Shokaku*. Most island invasions followed a uniform procedure—pulverization of the beaches by aircraft and by naval guns after which troops landed and fought battles in which defenders in concrete pillboxes usually preferred death to surrender.

MacArthur announced his return to the Philippines on October 20, 1944, and was photographed wading ashore on the island of Leyte in the wake of his assault forces. A truly courageous IJN decided to try for another decisive battle, even though such an attempt probably would be suicidal considering that the Americans

149

had concentrated over fifty carriers and two dozen battleships—the shipyards at home had more than fulfilled the goals of the 1940 appropriations—in the Pacific by late 1944. The Leyte battle was marked by the sinking of two American light carriers; a rare, old-fashioned sort of surface action in which battleships raised from the mud of Pearl Harbor leveled their heavy guns on a charging Japanese column, which lost the battleships *Fuso* and *Yamashiro* and the heavy cruiser *Mogami;* the sinking by planes of Japan's last four carriers; and a submarine attack that sank the 72,000-ton superbattleship *Musashi.* (Japan still had two of the three giant ships it had begun to build at the time the disarmament system ended in 1935. The *Shinano,* converted to the world's largest aircraft carrier, was completed in November 1944 and was sunk on her maiden voyage by the submarine *Archerfish;* air attacks sent the *Yamato* to the bottom in April 1945.)

MacArthur had completed reconquest of the Philippines by February 1945, and in the same month Nimitz's marines began their bitter struggle for Iwo Jima in the Bonin Islands. Tokyo and other cities had been bombed by fleets of Saipan-based B-29s since the previous November. Yet the enemy's will to carry on the war seemed undiminished; the invasion of Okinawa in the Ryukyu Islands in April and May took the lives of over 11,000 Americans and wounded 33,000 others, while thirty-six naval vessels were sunk—mainly by *kamikazes,* Japanese pilots who suicidally dived their planes into targets.

The closer the Americans had come to Japan, the more fanatic and bloody the fighting. Victory was no longer in doubt, but it was not with enthusiasm that the armed forces of the United States looked forward to invading the home islands.

While soldiers and sailors fought, everyone at home—according to the language of the time—was pitching in, doing his part, getting the job done. Like Rosie the Riveter, women helped build tanks and planes, hoping their war plants would win the prized E-for-Effort pennants awarded by the government. Or like the singing Andrews Sisters, they did their best to avoid apple trees until their men came home from overseas. Children collected scrap metal, bought war stamps, and paid for low-quality candy with ugly zinc pennies; Milky Ways, Hersheys, copper were gone for the duration, and food, gasoline, tires, and other necessities were strictly rationed. Slackers were scorned, and 4-Fs invented medical deceptions to try to get into the army or navy. The feeling of being in it together included the entire Allied world. Americans knew all about blitzed London, Mrs. Miniver, the RAF, and felt a close bond with the courageous British; the sacrifices of the Russian people were appreciated, and the Polish exiles, Free French, and "United Nations" large and small were considered linked in the common cause.

No ally could be more appealing than China. Pearl Buck's heroes were assumed to have been fighting the enemy since 1937, and now there was some guilt over not having helped the Chinese sooner. But better late than never. Nothing seemed more fitting than the current alliance—more a consummation, really, of those special feelings that had developed over four decades. No more the need to feel ashamed about unkept promises, for the United States, among its many duties in the war, was fighting for China's territorial integrity. And the Chinese were showing their gratitude, saving American lives in the Pacific by engaging huge Japanese armies on the mainland—or so the newspapers said.

The celebration of Allied harmony by press, radio, movies, and popular songs obscured the fact that the Chinese were slackers, that they had chosen the worst of times to justify their reputation for complexity. While Americans saw the war as a simple, two-sided thing, the Allies versus the Axis, Chiang's triangular view included his Nationalist government, the Japanese, and the Chinese Communists. His army had done little fighting since 1938, and he could see even less reason to engage the Japanese after the Americans and British entered the war in 1941. He was counting on the United States to defeat Japan while he hoarded the currency, gold, and Lend-Lease weapons delivered to him. These, he hoped, would ensure victory over what he had come to regard as his major enemy. "The Japanese are only lice on the body of China," he could say with more certainty after December 7, 1941, "but Communism is a disease of the heart."

The generalissimo understood the weaknesses of his regime,

many of which had developed out of his own refusals to initiate reforms. The structure rested on the loyalty of interest groups— army generals, warlords, scholars, and businessmen such as his in-laws, the Soongs. Chiang was a juggler, playing one group against another in a pattern of threats and payoffs that kept the system going. Generals pocketed funds intended for payment of their troops. Peasants owed high rents to landlords and high taxes to the government, and inability to pay was punishable by death in some provinces. The war had brought inflation, tax increases, strict press censorship, and other heavy-handed practices. Some Chinese stayed alive by eating cattle fodder and the country's ubiquitous cats and dogs. Chiang promised reforms, but millions of people were losing faith in a regime that seemed incorrigible.

According to rumor, the grass was greener over in Shensi province and adjoining areas that had come under the influence of the Chinese Communist Party. There were stories of low taxes, agricultural innovations, redistribution of land ownership, fair compensation for dispossessed landlords, freedom of speech and other civil liberties, and a happy, well-fed population willing and able to harass the Japanese. Some such tidings were true, for idealism has been present in the early stages of most revolutions, and others were propaganda; at any rate, descriptions of Mao's Shensi paradise spread throughout wartime China. Chiang feared the future and in his own best interests deceived the United States in order to strengthen his government against the coming storm.

American aviators were early discoverers of China's nonexistent war effort. The Flying Tigers, pre–Pearl Harbor volunteers, arrived with their P-40s in time to contribute the only Allied victories, symbolic as they may have been, during the Japanese advance of early 1942. After the Burma Road was severed, American transport pilots brought supplies to China in hazardous flights over the Himalaya Mountains. Both the Tigers and supply fliers, having risked their lives for China, were dismayed by what they found in Chungking. Chiang would never win an E-for-Effort award, they joked, but comments turned bitter after experience with corruption, profiteering, stealing of American supplies for the black market, and the shoulder-shrugging responses of Chinese officials asked about the war against Japan. The visitors came to despise China for the absence of all they had been led to believe that China represented. Someday the same elucidation would prove "a tremendous shock to the American public," wrote Leland Stowe, a writer traveling through Chungking in 1942.

But the public had no inkling of the truth, and the State Department took well over a year to accept it. Early in 1942 Brigadier General John A. Magruder, head of the first military mission to Chungking, reported that "the marvelous achievements and abilities of the Chinese Army . . . are absolutely without foundation. . . . The Chinese are great believers in the world of make-believe. . . . People in other countries swallow such glib untruths whole without realizing that they are being deceived." The report vexed the State Department, where Magruder was termed a cynic, dwelling on "unpleasant detail." But Clarence Gauss, the ambassador in Chungking, supported Magruder: "China is not now making any all-out war effort. . . . I agree that the American press has unwisely accepted and exaggerated Chinese propaganda reports of alleged military successes."

The fifth anniversary of China's invasion, in July of 1942, prompted Secretary Hull to congratulate Chiang on "the heroic fortitude and tenacity of the Chinese people." Roosevelt added, "All the world knows how well you have carried on the fight." Gauss added a private note: "This is rot."

With Washington growing suspicious, Chiang feared cutbacks in aid. He spurred his publicity corps to new heroics, and they manufactured stories for American papers in which the generalissimo emerged as the greatest tactician since Napoleon as he trapped and slaughtered hundreds of thousands of Japanese. Into the campaign Chiang threw his most valuable weapon; Madame Chiang's *Blitzkrieg* through Washington, New York, Chicago, and Hollywood in February 1943 accomplished all objectives—reinforcing her brother, T. V., in his negotiations for more Lend-Lease aid, inspiring United China Relief drives, and convincing almost all her listeners of the unbreakable bond of unity between the two countries and of China's dynamic fighting spirit. In her jewels, expensive frocks, and mink coats, she was not the typical

Pearl Buck heroine. She had brought along six dozen silk bed-sheets in her belief that American sheets were inferior. She demanded palatial suites in the best hotels, paid for by the United China Relief, whose funds had been intended to buy food for the Chinese people. Roosevelt admired beautiful women and was pleased by her visit to the White House, even if his wife, Eleanor, was not; the liberal First Lady was horrified by Madame Chiang's tendency to clap her hands loudly whenever she required the services of a waiter or maid. But for the American public, applauding her appearances and humming the new "Madame Chiang Kai-shek March," she fulfilled the image of glamour so long developed by magazine journalism. On May 1, 1943, *Life* described her speech before a joint session of Congress:

> It was almost as if a modern Sappho had charmed them with emerald phrases and her own pearly beauty. . . . Congressmen were wholly captivated by her personality, amazed by her presence, dizzied by her oratorical ability.

In 1943 Chiang's main enemy, apart from the Communists, was Lieutenant General Joseph W. Stilwell, the American commander of the China-Burma-India theater of war who had become chief adviser to the generalissimo. Stilwell saw himself as a problem solver, sent to Chungking to apply American know-how to those exasperating complications that were preventing China from getting on the ball. Understandably the war against Japan was his single-minded concern, and China tried his patience; he wanted to slap some sense into it and drill it into a model of dedication to the cause. The Chinese army need shaping up, and then Chiang must "re-engineer" his government so it would regain the loyalty of the people, a job Stilwell evidently considered no more difficult than building a pontoon bridge, though it might take a few days longer. He advised Roosevelt to get tough with Chiang, demanding reforms in return for further shipments of aid. He told Chiang to "patch things up with Mao" and fight alongside him against the Japanese in a new coalition government. As commander-in-chief of a united Nationalist-Communist army, Stilwell volunteered his own name. Not since the time of Willard Straight had a single individual assumed the burden of reshaping Asian history.

The elephant ignored the gnat, and unreformed China moved inexorably toward its destiny. Even if Chiang had been able to reform the country at that late date, he could not choose to eject his friends from power and relinquish his own job. Nor did he choose to strengthen the Communists by allowing them into the government, nor to hand over his hoarded divisions and weapons to an American who wanted to waste them against the Japanese. He considered Stilwell a simple man who could not see the dangerous future that lay beyond the end of the war, who had no understanding of Nationalist interests, who misread the intent of the movement centered in Shensi.

Perhaps Stilwell could not be blamed for pursuing the Japan-oriented interests of the United States, but his diplomacy hardly advanced those interests. He pushed too hard, and compromise became impossible after he let it be known that he considered the generalissimo "ignorant" and a "crazy little bastard." In letters he referred to Chiang as a "Peanut." American newspapermen came to admire Stilwell as a blunt, straight-talking hero in the shirtsleeves diplomacy tradition. They called him Vinegar Joe and praised his "salty remarks" and "peppery personality." Undoubtedly he had flavor even if his substance to this day remains an issue.

In spite of disappointing reports from Stilwell and others, the United States government kept trying to buy a war effort from the Nationalists. America's century-old extraterritorial privileges were renounced in 1943, along with the traditional immigration policy of Chinese exclusion. In late November of that year FDR and Churchill, on their way to the Teheran Conference with Stalin, stopped off in Cairo to talk with the Chiangs, who had flown there to meet them. The president promised that he would continue Lend-Lease, force Japan to surrender unconditionally, and see that China regained Formosa, the Pescadores, Manchuria, and all other territories lost since the Sino-Japanese War of 1894–95—with exception of Korea, which was to be independent. Churchill confessed that he could not understand Roosevelt's obsession with

155

China, and another British observer sourly blamed the knee-length slit in Madame Chiang's gown for the president's foolishness. But FDR was entranced by nothing Chinese. Earlier he had mentioned his "innumerable difficulties" with the Chiangs and the "corruption and inefficiency" of their government. Apparently he made another of his lesser-of-the-evils choices, preferring Chiang among the Asian alternatives and continuing the supply shipments in hope that some good might come of them.

A frustrated Vinegar Joe in 1944 asked Roosevelt to force Chiang to place him in command of all Chinese armies. The vigor of the generalissimo's protests instead forced Roosevelt to order Stilwell to return to the United States. Victory over a major enemy did wonders for Chiang's confidence; he fought no Japanese but increased Lend-Lease demands.

The next political engineer to arrive in China was the new ambassador, Patrick J. Hurley, whose mission was to arrange a coalition government that would unify China while keeping Chiang's party in control. The problem was not too difficult, Hurley surmised, merely one of persuading two brothers to shake hands and forget their little misunderstanding. He was proud of his "good personality, knowing how to get along with people," lack of which had led to Vinegar Joe's downfall. "Pat" Hurley never made the mistake of calling Chiang a crazy bastard; when the two met, it was always with a firm handclasp and "How do you do, Mr. Shek."

This master diplomat calculated that informality would work best with Mao Tse-tung and Chou En-lai, country folk who were less sophisticated than the Chiangs. Alighting from his plane at Yenan, he emitted an Indian war whoop and pounded the backs of the two revolutionaries. In the months of talks that followed, the Hurley personality lost its force, no diplomatic bridges were built, and he could begin to understand Stilwell's impatience with "the kind of people who never get things done." He privately referred to the Communist leaders as "Mouse Dung" and "Joe N. Lie."

It was not until October 1945—after Japan's surrender and a deflated Hurley's return to America—that Mao traveled to Chungking for coalition talks. Amid such dinner companions as the Chiangs, the Soongs, and "Daddy" Kung and his wife, who was Madame Chiang's sister, Mao seemed ill at ease in his blue denims. According to one story, he got himself locked in Chiang's gold-ornamented bathroom. "What a pity we let him out," T. V. Soong commented years later. The coalition talks were unproductive.

In view of later occurrences in China, writers have argued for years about the merits of Stilwell's plan for on-the-double reforms, Hurley's coalition gambit, Roosevelt's investment, and the advice of John Paton Davies and a few other Foreign Service officers that aid being sent to Chiang should be diverted to Mao on grounds that the Communists inevitably would win and thereafter be grateful to Americans and well behaved toward them. Such arguments have been based upon the assumption that failures in American diplomacy are caused by inability to find the right answers and not because some problems have no answers.

When the press broke the story of Stilwell's return to the United States in 1944, the American public received its first information on the true state of affairs in China. It was astonishing to learn that the Chiangs of all people and China of all countries were not pitching in, after all that had been done for them. Disillusionment started the pendulum of opinion in another direction, though it would not arrive at a new destination until later in the forties, after China had revealed the immense scope of its ingratitude. When modern history books mention George Washington's Farewell Address, they usually quote its least significant passages; Washington's most important remarks concerned the dangerous relationship of love and hate in foreign affairs.

The China muddle was only a part of the unwelcome complexity of the war's final year. With Allied victory certain, the final defeat of Germany appeared secondary to a race between Russian and Anglo-American armies to control as much as they could of the European continent. The Yalta Conference held in February 1945 was hardly a convivial meeting of victorious allies. It was a hard-bargaining confrontation of adversaries, with Stalin on one side and Roosevelt and Churchill on the other. Concessions were traded, among them a Far Eastern settlement in which Russia received the southern half of Sakhalin Island together with the Kuriles and seaport and railroad rights it had held in Manchuria prior to the defeat by Japan in 1905. Roosevelt had promised in Cairo in 1943 that Chiang's government would recover Manchuria; now, without consultation with the generalissimo, he broke that promise and was not overly distraught in doing so.

More important at Yalta than promises to Chungking—at least at the time—was to bind the Russians to a promise to enter the war against Japan, and this Stalin agreed to do. FDR's greatest military worry was the ferocity of Japanese defenders as they were pushed toward their home islands. Russian help would reduce American casualties—predicted to be from 500,000 to a million—in the final invasion that Roosevelt thought would be necessary.

FDR did not live to see V-E Day (Victory in Europe, May 8, 1945), which was more boisterously celebrated in London and Paris than in American cities. Europeans considered the war over. The fighting against Japan had been largely an American responsibility, a situation not expected to change. Instead of welcoming servicemen home, American families received foreboding letters describing transfer arrangements from Europe to the Pacific. The great hope was that the dreaded invasions of Japan, scheduled to begin with a Kyushu landing in November 1945, would be made unnecessary by a Japanese surrender.

Surrender would have to be unconditional, as Roosevelt had stated at Cairo in 1943; Japan must give up all its conquests and suffer occupation and punishment. American history's wisest Japanese policy, Theodore Roosevelt's, had acknowledged that Japan should have a place on the Asian continent for the sake of the balance of power and for its own economic sustenance. Even if this policy had been remembered, it would have seemed unthinkable in 1945—after Japanese attempts to take all of East Asia, the attack on Pearl Harbor, the Bataan death march and other atrocities, the war movies and songs, and the sacrifices and casualties of the long struggle. Americans had developed a bitter hatred for the Japanese, and the emotions of total war—felt as strongly by the losers as the winners—would dominate its final episodes.

B-29 bombers based on captured islands subjected Japan to devastating attacks in the spring and summer of 1945. Casualties could not be counted, so appalling was the loss of life. A vaguely estimated 40 percent—and much more in the Tokyo-Yokohama complex—of the country's sixty largest cities was turned to ashes and rubble. While the country burned, the Supreme Council for the Direction of the War, the most important military and government leaders, headed by Premier Kantaro Suzuki (Tojo having resigned the previous year), debated Japan's terms for a negotiated peace. The council's military faction wished to hold out for terms whereby the nation could avoid occupation, retain the emperor with full powers, and perhaps even keep Korea and Manchuria. It was hoped that the Americans would be afraid to invade the home islands, for the Japanese people had been ordered to defend their country to the last man, woman, and child; for this purpose the army had distributed ancient weapons taken from museums and millions of sharp-pointed bamboo spears. On the other hand the council's peace faction advised acceptance of unconditional surrender on the one condition that the emperor be allowed to retain his throne. The Foreign Ministry unsuccessfully sought Russian help—first through an idea for a Russo-Japanese alliance against the United States and then merely to aid Tokyo in arranging an honorable peace. Meanwhile minor Japanese officials conferred with the American government through agents in neutral Switzerland.

For Harry S Truman—president since Roosevelt's death on April 12, 1945—and for his cabinet and chiefs of staff, the reports from Japan were contradictory and confusing. Yet from diplomatic channels or decoded messages there was no indication that Japan's decision makers on the Supreme Council were close to a decision for unconditional surrender. Truman knew that the American people would accept nothing less than unconditional surrender and saw little hope that the Kyushu invasion could be avoided. This was his main concern in deciding to try to end the war through employment of the atomic bombs that had been developed by an international team of scientists. Some historians later came to believe that the decision to use the bombs was based upon a wish to impress Stalin with American power and thus gain an edge in the postwar difficulties that loomed between the Soviet Union and the United States. This view suffers from lack of proof and from the assumption that the human mind is a simple affair, forming decisions out of single motives. As long as Truman believed that dropping the bombs could save thousands of American lives—and there is no evidence that he did not believe this—then any number of corollary motives, if he had them, do not much matter.

The Allies demanded on July 26 that Japan surrender unconditionally. "The alternative," the proclamation said, ". . . is prompt and utter destruction." One clause in this proclamation allowed the Japanese some hope that they might be allowed to keep their emperor, but the subject was not specifically mentioned. The American government intended to maintain the imperial throne in a nominal sense, believing this would give the Japanese a feeling of continuity that would ease the problems of occupation and might even prevent a possible Communist revolution. But Truman, fearing public opinion in his own country, preferred not to spell out a point that might be interpreted as meeting a Japanese condition for peace. The Supreme Council in Tokyo formally rejected the Allied proclamation on July 29.

The B-29 *Enola Gay* destroyed the city of Hiroshima with an atomic bomb on August 6; estimates on the number of deaths have ranged all the way from 91,233 to 423,263. The bomb exploded over an army parade ground where troops were doing calisthenics. Two days later the Soviet Union declared war on Japan and invaded Manchuria. On August 9 the B-29 *Bock's Car,* carrying an atomic bomb, circled over Kokura, but the city's cloud cover promised to prevent good observation and photography, so the aircraft moved on to a secondary target. While the plane was flying over Nagasaki, a hole appeared in the clouds and the bomb was dropped.

The reports from Hiroshima had little effect upon debates in the Supreme Council, where military members still believed a negotiated peace was possible. Russia's declaration shook the council but the deadlock continued into August 9, when argument was interrupted by news of Nagasaki's destruction. This second attack implied—mistakenly as it turned out—that the United States had a large arsenal of atomic weapons and that a long series of such raids was in store. The council was summoned to an imperial conference in the bomb shelter of the palace. The emperor spoke with emotion on the "unbearable" suffering of his subjects. He gave no advice but his meaning was clear; some council members banged their heads on the table and sobbed uncontrollably. The government announced that it would accept unconditional surrender so long as this would not prejudice "the prerogatives of His Majesty as a Sovereign Ruler."

The reply, drafted in Washington, stated that the conditions of imperial authority would be "subject to the Supreme Commander of the Allied Powers." In Japan the council resumed debate. Chiefs of staff and the war minister could not entertain the thought of Hirohito taking orders from an American commander, but others felt that a subservient emperor was better than none at all. Arguments continued for three more days, until August 13 when Tokyo was bombed by 1,300 planes. At another imperial conference Hirohito broke tradition with a direct suggestion, stating a personal willingness to subject himself to a humiliating condition and advising the council to make peace immediately. Japan officially accepted the terms on August 14, and for the first time ever the emperor addressed his people by radio: "The war situation has developed not necessarily to Japan's advantage. . . . We have resolved to [gain peace] by enduring the unendurable and suffering what is unsufferable."

While the Japanese wept or in a few cases performed the ceremony of *hara-kiri,* the joyful V-J Day celebrations in American towns and cities were wildly uninhibited. A few editors injected gloomy themes; a noble cause had been tainted at its end by the use of a horror weapon that clouded the future, and the fragmentation of Allied unity in both Europe and the Far East promised challenges that would allow no long period of postwar relaxation. But mainly there was exultation. The fears of 1940–41 and of the months just after Pearl Harbor were not forgotten, nor was the grand manner in which difficulties had been overcome—through an industrial capacity that had produced armadas of planes and ships; a quality of weaponry attesting to technological superiority;

the courage and ability of twelve million men under arms, fighting all over the world, preserving or winning freedom for nations now voicing their gratitude and praise. Never had Americans been so aware of their country's greatness, omnipotence, unlimited capabilities. Proud memories of World War II were to have no small effect on the dreams of success and the torments of failure, both exorbitant, that lay in the future.

Commodore Matthew C. Perry's arrival in Japan, 1854, as shown by a contemporary artist. *U.S. Bureau of Ships*

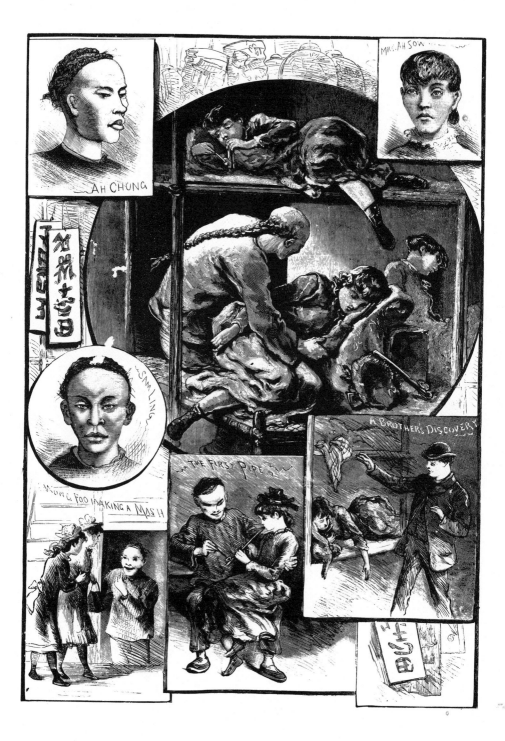

Left. Young girls were lured into Chinatown opium dens according to the *Police
Gazette* in 1883.

Above. An artist's depiction of Commodore (soon to be Admiral) Dewey at the
battle of Manila Bay.

Right. The Open Door as depicted in *Life,*
1900. Uncle Sam becomes a guardian.

U.S. artillerymen, part of an international expedition in 1900, attack Peking's Tartar Wall. *U.S. Signal Corps*

The *Connecticut*, flagship of Roosevelt's "Great White Fleet," in 1908 honored Japan but ignored China. *U.S. Navy*

A much-printed photo of a Japanese air attack on Shanghai in September 1937 helped increase American sympathy for China. *U.S. Office of War Information*

Japanese high school girls visited the American embassy in Tokyo to apologize for the *Panay* incident of December 12, 1937. *U.S. Information Agency*

The battleship *Arizona,* sinking at Pearl Harbor, December 7, 1941. *U.S. Navy*

Americans of Japanese descent, mainly in California, were sent to internment camps in the frenzied weeks that followed the Pearl Harbor attack. *Library of Congress*

"I am looking forward to dictating peace to the United States in the White House at Washington"
— *ADMIRAL YAMAMOTO*

What do YOU say, AMERICA?

Above. Yamamoto was misquoted on this wartime poster. In arguing against war, he had once warned colleagues that he feared America would not surrender until Japanese forces attained an impossible goal, the ability to "dictate peace in the White House at Washington." *U.S. Office of War Information*

Above right. A *kabuki* drama in Tokyo is interrupted by news of a Japanese victory early in World War II. *U.S. Information Agency*

Right. A *Mogami*-class cruiser was among Japanese ship losses at the decisive battle of Midway. *U.S. Navy*

Madame Chiang Kai-shek during her American good-will tour
of early 1943. *U.S. Office of War Information*

Chiang, Roosevelt, Churchill, and Madame Chiang discussed
China's wartime role at Cairo in 1943. *U.S. Signal Corps*

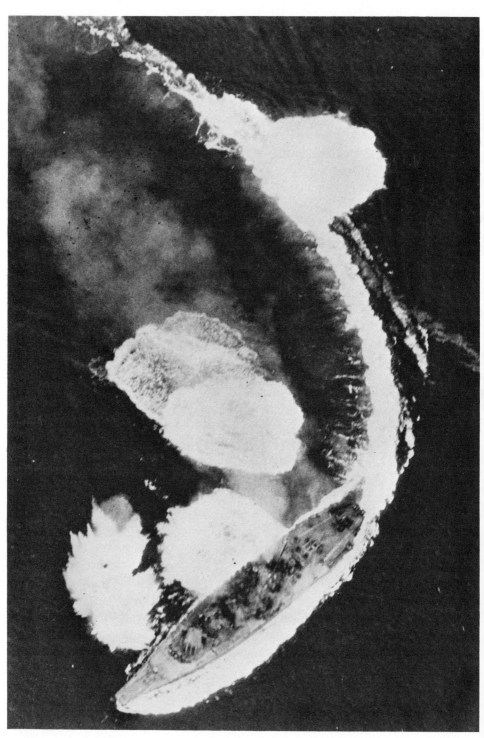

The superbattleship *Yamato* being sunk by American bombs in April 1945. *U.S. Navy*

Atomic cloud over Hiroshima, August 6, 1945. *U.S. Office of War Information*

Top left. Communist soldiers in Shanghai, 1949, celebrate their revolution's victory by displaying a "captured American plane." *U.S. Information Agency*

Left. Douglas MacArthur and the Emperor Hirohito at SCAP headquarters, Tokyo, as the American occupation begins. *U.S. Information Agency*

Above. John Foster Dulles and Dean Acheson still spoke to each other in September 1951, when the Japanese peace treaty was signed. *U.S. Information Agency*

Christmas in Korea, 1950— the long American retreat from the Yalu River. *U.S. Information Agency*

U.S. Marines in the city of Hue, February 1968, during North Vietnam's "Tet offensive." *Defense Department (Marine Corps)*

X

The New
Balance

A FAST RESHUFFLING of friends and foes, standard procedure in
the equilibrium-minded eighteenth century, is not easily accepted in the twentieth, with its ideologies, emotions, and democratic participation in diplomacy. Most Americans needed several
years to get used to the idea that Germany and Japan, bereft of
their wartime leaders, were desirable as allies. In contrast was the
sudden comprehension in 1945–46 that yesterday's ally, the Soviet
Union, had become the grave concern of American foreign relations. Confrontations with Russia and disturbing reports from a
part of the world considered more than ever before to be
"America's Asia" produced tension and confusion.

As if by instinct, ancient simplicities emerged in a din of argument. Senator Robert A. Taft and others called for a new isolationism, but a majority of Americans understood that another long
period of hibernation was not the answer. Some were comforted
by Eleanor Roosevelt's faith that this time, unlike the last, international cooperation would end the world's troubles; but idealism
diminished with every use of the veto power that indicated the new
United Nations could be no more effective than the old League.
For many Americans the answer lay in another military crusade for
freedom, apparently to be led by Congresswoman Clare Boothe
Luce, whose demands for a manly policy were endorsed by the influential publications of her husband, Henry; it was sometimes
forgotten that the armed forces of the United States, unlike those
of Russia, had been demobilized and that America's atomic bomb

1 6 3

monopoly, which would last until 1949, lacked feasibility as a method of liberating eastern European countries occupied by the Red Army. Remembering their potency in World War II, Americans fumed, frustrations mounting until they neared a condition of apoplexy by the late forties.

Meanwhile the Truman administration (1945–53) was fortunate enough to be endowed with able diplomats. They did much to develop a new balance of power in Europe, and in the Far East—though not entirely through intention—they also managed a kind of balance. Assailed by writers of the 1950s for being soft on communism and by those of later years for having been too hard on communism, Truman's diplomats have a good chance to be remembered for moderation.

Blame or credit for postwar policies usually is distributed among four individuals of widely varying backgrounds. The machine politics of Kansas City had taught Truman certain techniques of power; he was proud of his ability to make decisions and reputation for "tough talk," but he was eager for instruction from the history books he liked to read and from the advisers whom he selected with considerable wisdom. George C. Marshall, secretary of state from 1947 to 1949, had been Roosevelt's army chief of staff and a reliable consultant on diplomatic as well as military strategy. Marshall's own chief adviser in the State Department was George F. Kennan, a veteran Foreign Service officer and the philosopher of the containment policy, at least as it was employed during the Truman years. Dean Acheson, who became secretary of state in January 1949 after Marshall resigned because of illness, is best known for development of the NATO alliance and for his guardsman's mustache and the London tailoring; having graduated from both Yale and Harvard, Acheson started with two strikes against him insofar as public opinion was concerned. A machine politician, an army general, a specialist in diplomacy, and an elitist—such types, along with their moderate policies, could hardly endear themselves to ideologists either buttoned-down in the fifties or blue-jeaned in the sixties.

The "Cold War mentality" of Truman's advisers was circumstantial. They were professionals, understanding their job to be the protection of national security, and would have given their attention to any concern of their era, be it communism, fascism, resurgent monarchy, or flying saucers. Indeed, all had performed usefully in the war against fascism. But that was yesterday's difficulty and times do change. The new difficulty was communism. Of course they had Cold War mentalities, just as President Lincoln had a Civil War mentality.

At least in Truman's time the Cold War was an unavoidable presence. The devastation of World War II had allowed only the United States and the Soviet Union to emerge as strong nations, creating a temporarily bipolar condition in the world. In later years each nation would try to expand its influence, but in the Truman-Stalin period most of the pressure came from the Communist side—Soviet activity in Iran, reappearance of the Comintern under the new name Cominform, pressure on Turkey and Greece, institution of Communist governments in eastern Europe, Moscow-oriented political parties thriving on economic hardship and growing more powerful in western Europe, Stalin's blockade of West Berlin, communism's tremendous victory in China, and the invasion of South Korea. When one "added it all up," as a television newscaster said in late 1950, the tide appeared to be "shifting against the free world for the second time in a decade."

But analogy could be dangerous. Problems of the late forties were far more complex than those at the beginning of the decade. Was hostility the simple result of diplomatic circumstances or the inevitable result of political differences? Was Russian expansionism propelled by Marxist doctrine or national heritage? Would it stop when Russia had achieved a buffer zone, or would buffers require buffers ad infinitum? Was communism a Kremlin-controlled monolith, or was it the natural ideological preference of some nationalist and anticolonial movements? What of its bewildering mixture of tactics—military threats, arms aid, internal subversion, political agitation, economic appeal to hungry populations? While communism appeared to be gaining, it lacked the palpable quality of tank columns moving across France and China or bombers over London and Pearl Harbor. The uncomplicated question of 1941 had been whether to fight, a test of nerve more

than of analytical ability. A great many Americans were still eager
to fight in Truman's time, perhaps too eager in view of their
perplexity over what, how, and where to fight. The new situation
demanded thought as well as courage.

Any policy based upon patience and respect for intricacies was
not likely to win popularity in the midst of a public debate over
isolationism, internationalism, or a crusade against evil in its latest
form. Yet with tentative composure the administration instituted its
containment policy in 1947. It worked well even if the statesmen
who devised and manipulated it—Truman, Marshall, Acheson,
and Kennan—did not agree upon all its premises and applications.
The 1947–53 version of containment was based upon flexibility, a
diversity of procedures designed to confront a diversity of Soviet
tactics in hope of maintaining both balance and peace in Europe.
On that continent the Cold War became a chess match rather than
a championship prizefight. With shipment of arms to Greece and
Turkey, the Marshall Plan's massive economic aid to western European nations, the Berlin airlift, and development of the NATO
alliance, versatility of response blocked a variety of pressures and
the European situation was stable by the early 1950s. These were
relatively quiet achievements, but they occurred in the region of
highest priority, as judged by interest-weighing diplomats. If the
American people had paid more attention to the State Department's successes in Europe, they might have remained calm and
avoided the troubles associated with the late forties and early fifties.

Unfortunately Asia retained its fascination, its ability to draw
American attention, all the more because of spectacular changes
there. The volatile Far East was no place for the intricate adjustments of containment that were working in Europe. To imagine
the sort of response needed to check the Chinese upheaval is akin
to regarding the sky on a clear night and contemplating infinity.
Yet when the Truman people left office in 1953, they could
claim—if anyone bothered to listen to them by that time—a stabilized result for their many experiences in Asia; they could weigh
disaster in China against surprising success in Japan and could

point out that a literal line of balance—38° north latitude—had been the original purpose and the final effect of their war in Korea.

Disenchantment with Chiang as a wartime ally could not deter American efforts to keep him in control of postwar China. The northeast region of that country saw a scramble of troop movements in late 1945. Japanese soldiers, looking for someone to accept their surrender, were ordered by American officers to help hold back Chinese Communists marching eastward from Shensi. Meanwhile in a logistical operation covering all of China, American planes and truck convoys helped bring a none-too-eager Nationalist army to the critical northeast. At last the tired Japanese were allowed to go home. Soviet armies had occupied Manchuria at the end of the war, but a wary Stalin wanted no part of the Chinese showdown until he was sure which side would win; he preferred Mao's ideology but preferred the inefficient Nationalists as next-door neighbors. After presenting the Chinese Communists with weapons captured from Japan's Kwantung Army, the Russians pulled out of Manchuria, taking with them over two billion dollars' worth of factory machinery and railroad supplies. Until 1948 the civil war would be fought mainly in Manchuria, the CCP with their Japanese weapons controlling the countryside and the American-equipped Nationalists holding the cities.

Not hopeful that Chiang could win a war, Washington wanted a coalition that would allow him to retain some if not most of his power. General Marshall spent nearly all of 1946 in China, seeking to persuade the adversaries to cooperate in a government in which both would be represented. This was a mission reminiscent of earlier projects, but Marshall was not a fist shaker like Stilwell or a hand pumper like Hurley. Reserved but tactful, he won the respect of both leaders, and for a time in early 1946 prospects improved; there were mutual concessions, and fighting virtually stopped. Yet neither Chiang nor Mao could agree to types of concessions that might have impeded ultimate goals of victory. The talks broke down, the war resumed, and Marshall headed home to assume new duties as secretary of state. He was not enormously disappointed, for by this time reports from eastern Europe were teaching Americans that coalition governments could not long endure when they included Communist parties. At least his mission had proved that even a skilled American negotiator was unable to affect the Chinese struggle; had such efforts ended with Stilwell and Hurley, there would always have been doubts.

Some two billion American dollars, sent between V-J Day and 1948, were intended to provide a payroll for Nationalist soldiers and stop inflation by supporting Chiang's worthless currency. It was probably history's poorest investment, doing more harm than good. Increasingly dependent upon financial infusions, Chiang grew weaker in his own attempts, which had never been strenuous, to improve economic conditions. American money merely offered added opportunities for corruption among government leaders, whose dealings were flaunted in ways that helped divest the regime of its remnants of support among middle-class people, who were being ruined by an inflationary rate that had doubled sixty-seven times since January 1946. It was said that ten million American dollars could have stabilized the currency in 1948, yet thirty times that amount was being hoarded in the treasury or was already in transit to depositories on the island of Taiwan (Formosa), where the government was preparing a hideaway. In the same period, 1945–48, American weapons worth over a billion dollars reached the Nationalist army—these in addition to equipment left behind when United States personnel had left the country in 1945 and 1946. Aid of all kinds between 1938 and 1948 totaled between five and six billion dollars.

In terms of counterproductive activities, weapons shipments were even more significant than money grants. If the United States ever "betrayed" Chiang, as was later charged, it was by sending him too much help. He had garrisoned his best troops in the Manchurian cities, but the Communists controlled the surrounding country. Nationalist soldiers were seldom paid, and in any case their loyalty had never approached fanaticism. In a series of surrenders Manchuria fell in 1948, and the Communists now possessed so many late-model American weapons that their rusting Japanese equipment could be thrown away.

Unsupported by soldiers at the front or by civilians in the south, the Nationalist cause crumbled in 1949. January saw the fall of Peking and Tientsin, the latter city taken by regiments equipped entirely with American automatic rifles, machine guns, artillery, Patton tanks, and even C-ration kits. Mao's legions swept south, joking about "Supply Sergeant Chiang" and the stores of American hardware they collected every time a Nationalist division changed sides. Distressed by news of the rapid advance, Americans could not even take solace from the effectiveness of their military technology, for they had assumed that the Communists were being supplied with Russian weapons.

Truman and Marshall, comprehending the truth, shut off all aid taps by early autumn of 1948. For the purpose of saving Chiang they had tried about everything—logistical help in 1945, diplomacy in 1946, shipments of money and weapons. One other possibility, the sending of American troops to fight in China, was not really discussed in 1947 and 1948. Influential elements in the press and Congress, not to mention Republican candidate Thomas E. Dewey in his 1948 presidential campaign against Truman, were insisting that the United States must not abandon China to communism. But even such ardent China enthusiasts as Senator William Knowland of California never for a moment considered military intervention. And President Truman's diplomatic and military advisers strongly opposed entering the war in China. The State Department believed that China with its unpromising industrial potential was not worth the fantastic effort that would be needed to try to keep its government in friendly hands. Kennan, the department's chief of policy planning, advised his superiors to "liquidate unsound commitments in China and try to recover our detachment and freedom of action with relation to that situation." Shades of Theodore Roosevelt and his open door attitude.

Military advisers were even less enthusiastic about the idea of fighting in China. During World War II, they recalled—even when the United States had possessed strong allies and huge armies that would have been welcomed by the Chinese people—the idea of major involvement on the mainland had been rejected. Now the odds were prohibitive. Assuming public opinion would permit the drafting of another multi-million-man army, such an army could not be trained until after China was in the hands of the CCP. Thus an invasion would be necessary, followed by thrusts into endless territories. Even if a battle line with protected flanks could be established, a hostile people behind the line would engage in guerrilla warfare. Assuming China could be conquered, what would be done with it? How long would Americans have to stay there to protect Chiang's government against a population that detested it? Would the United States have to rebuild the place and feed its six hundred million people, all the while facing Russia on the northern border?

If reality demanded no defense of the administration's limited effort, politics did. In August 1949 the government published its China white paper, a bulky explanation of the reasons for Chiang's defeat, American attempts to help him, and why those attempts failed. Acheson, secretary of state since January 1949, summed up the white paper's arguments:

> The unfortunate but inescapable fact is that the ominous result of the civil war in China was beyond the control of the government of the United States. Nothing that this country did or could have done within the reasonable limits of its capabilities could have changed that result. . . . It was the product of internal Chinese forces, forces which this country tried to influence but could not.

The Communists crossed the Yangtze and entered Shanghai in May 1949, Canton fell in October, and a fast-moving column of Patton tanks took Chungking in November. The victors could not prevent the exodus to Taiwan of the Chiangs, the Nationalist government, the loot, and about 500,000 troops. Hoping for additional funds, a suddenly ferocious Chiang sent the first of his messages to America telling of plans to invade China.

The unworried comrades of the mainland proclaimed a Chinese People's Republic on October 1, 1949, and Peking reassumed its old name as the country's capital. The first stage of revolutionary

170

control was largely ceremonial, including firecracker and paper-dragon festivals, threats to foreign enemies, warnings against internal dissent, and symbolic executions of certain landlords and capitalists perhaps not numbering more than some thousand. The great changes in Chinese life would come later. The Russians, now friendly, offered valuable advice; in December 1949 Mao began a nine-week collectivization study in Moscow and while there signed a Treaty of Friendship, Alliance, and Mutual Assistance intended to be in effect until 1980. The Soviets, more thrifty than the Americans, agreed to lend their Chinese protégés the equivalent of $60 million a year until 1955.

Foreign nations began the normal process of recognizing a de facto regime, but the United States reaffirmed recognition of the Taiwan Nationalists as the government of China and in so doing embarked upon another episode in the Wilson-Stimson tradition, which holds that evil governments have no official existence. Even if Truman had wanted to recognize Peking or allow the America-associated bloc of United Nations members to approve its entry into that organization, he knew that such actions would have infuriated a majority of Americans. The long freeze began, one that would prevent the United States from gaining clear information on momentous changes taking place in China. Communist brutalities would make those of Chiang seem random and petty by comparison, thus encouraging the American stance, but history records that moralists are adept at hurting themselves more than others.

Americans took nonrecognition for granted. Indeed, it was a most inadequate expression of an opinion that had reversed itself since the bilateral embrace just after Pearl Harbor. The Yellow Peril, with its several synonyms and cartoon depictions of awakening dragons, was back again. Along with fear appeared the ancient terms of loathing for China, its insidious cunning, subhuman cruelty, and other Fu Manchuisms. A few Pearl Buck fans might prefer to believe that the Chinese people were once again the hapless victims of an alien force, this one Russian, but the ridiculous ease of the revolution forced general admission that China's masses probably were not opposed to the new system. Perhaps it was the irony that hurt most, based on the old feeling that America

171

was China's historic benefactor and that the two countries had enjoyed a special relationship. China's dilatory war effort of the early 1940s might have been forgiven, but its choice of communism seemed a direct affront, an obscene gesture at an old friend, an ultimate form of mockery for every time-honored hope that the Chinese would be good customers, Christian converts, and democratic pupils forever grateful and loyal.

Indignation over the betrayal was not expended entirely upon China. Acheson's frank statement that the civil war had been too much to handle was unacceptable to the national self-confidence, an insult to the tradition that no job was too big to be done. It was preferable to think that the failure had not been national but one of individual weaklings, blunderers, traitors. In its early stages the hunt for scapegoats was conducted by the "China Lobby," a group of publishers, former missionaries, businessmen, and congressmen whose common interests included vigorous anticommunism, unwavering loyalty to Chiang, and defeat of the administration in the next election. Questions were incessant. Whose advice had been instrumental in decisions that had limited aid to the Nationalists? Who had betrayed Chiang? Who had lost China? John Paton Davies, John S. Service, and other Foreign Service officers came under suspicion for their wartime reports—some naive and some realistic—which stressed the "agrarian reform" intent of Mao's movement or suggested that it was strong enough to defeat Chiang. Marshall's coalition effort of 1946 was condemned as having been an attempt to compromise with communism, and Acheson, with his slur on American know-how and his Ivy League mannerisms, seemed an alien presence. It was difficult to see anything sinister in Truman, but at least he could be charged with ignorance of what was going on in his administration. Insinuations of the lobby gained attention in a country perplexed and bitter over "America's loss of China." The furor puzzled European commentators, who wondered why Americans believed China had ever been theirs to lose.

The China watchers of the Truman era might have calmed themselves by paying equal attention to Japan and the prospering of

American interests there. Japan, though defeated, had not lost its importance, nor could a successful occupation be taken for granted. The occupation forces were not Augustan Romans or Victorian Englishmen, trained in the rule of conquered populations. In their own national tradition they might have acted as self-righteous avengers or over-eager reformers; they might have bungled the experience in any number of ways, turning a temporary enemy into a permanent one. But they did not. For the most part their power was wisely used, surprising the Japanese and eventually serving Japan's interests along with those of the United States.

In late August 1945 advance units of the Eighth Army entered the ruined city of Tokyo. Electric trains were running on schedule but without passengers. Except for a few frightened traffic policemen standing in empty intersections, Tokyo appeared to be uninhabited. Following some first assumptions that the air raids had killed everybody, it became clear that the Japanese were hiding. They feared the bayonets of revenge-minded conquerors, and most of the women had been evacuated to the country. Brave individuals emerged, then groups, to receive the food, medical care, and housing consultation being offered by the army of occupation. The first signs of mutual amity were based mainly upon surprise. The Americans had expected sniper fire, bamboo spears in the back, and stony-faced hatred; instead they found politeness, mostly formal but sometimes friendly. The Japanese, who had been taught to expect horrible brutalities, were mystified by the exemplary conduct of the victorious army.

General Douglas MacArthur received Japan's formal surrender aboard the battleship *Missouri* on September 2, and then moved into his Tokyo headquarters as Supreme Commander for the Allied Powers (SCAP became the abbreviation for the commander, his staff, and the GHQ building across the moat from the imperial palace.) MacArthur was cold, arrogant, egotistical. During monologues on the glories of the Roman Empire he brandished his corncob pipe as if it were a scepter. Staff members referred to him as J. C., most often meaning Julius Caesar, but a few individuals insisted that they had seen him strolling on the palace moat in the early morning mist. The general's personality had not contributed to command harmony during the war, and it would bring about his downfall in another war. He was not a man for all seasons, few of them in fact, but in postwar Japan he found the time and the place for which his nature had been designed.

The Japanese admired such traits as dignity, austerity, and authority. Even arrogance, from which might be inferred confidence, was not unwelcome in a time of confusion and low morale. MacArthur lent style and prestige to the occupation, giving it a ceremonial flourish. Crowds gathered each morning to cheer the arrival of his limousine and stare at the tall commander, inscrutable in sunglasses, as he entered SCAP between rows of snappily drilled and decorated MPs. He did little to discourage rumors that he was a demigod or at the least a form of Tokugawa shogun—the true ruler of pre-Restoration Japan even though an emperor was tolerated for ceremonial purposes. The general's style worried the State Department, where it was felt that he was something less than the perfect example of democracy in action. One can only guess at how the Japanese would have responded to an eager-to-please civil administrator shaking hands, passing out gum to children, fighting the battle of men's minds through pleading dialectic on the virtues of democracy. This sort of approach to Asia, standard procedure in later years, would become notorious for its failures. As Ambassador Grew had once said, the Japanese respected power. MacArthur was its perfect symbol.

The occupation's first phase, 1945 to early 1948, was aimed at reforming a troublemaker. In teaching the Japanese never again to repeat their recent behavior, the Americans meant to punish "war criminals," eradicate militarism, destroy the power centers of Japanese society, and establish democratic practices. According to one directive, the emperor must be humanized. Antidivinity propaganda included the distribution of a photograph that showed Hirohito and MacArthur, the latter's casual attire and hands-on-hip pose suggesting indifference to the imperial presence. Hirohito cooperated in all that was asked, renouncing his divinity and appearing on the street in a baggy suit for the purpose of chatting casually with the people. "We'll turn him into Charlie Chaplin," said one SCAP official. But Hirohito's subjects understood his position and sympathized with his efforts to "endure the unendurable.'' His example, in realistically accepting change, encouraged the nation to do the same, and when the Americans perceived his value, they wisely ended their program to degrade him.

The International Tribunal that sat for two years in Tokyo dispensed victors' justice through procedures alien to those persons on trial, but it was hoped that the Western judicial system would appear impressive through its meticulous attention to rules of evidence. No matter what the Japanese thought of the trials, they cared little about what happened to former leaders who had led them to defeat and destruction. The most important defendant, General Tojo, who had tried to kill himself and failed, appeared more a fool than a martyr. Prince Konoye had succeeded in ending his life before the start of the showcase trials, which finally resulted in execution of Tojo and six others and eighteen prison sentences. Away from the public eye, in the Philippines and other parts of Southeast Asia, some nine hundred "minor war criminals" were hanged or shot after courts-martial in which wristwatches had been consulted more often than evidence.

SCAP designed a political and cultural revolution for Japan, some of it embodied in a constitution written by MacArthur and his staff and promulgated in October 1946. The emperor was defined as a symbol of the state, subject to the will of the people through their elected Diet, and there were twenty-nine *jinken* (''human rights''), including women's suffrage, freedom of speech and press, and other specifics inspired by the American constitution. It has been too often assumed that the United States presented Japan with liberties it had never heard of; a movement toward democracy had been a strain in Japanese history, though not always a strong one, since the late nineteenth century.

Many reforms—contained in the constitution or otherwise decreed by SCAP—were aimed at preventing a recurrence of militarism. Article nine of the constitution renounced war forever, and maintenance of armed forces was outlawed. Some 200,000 persons were fired from the Diet, civil service, educational system, and private business on the ground that they had held their positions during the war. To discourage regeneration of national power in any form, the Americans ordered decentralization of the ad-

175

ministration, judiciary, land control, national police force, and education. Steps were taken to dissolve industrial monopolies and to encourage development of American-style labor unions.

In wanting to rid Japan of "feudal customs," SCAP officers sometimes brushed aside ancient and revered traditions; in working with Japanese officials, they sometimes ignored etiquette and conversational elaboration designed to preserve dignity. But postwar Japanese were in no position to stand on pride, and many of them were honestly appreciative of the considerable numbers of occupation officers who sought to improve their diplomacy by studying a difficult language and a complex culture. In any case the Japanese were sick of militarism and approved of most of the American reforms.

It was in 1947, a year of troubles in Europe and China, that Marshall, Kennan, and others in the State Department awakened to the fact that a weakened Japan did not fit the changing needs of American foreign policy. No matter what Japan had done in the past, its islands remained the greatest industrial complex in the Far East, a crucial factor in the area's balance of power. Why wreck the efficiency of that industry by breaking up monopolies? Why encourage labor unions, which were already showing signs of Communist influence? Why purge experienced administrators and teachers, weaken the police, prohibit armed forces? Nothing could be done about China, as Kennan told Marshall, but the United States was in physical control of the Far East's strongest nation, and every advantage should be taken of that fact.

The occupation's second phase, one that viewed Japan as a future ally rather than as a recent enemy, began early in 1948. Kennan arrived in Tokyo in March, somewhat fearful of the potentate who had so often told the State Department to mind its own business. MacArthur entertained him at dinner with a two-hour monologue on Caesar in Gaul. After sizing up each other for several days, the diplomat and the general decided they were in perfect agreement. As it turned out, MacArthur had already done some thinking about phase two.

Most SCAP officers had figured on a short occupation—that a reformed Japan could be left to its own devices, no matter how feeble and disorganized, as early as 1948. Now it became clear that the occupation must continue until the country had established its economic health, internal order, and attitude on world politics. The reformer became a rebuilder. Thousands of civil servants and teachers were rehired even if they had held leadership positions in the war against the United States. Business monopolies, not yet entirely fragmented, were helped to regroup and raise production schedules. The union movement, having shown more interest in politics than collective bargaining, was discouraged with partial success. By 1950 the occupiers were aiding in the development of a National Police Reserve of 70,000 men armed as infantry soldiers and were discussing plans for a new "self-defense" system to include an army, navy, and air force.

Some Japanese, studying the document written by the American founding fathers in 1946, puzzled over the constitutionality of the occupation's second phase. In the United States the policy change was generally attributed to a good-hearted wish to help Japan get back on its feet. But humanitarianism had been a less important motive than American interests. Worry over Communist nations, exaggerated or not, had fortunate effects upon relations with Japan as well as Germany, where goals were similar. There was no repetition of the Versailles blunder in which the desire to punish and weaken a former enemy had produced disastrous results.

Trailing policy by several years, the American people gradually came to realize that yesterday's enemy could be today's friend. The early 1950s saw the beginning of a Japanese vogue, the first since the wave of good feeling that followed the surprise attack on Port Arthur in 1904. Soldiers brought home fans, tea sets, kimonos, and other reminders of old quaintnesses. They told extravagant tales of geisha houses and communal baths, and a few were able to speak of social relationships with Japanese families. Journalists re-created the flattering emulation theme, reporting "crazes" for American food, clothing, household gadgets, popular songs, obscene magazines, pinball machines, monster movies, and *besu-boro* (though baseball had been popular long before the war and had been a favorite recreation for Japanese aviators between sorties). In the fifties Americans developed interests in jujitsu, origami, sake, and flower arranging. Movies such as *Teahouse of the August Moon* recaptured the *Mikado* theme of a funny but likeable little people, while the *Sayonara* type of film was sheer Butterflyism involving American servicemen with geishas and Takarazuka dancers in ways that did little honor to ancient institutions. It has been suggested that Americans, on the rebound from China, were seeking another Oriental object of affection. Happily the vogue remained moderate, for, like the Chinese, the Japanese preferred mutual respect to mushier forms of international relations.

A peace treaty signed at San Francisco on September 8, 1951, and ratified early the next year included no punishments or restrictions, but it formally established Japan's loss of all former territories with exception of the Bonins and Ryukyus, which would temporarily remain in American hands. At the same time the two nations signed a Security Pact, which stated that Japan requested, in the interest of its defense, American military bases in the home islands. In 1954 a Mutual Defense Assistance Agreement completed the making of a military alliance.

The occupation officially ended with ratification of the peace treaty. Japanese parties of the left celebrated with anti-American riots, and conservatives were relieved, for they had come to deplore the pinball-honkytonk atmosphere, the decline in standards of courtesy, especially among young people, and other results of the American presence. Incidents of GI misbehavior had increased during the later stages of the occupation as young recruits, who expected too much of what they had heard of Japanese friendliness, replaced the disciplined veterans who had performed so well in the beginning. SCAP officers increasingly abused their great power, at the least developing ''infallibility complexes'' that annoyed Japanese no longer in awe of the organization. ''They all smoke corncobs now'' was the hyperbole of one civil employee at SCAP. Even after ratification the GI uniform was slow to disappear, because of the base arrangements and because Japan was the staging area for the Korean war.

The Americans overstayed their welcome, but the broad moderate element of Japanese society would remember them with approval. The occupation had not been a happy time, with its hardships and humiliation, but it was far from the calamity it might have been. As it ended, Japan was entering a period in which it would become the Far East's most stable democracy and the economic envy of the world, results due mainly to Japanese abilities yet owing something to occupation policies. The result for the United States was the transformation of a strong enemy into a strong ally.

Goodbye China, hello Japan. The exchange was not at all harmful to the United States and for many reasons might have been desirable much earlier in the century. But the Truman government had not intended to achieve balance by trading off China and still faced the domestic political consequences of that fateful event.

XI

Drawing a Line

THE ORIENTAL DIPLOMACY of the United States, historically concerned with China and Japan, faced complications brought about by the post–World War II demise of colonialism and the emergence of new sovereignties. Colonialism had not fared well in the twentieth century. For years the capitals of empire had been tormented by rising costs of caring for overseas subjects, by moral issues argued in an era of increasing liberalism and fashionable feelings of guilt, and by independence movements throughout their domains. Easy Japanese victories in 1942 had inspired other Asians to think that they too could defeat the once feared Westerners, assuming the latter would even bother to fight. Numerous Americans, including Presidents Wilson and Franklin D. Roosevelt, had added their influence, shaming the colonizers by pressing their ideal of "self-determination of peoples."

Americans tended to identify self-determination with democracy, imagining that the end of colonialism would automatically produce an array of antipodal constitutional conventions styled after Philadelphia's in 1787. It was saddening to learn that self-determination usually substituted local tyrannies—left, right, or exotic specimens not easily classified—for that orderly and often well-meaning rule once emanating from the colonial ministries of Europe. It was enough to make some Americans yearn for the good old days of imperialism. But there was also the temptation to promote democracy, employing American influence to fill the vacuum that American influence had helped to create. Newly independent nations varied in their importance to American interests, thus posing new tests for the country's sense of proportion.

Pandora's box was opened by the Truman administration within a year after the war's end with a grant of independence to the Philippines. Publicized as example setting, the act fulfilled a historic wish to bid the Filipinos a fond farewell. Possession of the islands had tainted the sincerity of every self-determination lecture to Europeans. Hundreds of courthouses, schools, sanitation plants, and other services intended to mark the United States as a model imperialist power had represented a continuous financial drain, and in seeking to avoid mercantilism, the government had allowed colonial traders to profit more than those in America. It had proved difficult to interest the Filipinos in independence. The Wilson administration tried hard to lay down the white man's burden, but Manuel Quezon and other leaders in the islands secretly insisted they were not ready for self-rule. The Tydings-McDuffie Act of 1934 provided for independence in 1946 under terms acceptable to the colonials, and World War II ended in time for the plan to be carried out on July 4, 1946. War had destroyed the Filipino economy, and the Communist-led "Huk" revolution was gaining, yet Washington resisted all attempts to postpone the date of liberation. But military and financial aid to the new nation was not withheld; that and the efforts of Ramón Magsaysay, a strong, reform-minded president elected in 1953, helped Filipino democracy weather its storms for at least a few more years.

In the initial year following Filipino independence, impoverished Britain began the process of divesting itself of India, Burma, Malaya, Singapore, and other holdings. Malaya and Singapore united with former British areas of northern Borneo to form the Republic of Malaysia in 1963, but Singapore dropped out two years later. Considering what empire once had meant to the British, they showed considerable class in accepting the change. The Netherlands refused to accept the inevitable and with small military gestures tried to regain the East Indies. The Dutch were forced to recognize the Republic of the United States of Indonesia in November 1949.

Deprived of their military reputation and uncharacteristically insensitive to elements of farce, the French were intent upon retaining the status symbol of empire. During the war Roosevelt had viewed French imperial pretensions with special distaste and stated that he wanted independence at least for Indochina. "France has milked it for one hundred years," he said in 1944. "The people of Indochina are entitled to something better than that." He made the same point at Yalta but died two months later, and the busy Truman administration showed little interest in 1946 when French forces began efforts to reestablish their Southeast Asian colony. Confronting them was their prewar revolutionary enemy, Ho Chi Minh, whose followers called themselves the Vietminh. Ho was a Communist of the international variety, having served the Comintern since the mid-1920s, but he was also a hero of Vietnamese nationalism and had led a guerrilla war against the Japanese that made him a former American ally. He represented complexity and one day would become a topic of debate in the United States. But in Washington's lurid political climate of the latter 1940s, the State Department could not afford to debate issues involving communism. Ho soon was classified as an "agent of world communism" and the French praised for their part in the "world-wide resistance by the Free Nations to Communist attempts at conquest and subversion." In supporting the French with limited funds beginning early in 1950, Truman and Acheson were unaware that history would endow this action—a small matter in comparison with that year's important activities—with any special significance.

Japan's pre-1940 empire meanwhile had fallen mainly to the Chinese Communists, although Chiang wound up in control of Taiwan, and Russia in 1945 received the Kuriles and southern Sakhalin. Korea, like Indochina, had been a special object of Roosevelt's self-determination program, and the wartime president had pledged its independence as early as 1943. At the Yalta conference he agreed that Russian and American troops would occupy the country until the Japanese army and government could be removed, free elections held, and a constitutional regime established. Following V-J Day the Russians arrived on the scene more quickly than the Americans. To preserve the joint occupation agreement, Washington insisted that the Soviets confine their zone to the northern half of the country, choosing the thirty-eighth parallel as the line of demarcation. The Americans moved in to occupy Korea south of that line, a border that would attain an unintended permanence as the years passed. From 1945 to 1948 Russia rejected several United Nations unification plans and refused to allow its zone to participate in a national election.

Tired of waiting, the UN conducted a South Korean election in 1948, which established a constitutional democracy called the Republic of Korea (ROK). Its seventy-three-year-old president, Syngman Rhee, had spent most of his adult life in the United States promoting his country's freedom. He loved democracy, he often said, yet anyone who voiced opposition to his wishes risked throwing him into a tantrum of screaming and furniture kicking. Despite foreboding signs, democracy seemed to be functioning when American forces departed in 1949, after a grant of $300 million in economic aid and the first $10 million in a program designed to equip the ROK with an army and a navy. In the north the Russians also withdrew, leaving behind a Democratic People's Republic of Korea, more effectively indoctrinated in politics and much better subsidized and trained for war than was its neighbor to the south.

North Korea invaded South Korea on June 25, 1950. Six well-coordinated thrusts, from one side of the peninsula to the other, easily routed the ROK army. As Communist tanks approached the capital city of Seoul, the government fled south, with President Rhee limping, it has been said, after a barefooted assault upon a grand piano.

The causes of the war are not precisely understood because of the inaccessibility of North Korean and Soviet documents, but historians of sundry political leanings agree that Russia knew what was coming and helped prepare it. Indeed, Nikita Khrushchev in his reminiscences took it for granted that the Soviet Union had sponsored or at least approved the invasion. Moscow's prestige could prosper from a victory of its protégé over that of Washington, coming at a time when Cold War sensitivities were at their peak and most countries in the world expected to identify with one ideology or the other. The Soviets had been discomfited by the tough but peace-minded techniques of containment in Europe; would American resolution weaken when confronted by a pressure that was military? If so, would NATO nations realize that they could not depend upon promises by the United States to support them? Would the Japanese, noting a Communist success so close to their islands, conclude that they were choosing the wrong side and resist further American efforts to turn them into allies? And what of Russia's recent alliance with Peking; did China need an early demonstration of which nation was senior partner and prime mover of Communist strategy in the Far East?

Whatever its main motive, Moscow had reason to think that a North Korean victory could be accomplished quickly and easily, probably without an American attempt to defend its ROK client. Under attack by the Republicans, the administration was being pressed to explain why it had not done more to help Chiang, and one such explanation discounted the Asian mainland as a primary region of national interest. America's "defense perimeter," Acheson had announced in January 1950, extended no farther than Japan, Okinawa, and the Philippines. The strategy was wise, drawing a line through water and relying upon the naval advantage enjoyed by the United States, but its advertisement served to invite attack in Korea. What if the Americans, in spite of Acheson's strategy, decided to respond? In keeping with peacetime tradition their army strength was minimal; their occupation force in Japan comprised mainly administrators and clerks, with no recent battle training. What if the United Nations decided to protect the political arrangement it had sponsored in Korea? Russia could not veto such action because its delegate to the Security Council, Jacob Malik, had been boycotting the UN over its refusal to admit mainland China in place of Chiang's Taiwan. Malik's absence might indicate that Russia did not know in advance of the North Korean invasion. But he was never more than a few city blocks away from the Security Council during the two days of debate that preceded its decision; he could have brought his veto power into the council chamber at any time. It was more important to Moscow not to appear weak in Chinese eyes by giving up on the UN boycott. It expected the North Korean army to conquer the peninsula long before any effective defense could be mustered by the United States and/or the United Nations.

On Sunday, July 25, within hours of the crossing of the thirty-eighth parallel, the Security Council ordered a cease-fire and withdrawal of the North Koreans, but there was no mention of means through which the edict could be enforced. After flying back to Washington from Independence, Missouri, Truman met with the secretaries of state and defense, their top advisers, and the Joint Chiefs of Staff. The conferees pondered how far the UN would be willing to go, the current state of American military strength, and the odds for fighting a successful war on Asia's mainland. But what concerned them most were the probable ramifications of inaction. South Korea was a symbol that—considering nervous uncertainties in Japan and Europe—was judged important enough for a decision to "draw the line," as Truman put it, even though the line would be well forward of the perimeter defined by the State Department.

The decision to act was not announced publicly, for the means of carrying it out remained hazy, in some part dependent upon events in the Security Council. On Monday the China Lobby demanded action, congressmen debated, and the press in Europe and the United States tried to guess what Truman would do. Argument raged over an anonymous but widely publicized comment by a European diplomat in Washington: "The time has come when Uncle Sam must put up or shut up, and my guess is that he will do neither."

Shortly after noon on Tuesday, July 27, Truman announced that he had pledged air and naval forces to the defense of South Korea. A journalist in Washington, Joseph C. Harsch, felt "a sense of relief and unity pass through the city," even if UN and presidential statements still fell short of all-out commitment to the country under attack. A meeting of the Security Council was set for Tuesday afternoon, and the American government had prepared a strong resolution. Shortly before the session Trygve Lie, the

UN Secretary-General, had lunch with Malik and felt a duty to invite the Russian delegate to return to his seat on the council. "No, I will not go there," Malik answered, to Lie's great relief. Debate on the American resolution lasted throughout the afternoon and evening. Delegates often turned to glance at the chamber door, but Malik did not appear. The council passed the resolution, which summoned member nations to "furnish such assistance to the Republic of Korea as may be necessary to repel the armed attack." On Thursday the twenty-ninth General MacArthur communicated from Tokyo, asking that he be allowed to send American ground forces from Japan to Korea. Truman authorized the move as part of a UN "police action."

Americans would have little reason for fond memories of Truman's war. It produced high casualties—33,647 killed and missing and 103,376 wounded, most of them draftees—and contributed to the American political crisis of the early fifties. Yet most historians have rejected an analogy that became popular during a later war, the temptation to lump Korea and Vietnam together as a double example of meaningless Asian involvement. For there were differences between the two wars. The symbolic nature of the Korean stand had value at a time of great uncertainty among important allies in Europe and Asia. While the United States played the major military role in Korea, this was not a lonely role that could make the country vulnerable to ridicule and hatred in case the war went badly; hiding its conception of national interest in official UN sponsorship, Truman's government had sixty-four active allies, fifteen of them contributing troops and the others supplies. Even the old rule that insists upon the folly of war on the Asian mainland found exception on Korea's narrow peninsula, where Americans could fight in the ways they knew best, on Western rather than Asian terms; a front could be established and flanks anchored on the coasts and guarded by naval superiority, creating that frontal definition necessary to effective use of air power. Eventually the war was won—at least in terms of its original objective—in accord with the strategy based upon Korea's unique geography.

The original objective as stated by Truman in June 1950 was limited to preservation of the Republic of Korea and the reestab-

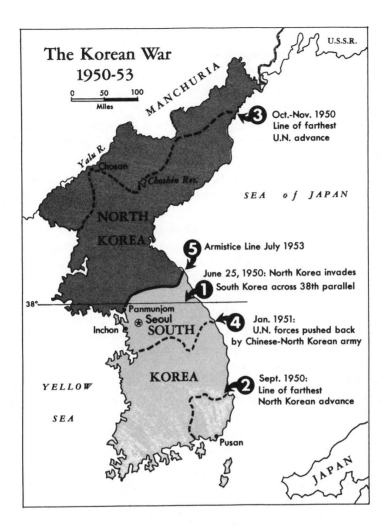

The Korean War
1950-53

0   50   100
Miles

U.S.S.R.

MANCHURIA

Yalu R.

Chosan

Choshin Res.

3 Oct.-Nov. 1950
Line of farthest
U.N. advance

SEA of JAPAN

NORTH

KOREA

5 Armistice Line July 1953

June 25, 1950: North Korea invades
1 South Korea across 38th parallel

38°

Panmunjom

⊛ Seoul

Inchon   SOUTH

4 Jan. 1951:
U.N. forces pushed back
by Chinese-North Korean army

KOREA

2 Sept. 1950:
Line of farthest
North Korean advance

YELLOW

SEA

Pusan

JAPAN

lishment of its border at the thirty-eighth parallel. There were no plans to invade North Korea, no designs upon Chinese and Russian territories that lay beyond. The president often repeated these limited objectives in hope that the major Communist powers would find no reason to enter the war. For the same reason Truman rejected Chiang's offer to send Nationalist Chinese soldiers to Korea and ordered the United States Seventh Fleet to assume a stabilizing position in the strait between Taiwan and the mainland.

In the war's early weeks the North Koreans, trained to fly MIG jets and maneuver the latest models of Soviet tanks, swept south as the ROK army retreated in panic. Americans were confident the tide would turn once their troops arrived on the scene, but the first units flown in from Japan performed no better than the South Koreans. Most had been trained mainly for their desk-jockey duties of the occupation; then too they were overwhelmingly outnumbered by their enemy. In July and August the northerners took all of South Korea except for a small perimeter around the southeastern port of Pusan. There the battle was stabilized by the increasing numbers of American troops ferried across the Tsushima Strait from Japan.

With the Pusan buildup continuing, MacArthur surprised the North Koreans on September 15 by landing troops at Inchon on the west coast not far below the thirty-eighth parallel. The amphibious operation, which reminded Americans of the land-sea-air island victories of World War II, was coordinated with an offensive out of the Pusan perimeter. MacArthur had found his Gaul, for the Inchon legions took Seoul and divided Korea with a swift eastward movement toward the other side of the peninsula. Forced back by the Pusan drive and fearing entrapment by the Inchon maneuver, the North Koreans broke and ran, a few remnants of their army managing to get back across the thirty-eighth parallel before MacArthur closed the last escape routes.

That bright and fleeting moment, September 1950, invites indulgence in the game sometimes played with the "ifs" of history. What if the Truman administration, in the manner of eighteenth-century statesmen, had been satisfied with balance, attained through achievement of those limited objectives that had prompted the decision for war? What if the war had been allowed to end in September, with the invaders humiliated and thrown back to their side of the line? Truman's symbolic war had been won with brilliance, ease, and few American casualties. Had this been its final result, what calming effects might it have had on future aggressors, the country's allies, and those Americans then seething over the administration's past failures to win against communism?

But September passed and the war went on, becoming symbolic of other things—fifty years of inordinate expectations for success in the Far East; the twentieth-century view that total victory is the only acceptable purpose of combat; and an ambitious leader who wanted to drive ahead, finish the job, and raise his flag over the capital of a beaten enemy. Small symbols were important too. The corncob pipe and sunglasses—ubiquitous in the photographic record of a general whose name was synonymous with victory, as commander of great campaigns in the big war, as the lordly SCAP, as the mastermind of Inchon—were present again as cameramen recorded a MacArthur-Truman conference at Wake Island on October 15. Who was really commander-in-chief? Was it the little man in the double-breasted business suit, looking about as assertive as had Hirohito in his 1946 photo with MacArthur? Or was it the latter, tall in stature and larger than life in reputation? Hands on hips and wearing dark glasses, MacArthur gave the impression of supreme indifference as he looked down at Truman, perhaps preferring to regard his wristwatch. In having asked for this conference, the civilian from the White House was taking up valuable time, time better used in Korea, where MacArthur had been conducting an invasion north of the thirty-eighth parallel. Informed of this decision, Truman from Washington had raised doubts. What if Chou En-lai, the foreign minister in Peking, had not been bluffing in warnings that China would enter the war if UN troops carried it into North Korea? MacArthur had scoffed at such warnings, but Truman, seeking reassurance, had asked for the meeting at Wake. The general brusquely provided reassurance—yes, he was sure that the Chinese would never dare attack a well-equipped American army—whereupon he was flown back to his Rubicon while Truman departed for Washington in the realization that he had not experienced the finest hour of his decision-making career.

Truman later claimed that MacArthur's confidence had been misleading, but the general by no means deserves all blame for the sudden end of the restrained policy that had controlled the war's beginning. After Inchon both Democrats and Republicans in Congress were demanding total victory, the reunification of a Korea to be ruled from Seoul. This goal was reasonable and desirable, the UN General Assembly concurred in a vote of October 7. A two-thirds majority of the American people wanted to "finish the job," according to a national poll released on October 13.

Journalists were excited too, depicting the slashing offensives from Inchon and Pusan with great black arrows on newsprint maps, action headlines, and vibrant reports on radio and television. The nation was simply reliving World War II, that proud time when frustrations had been swept aside by American military power. Caught up in the euphoria, Truman could not stop the march north and there is no evidence that he wanted to. By late November the UN army had taken most of North Korea, and one regiment was so close to the Yalu River that its officers with the help of binoculars could see across into Manchuria.

Then came the disillusionment, as it so often has come for Americans in the Far East. Chou had not been bluffing. China was disinclined to allow the fall of a buffering ally, accept American presence on the Chinese border, and lose face with its population—not to mention with Russia—after only a year of Communist rule. Had an American embassy existed in Peking, it might have gauged the mood there and sent reports to Washington.

The Chinese government sent several units of "people's volunteers" into North Korea in October, but their numbers were limited. MacArthur considered them to be a token force, and he assured his own soldiers that they would be home by Christmas. Engaged in a relaxed "mopping up" exercise, American troops were not prepared to engage the large Chinese army that crossed the Yalu and began a major offensive on November 26. Masses of soldiers in quilted uniforms, urged on by blaring bugles, overran their objectives. American casualties soared, many of the wounded froze to death, and the Chinese were inclined to take few prisoners.

The war's third pell-mell retreat continued through the holiday season, a time of mortification for Americans. It was not easy to adjust to being beaten by Chinese, whose military ability had been a subject either of laughter or of lamentation since the Opium War of 1839. Excuse-making relied upon an old image reminiscent of the summer of the Boxer Rebellion—Chinese armies as human seas, human waves, yellow tides, ocher hordes, from a land where life is cheap, automatistically moving forward to inundate small groups of brave defenders usually running low on ammunition.

While there was some truth in this view, several United States army officers would write later that it failed to show the frequent skill of Chinese tactics and effective use of artillery. In the winter of 1950–51 there was also some solace in emphasizing that this was a UN defeat, but European commentators were by now insisting that the war was an essentially American operation.

The shock of defeat produced addled debates in Congress and among journalists, one side calling for total effort for total victory and the other demanding an immediate pullout, with the consequences of either extreme seldom entering the argument. Through it all Truman seemed undisturbed, intent upon a middle course that furious partisans called indecision.

Chinese forces moved far to the south of the thirty-eighth parallel, but the retreat ended in January 1951 when a line was formed, anchored on the coasts, and American planes and tanks began to prove effective against Chinese infantry. Again the war moved north, this time slowly and with bitter loss of life. In the vicinity of the thirty-eighth parallel the UN push halted, there being little inclination in the White House for another drive into North Korea. A strong front, established across the peninsula at its narrowest width, would withstand enemy assaults for the remainder of the war. The original purpose had been attained for a second time, but by another name balance was stalemate, and its frustrations fed the continuing debate in the United States.

MacArthur became the idol of the victory enthusiasts. In a letter to the Republican congressman Joseph W. Martin, Jr.—which Martin made public—the general emphasized the menace of communism in Asia and coined a slogan, "There is no substitute for victory." He had found a substitute in his post-Inchon strategy, but such a man could easily ignore his own mistakes and dwell instead upon Promethean concepts, the handicaps imposed upon him by the administration's weak-kneed policy of limited war. In press conferences MacArthur ignored government policy and called for victory through another northern offensive, the bombing of China, and an invasion of the mainland by Chiang. Truman did not want unlimited war with China; he and his chairman of the Joint Chiefs of Staff, General Omar N. Bradley, believed such a war would waste the country's men and resources at a time when a strong posture against Russia in Europe should remain the primary concern. Truman knew that MacArthur had every right to hold opinions on policy—but no right to make policy, as he seemed to be trying to do in his press conference warnings to China. The Constitution assigns decisions on policy and war to civil heads of state and to Congress, not to generals, and on grounds of insubordination Truman dismissed MacArthur from his commands in Korea and Japan on April 11, 1951.

The "weakling" in the White House had fired a great hero. Popular disbelief gave way to rage, which, mixed with adulation for MacArthur's past exploits, produced the most tumultuous homecoming welcome in the country's history. The general had not set foot in his native land for fifteen years, so busy had been his career, and with his return confetti filled the sky as millions cheered or wept along parade routes in major cities. Teenagers danced to a song called "General Mac," which disk jockeys played again and again along with "God Bless America" and the barrack-room ballad "Old Soldiers Never Die." Throughout the country Truman was hanged in effigy, and senators threatened him with impeachment. The hero-martyr's televised speech to Congress criticized government policy in the Far East and ended on a sentimental note: "I now close my military career and just fade away, an old soldier who tried to do his duty as God gave him the light to see that duty. Good-by." As the parades and press conferences continued, MacArthur received letters urging him to take advantage of his popularity and cure the country of its ills. Most letter writers wanted him to run for president in 1952, but a few urged him to become "the man on horseback," leading a coup against the Truman administration. There is no evidence that the wilder suggestions were received with anything but repugnance by MacArthur; his decision to keep the promise to "fade away" was one of the more commendable of a remarkable career.

After the Chinese failed in two offensives during the spring of 1951, they and the North Koreans agreed to open truce talks, but these would not succeed in bringing about an armistice until July 1953. Thus desultory warfare along the thirty-eighth parallel continued through the remainder of Truman's term of office. History records his war, despite the blunder of autumn 1950, as a successful fulfillment of its first intent. Yet its costly prolongation was understandably unpopular, and administration suggestions that the war, taken as a whole, was a victory were considered outrageous in the early 1950s. Truman endured his last months in office with a popularity rating of 23 percent, the lowest for any president in the history of poll taking and one point lower than the rating assigned President Richard M. Nixon in the week prior to his resignation in 1974.

Hindsight would suggest that the administration most despised during its time in office had performed well during a complex and perilous era. Its Marshall Plan and other containment measures had brought stability to western Europe and diminished the chances of a third world war; Japan was an ally and Korea's dividing line remained the thirty-eighth parallel. But these results were obscured by others. America's alleged loss of China, loss of its atomic weapons monopoly in 1949, and inability to win a smashing victory in Korea induced fear, frustration, anger. Yearning for a simple answer to the problem of communism, Americans were tired of diplomats who achieved mixed results, who talked of balance, patience, flexibility, defensive containment, and other wishy-washy ideas that seemed little more than excuses for failure. Aggravations mounted as the nation prepared another of its overreactions to affairs in the Far East.

In the early fifties the clouds of suspicion darkened and the language of accusation became hysterical. What had caused the failures? Were some world events uncontrollable, as the State Department insisted? This was difficult to understand, especially in the period just after World War II. Had Uncle Sam as an entity—the people, the ideals, the vaunted strength—somehow not measured up to the job? This too was unacceptable. The blame must lie with certain individuals who had been entrusted with responsibilities, major and minor, in the State Department and other areas of government. The China Lobby investigators of the late forties were joined by congressmen, journalists, authors, historians—influential if limited in number—who were either sincere in their beliefs or seeking fame through the creation of sensational headlines. Name-calling intensified. It was no longer enough to charge that suspects were failures, blunderers, weaklings, or diplomatic sissies in striped trousers; rather, they were soft on communism or in some cases traitors or enemy agents. The list of their conspiracies grew longer with every hastily contrived investigation. It was said that FDR had conceived a Pearl Harbor plot for the purpose of bringing the United States into a war to aid world communism; he had sold out to Stalin at Yalta; in wanting to lose China the Trumanites had betrayed Chiang; then they had leashed him with the Seventh Fleet for the purpose of saving Mao's regime; and they had not wanted to win in Korea and therefore had deposed the general who had called for victory there. Shocking revelations emanated from books, newspapers, and especially some busy committees in Congress—the House Un-American Activities Committee, the Senate Internal Security Subcommittee, and the Senate Permanent Investigating Subcommittee, which became home base for the champion maker of headlines, Senator Joseph R. McCarthy of Wisconsin.

McCarthy, who gave his name to an era, first gained attention early in 1950 with a series of unsubstantiated charges that the State Department was infested with Communists. He went on to call Truman a moron, Acheson soft on communism, and General Marshall a traitor, while applying terms shaded from pink to red to a number of Foreign Service officers who had been connected with Far Eastern policies over the past decade. Having disposed of the State Department, he took on other senators, the science establishment, the army, and virtually the entire Democratic administration and its "twenty years of treason." His tactics in committee hearings—innuendo, guilt by association, manufacture of physical evidence—proved none too useful in catching Communists; yet the sliest of insinuations could raise suspicion, and in this manner hundreds of government employees lost their reputations, friends, and jobs. The term *McCarthyism* referred to the senator's methods as well as to their emulation by other congressional committees, the attorney general's office, agencies in states and cities, school and library boards throughout the country, the entertainment industry, and other types of private business. Before McCarthyism lost its force in 1954, it had destroyed the careers of countless Americans through vague allegations, posed a serious threat to freedom of speech and press and other civil rights, and created lasting impressions that would affect the future in a number of ways.

Born out of diplomatic troubles, McCarthyism also had its effects upon the country's foreign affairs. A particular case was that of Tsien Hsue-shen, who in 1935 had come from China to the United States to study at the Massachusetts Institute of Technology. He had won a distinguished reputation by the early fifties, when he was a professor of jet propulsion at the California Institute of Technology and held an inner-circle role among scientists working on government-sponsored research in nuclear weapons and missiles. During the height of the McCarthy furor Tsien was declared a "security risk" and lost his key positions. Naturally resentful, he decided to take his talents elsewhere, and it is remarkable that he was eventually allowed to do so. When last seen, Tsien was headed for Lop Nor in China's western desert, soon to become famous as the site of rapid accomplishments in nuclear fission and fusion and in missile development.

McCarthyism's other diplomatic effects were more general. Foreign nations lost respect; the tone of western European journalism was one of dismay over a society gone berserk. At a time when Americans professed leadership of the free world, they seemed intent upon wrecking their own freedom. And in their exaggerated concern over the menace of internal communism, they were creating bitter divisions among themselves, ruining morale in the State Department and armed forces, and weakening their nation's position on the international scene where communism was a reality. Crucial changes in foreign policy were also influenced by McCarthyism, which was furiously present in the election campaign of 1952. When the Republicans won that election—General of the Army Dwight D. Eisenhower defeated the Democratic nominee, Adlai Stevenson, Jr., in a landslide—they had good reason to believe that the American people were demanding policies far different from those of the Truman administration.

XII

Positive
Thinking

THE FIRST TWO YEARS of the new Republican diplomacy, 1953–54, coincided with the rise to the top of the best-seller list of the Reverend Dr. Norman Vincent Peale's *The Power of Positive Thinking*. President Eisenhower preferred novels about the Old West, but his secretary of state, John Foster Dulles, may well have read Dr. Peale's book, finding in it nothing he did not know already. At times administration leaders professed scorn for the McCarthy tactics that had helped win the election, but they were convinced that the foreign policies of their predecessors had been at the very least negative. Through conviction and political need, they were determined to provide the sharpest of contrasts. Words and slogans were important. Containment, balance, defensive perimeter, stalemate—these and other lackluster ideas must be replaced by mission, besiegement, liberation, victory. But 1953 was not 1898, 1917, or 1941. The world of the fifties was a political wilderness in which the enemy, its strategy and even its nature, was indistinct at best. Bold crusaders might lose their way, confronting only exhaustion and self-defeat. In some cases missions were threatened but bugles never blown; in others, the Far East included, new policies were pushed so far forward that there was little chance of saving the future from their effects.

The United States and the Soviet Union appeared to be exchanging strategies in early 1953. The Eisenhower administration, talking of bipolar struggle and the need to win it by taking the offensive, entered office in early January. Two months later Stalin died and his successor, Georgi Malenkov, called for "a peaceful coexistence of two systems.'' An increasing number of Kremlin leaders had come to view the Stalinist pressure tactics as dangerous, and the failure of those tactics had embarrassed the Soviets on several occasions between 1947 and 1952. When Nikita S. Khrushchev emerged as the government's dominant figure in the mid-1950s, he attacked Stalinist policies, repeated the coexistence theme, and based his country's strategy on hopes for its long-range ability to outperform the capitalist economic system. Russian interests remained the same, but they were advanced with tactics more subtle than in Stalin's time. Moscow seemed more aware than Washington of the manner in which the world was changing. It would be ''futile and dangerous,'' Khrushchev said, to try to force reluctant nations into one Cold War camp or the other; pushing them too hard could turn them into enemies. If the Americans wanted to try, let them.

The new policies in Washington, moving from complexity toward simplicity, were poorly timed, to say the least. Perversely the rest of the world was moving in the opposite direction toward a condition variously described as multipolar, polycentric, or pluralistic. American domination of its alliance system weakened as countries in western Europe recovered strength and confidence, forgetting that feeling of dependence in the years just after the Second World War. Latin American nations, located in an area usually taken for granted, could prove disagreeable, and the Japanese sometimes voiced unhappiness with an alliance in which they could make no important decisions of their own. Nor could the Soviet system avoid fragmentation. Yugoslavia had remained Communist while turning a cold shoulder to Russian leadership, and there were riots in East Berlin in 1953 and revolutionary efforts in Poland and Hungary in 1956. What Dulles called the ''unholy alliance'' between Russia and China endured until the late 1950s, but the relationship was awkward and marked by cold civility.

Diversity within the Russian-American ''blocs'' was confusing but not nearly so much as in those regions that the State Department—searching for a tactful way to describe recipients of its AID programs—called undeveloped, underdeveloped, then developing, then emerging. Other terms such as *Third Force* and *Third World* came into being, but no single classification could describe the aftermath of colonialism in the Middle East, Africa, and Asia. New nations emerged every year, sometimes singly and often in bunches, displaying a multiplicity of nationalist themes and curious political brews. Never had the world seen so many sovereignties, so many recipes for national experience. And never had American diplomacy, if it was to be effective, been more in need of flexibility, of professionals trained in dozens of languages, cultures, histories, and current political attitudes. Conducting his single policy, Secretary Dulles was perpetually astonished by nations that showed disinterest in the Cold War and pursued policies with no reference to "our side" or the "other side."

President Eisenhower achieved an extraordinary popularity based upon admiration for his wartime leadership, a radiant smile, and a next-door-neighbor style of verbal communication. He had kept himself apart from the mud-slinging department of the campaign, and as chief executive he often seemed apart from the affairs of government, preferring to delegate responsibility to cabinet members regarded as experts in their fields. For this reason the conduct of American foreign policy has been associated less with Eisenhower than with his secretary of state. The president considered Dulles to be a "mastermind of diplomacy" with an "encyclopedic knowledge" of world problems, and the secretary did not quarrel with this assessment. In the administration's early days, according to White House aide Emmet J. Hughes, Dulles assured Eisenhower that "with my understanding of the intricate relationships between the peoples of the world and your sensitiveness to the political considerations involved, we will make the most successful team in history."

Although a Republican, Dulles had served in the State Department during the administrations of Wilson, Roosevelt, and Truman, his latest accomplishments being the negotiation of the peace treaty with Japan and the mutual security treaties with Japan, the Philippines, Australia, and New Zealand. He had not been happy with trends in policy and early in 1952 had resigned from the Truman administration in order to campaign against it. Refusing to lower himself to the level of McCarthy and other campaigners who charged the incumbents with treason, he nonetheless contributed to the thorough discreditation of the Truman foreign policy. In speeches and magazine articles Dulles called for a "new dynamism," a "policy of boldness" that would bring about the "liberation" of peoples in eastern Europe. He wanted Chiang to be "unleashed" for the purpose of liberating China. In the Republican platform he promised to do away with "the negative, futile, and immoral policy of 'containment' which abandons countless human beings to despotism and Godless terrorism."

Throughout his career Dulles would employ a somber language strewn with such terms as *righteousness, crusade, mission, moral dynamism, moral zeal, absolute right,* and *absolute wrong.* Like Woodrow Wilson, he had been reared in the Calvinist-Puritan-Presbyterian tradition. Occasionally he was called upon for sermons in his church, and there was something of this in his diplomatic manner. Foreign statesmen sometimes complained that they felt superfluous at conferences because the secretary seldom looked at their faces; his glance was upward as he seemed to address the cosmos. Dulles's defenders have stressed his experience and knowledge, depicting a reasonable man pushed forward by the feverish state of public opinion during the early 1950s, forced to make the kind of pronouncements that would serve his party and tell worried Americans what they wanted to hear concerning the health of national ideals and capabilities.

Upon entering office, the secretary began the job of liberating eastern Europe by ordering the United States Information Service to send freedom messages, conveyed by radio and penny balloons filled with helium, across the Iron Curtain. Within a year he was talking about another policy, referred to as "massive retaliation," which he hoped might solve most of the country's diplomatic problems. Assuming that Communist activities throughout the world were promoted in Moscow, he warned the Russians to desist or face the possibility of a hydrogen bomb attack. There would be no war, he judged, for the threat against Moscow would act as a deterrent to Communist pressures everywhere, in the jungles of Africa and Asia as well as in Europe. Reliance upon nuclear weapons would allow the United States to cut back the size of its military forces with their expensive array of conventional weapons. A nuclear policy, as Eisenhower's friends put it, meant

199

"more bang for the buck" and coincided nicely with Republican promises to cut government spending.

Global pluralism ruined the massive retaliation idea. While Dulles knew that Communist movements existed in Africa and Asia, their origins were hazy, their definitions vague in mixture with local nationalisms, their threat too remote to justify his serving the Soviet Union with a nuclear warning. In turn the massive retaliation policy destroyed any hope, if one had seriously existed, of liberating eastern Europe. The pathetic condition of conventional military forces made it certain that Washington must watch helplessly in the autumn of 1956 when rebellions in Poland and Hungary were crushed by the tanks of the Russian army. By 1957 Dulles was agreeing with military officers that, despite the cost, the United States must rebuild its conventional forces. American and Russian nuclear stockpiles had grown ominously, and it was not reasonable that statesmen could discuss their use even in the day-to-day bluster of Cold War diplomacy. Without an adequately equipped army and navy Dulles could not even achieve containments and stalemates, much less go on the offensive against communism and besiege it.

While two poorly conceived policies—massive retaliation and liberation of eastern Europe—were heading for failure, Dulles was on the offensive in the Far East, pressing siege lines forward. This was accomplished through a series of alliances and commitments that drew a new boundary for what the secretary called the free world. Acheson's "defensive perimeter" of 1950 had been drawn in water so that the United States, with its advantages in sea and air power, could hold it easily. There had been no alliance with South Korea; an obligation of this sort had not been among Truman's reasons for going to war there. The Truman administration had limited its Far Eastern allies to Japan, Australia, New Zealand, and the Philippines. Dulles had negotiated these security pacts with patience, skill, and strategic understanding of why the four countries were good bets in terms of American commitment; three had stable governments and strength that was important to the United States, and the insular nature of all promised no problems in defending them against mainlanders. It was the same strategy that had kept navy-conscious Britain uninvaded for nearly a thousand years. The intelligent Dulles understood such matters but was not much interested in them. More important to him were moral values. The four alliances, he often said, represented "victories for the free world." In these places the United States was "solemnly pledging itself to the defense of freedom." A fine idea except that, viewed in terms of principle, the Japanese and Australians were no different from weak, undefendable peoples who also deserved to be free. This became apparent after Dulles became secretary of state and pushed the line of commitment close to the mainland and onto it.

The brave secretary began signing alliances and agreements in 1954 that offered severe liabilities and few assets. His game of choose-up-sides in the Cold War drew the attention of cartoonists in Europe and a few in the United States, who depicted Dulles poised over an adding machine, mistaking quantity for quality as he totaled up more allies than had Russia and China; as a squirrel gathering nuts for the winter; with a butterfly net collecting rare species of commitments; or as a General Custer riding deep into the diplomatic wilderness. Now and then editorial writers were reminded of the days of McKinley and Taft, of high-minded but unstudied lunges to the Philippines and China. But critics in America were few in the mid-fifties. There was general satisfaction in knowing that the country had not lost the ability to move forward, and those who fussed over small strategic details were no better than Trumanites.

Eisenhower and Dulles made good on campaign promises to end the fighting in Korea, where truce talks that had dragged on since the summer of 1951 ended in the armistice of July 1953. President Rhee was furious with the Americans for having failed to conquer North Korea, but he was mollified by more payments in a continuing program of military and economic aid—and by a mutual security treaty that the United States Senate approved in January 1954. The war that Truman had judged necessary to the needs of 1950 thus turned into a permanent commitment that failed to acknowledge the possibility of changes in South Korea's relationship to American interests.

An alliance with Chiang resulted from occurrences in the region of Taiwan. Beginning with the generalissimo's arrival on the island late in 1949, both he and his ejectors had threatened to invade each other and Truman had interposed the Seventh Fleet between them. Restrained, Chiang grew bold in describing the awful fate that would have befallen the Communists had his military prowess not been thwarted by the Americans. He exaggerated the strength and size of the 500,000-man army he had brought to Taiwan, and in a fascinated American press it became a force of 600,000, 800,000, and eventually well over a million. At its then rate of growth, commented A. J. Liebling in the *New Yorker* magazine, it would have reached six billion by 1958. Liebling called it a rubber army, expandable and contractable according to political needs. During the 1952 campaign the Republicans praised Chiang's troops as a mighty force capable of retaking China were it not being kept from doing so by the pro-Communist Truman administration, and Dulles made his "unleashing" promise. After the election the United States would no longer "shield" Red China from Chiang.

One of the Eisenhower government's first acts was to remove the Seventh Fleet from the Formosa Strait, whereupon it turned out that Chiang had not really wanted to be unleashed. He complained of shortages in weapons and money. His army was deflated to 500,000, then kept shrinking to a condition estimated to be no more than 12,000 combat-ready troops. The generalissimo so insisted upon his weakness that Peking was encouraged to prepare a sortie of its own. Taiwan must be liquidated, Chou En-lai declared in August 1954, and the Communists used heavy artillery to shell Nationalist-held islands—the Tachen, Matsu, and Quemoy groups close to mainland China, the Quemoys lying off Amoy just five miles from shore.

Disappointed by Chiang's loss of élan, Dulles nonetheless considered him worthy of protection. The Seventh Fleet returned to the strait, and Taiwan and the United States in December 1954 signed a treaty pledging to defend each other's territory. The treaty defined Chiang's domain as Taiwan and its nearby Pescadore Islands, making no mention of the islands that lay within shooting distance of the mainland. Yet in early 1955, as one of the Tachens fell to the Communists and the bombardment of the Quemoys and Matsus continued, both Eisenhower and Dulles warned that these coastal islands *might* be considered vital to the defense of Taiwan and *might* then be interpreted as protected by the treaty. The statements were purposely vague, and Peking apparently decided not to risk a major war by taking the Quemoys and Matsus. Dulles later said that he had gone to "the verge of war. . . . If you are scared to go to the brink, you are lost." His gamble had paid off and he expected congratulations, but "brinkmanship" drew only criticism from European and Japanese allies who saw Dulles as too awkward a statesman to be able to tiptoe forever along precipices without falling off and, in a nuclear age, taking the rest of the world with him. Any diplomat must be prepared to take a calculated risk if such is warranted by important circumstances, but the tiny islands seemed so useless, even to Chiang, even as symbols. But to a man of principle Matsu is every bit as important as Japan, Hawaii, or Catalina.

The renewed bombardment of the Quemoys in 1958 produced another flurry of nervousness as the islands retained their interest to Americans. They were prominent in the 1960 television debates between presidential nominees John F. Kennedy and Vice President Nixon. Kennedy questioned the relationship of the islands to American security, but Nixon declared that the United States must not abandon even one "island of freedom."

American activities around the rim of China, along with other factors, affected the unnatural Sino-Soviet alliance of the 1950s. During the first decade of Chinese communism, while the system was not yet firmly established, Peking needed Soviet diplomatic support and whatever technological aid the Russians were willing to supply. Meanwhile the Chinese Communist Party worked strenuously to develop unity, a term never before associated with the modern history of that country. Millions of nonconformists were sentenced to "deprivation of existence." * The regime decreed

---

* In describing the awesome miseries of China—floods, starvation, Taipings, or modern purges—historians have had to resort to vague references of "mil-

group activities, providing patriotic organizations for workers, peasants, women, and children; imposed ideological regimentation through the schools, the arts, and pageantry; abolished formal religion; instituted a commune system for agriculture that, for the double purpose of efficiency and eliminating the "danger of privacy," meant burning individual farmhouses and building large dormitories; increased state ownership of the means of production and distribution; and promulgated the Five Year Plans of 1953 and 1958, which were aimed at improving industrial production. Not always did theory accord with reality. Many plans and projects required the services of individuals of talent although their employment was repugnant to the Marxist ideal of equality. The Russians had learned to cheat on Marxism, understanding that some people are more equal than others, unofficially accepting the natural laws associated with Darwin. Such acceptance was impossible in a revolution that was young and pure; leaders of the CCP used the services of ideologically impure individuals with reluctance, and knew that someday this puritan dilemma would have to be resolved.

In spite of disappointments, especially in the industrial results, Chinese strength and confidence had grown so impressively by the late 1950s that the CCP could afford to quarrel openly with the Kremlin. Peking was contemptuous of Russia's impure communism and resented changes in that country's foreign policy since Stalin's time. Khrushchev's criticism of Stalin seemed implicitly a criticism of Mao. Moscow was accused of diplomatic conservatism and weakness, of betraying the tenet of Marxism that was the unrelenting promotion of world revolution. The "revisionist" split meant contests over leadership of the Communist world and over tactics to be used against the United States and other capitalist na-

---

lions'' of deaths. No one knows how many people lost their lives in the liquidations of the 1950s or in the Great Cultural Revolution of the 1960s. The Peking government placed the figure at 2,326,000 from October 1949 to May 1952, but the French government estimated three million for the same period. The Soviet government, at odds with the CCP by 1960 but whose observers had been in China during the previous decade, reported a 1949–60 total of 13,300,000.

tions. Doctrinal argument might have been resolved had interests so demanded, but the increasing antagonism was one of nations as well as parties. The main problem was geographical contiguity, the 4,500-mile-long Sino-Soviet border that had been a source of troubles throughout modern history. Peking could not forget Russia's seizure of Chinese territories in tsarist times and its subsequent retention of them, while Moscow feared that sparsely populated eastern Siberia might some day prove too tempting for China to ignore.

It was against the law of averages that all of Dulles's commitments, some of them stemming from ideological vanity rather than practical need, could avoid eventual disaster. To the South Korean and Taiwanese pacts of 1954 was added SEATO (Southeast Asia Treaty Organization), which established an American commitment totally unrelated to past strategies either insular or peninsular, and therein lay the rub.

The secretary's Southeast Asian policy perhaps represented an excited reaction to the failure of France's colonial war against the Vietminh. From 1946 to 1954, fighting a guerrilla conflict they did not know how to win, the French tried to maintain at least a token form of imperial status. As their military position worsened, they offered concessions to the precolonial components of Indochina—Vietnam, stretching along the east coast, Laos in the northwest, and Cambodia in the southwest—and in 1950 went so far as to grant the three states independence within a French Union intended to resemble the British Commonwealth. This arrangement was agreeable to Bao Dai, a leader of non-Communist Vietnamese nationalism who called himself an emperor, and the French began training an army for him in the hope that it could assume a major part in the war. The training went slowly, Bao Dai had trouble promoting the French Union even among anti-Communist elements in his country, and his efforts were never vigorous; he preferred the nightclubs of Paris and the Riviera to Vietnamese politics.

While it waited in vain for "indigenous reinforcements," the

French army kept losing to Ho Chi Minh's Communist version of nationalism in northern Vietnam. American aid, begun by Truman and Acheson in 1950 and comprising 78 percent of France's Indochina war budget by 1954 (a four-year total of $2.6 billion), was offset by strategic advantages enjoyed by the guerrillas as well as by aid they received from Russia and China. The end of the Korean war in 1953 enabled China to send larger stores of weapons, including field artillery, to the Vietminh. By early 1954 a large French force was surrounded at Dienbienphu in northwest Vietnam near the Laotian frontier. In France the war was exceedingly unpopular, the government in danger of falling, and many of its members hoping for a diplomatic settlement as the only honorable means of pulling out of *la folie* in the Far East. An opportunity for negotiation would come in April at Geneva, at an international conference scheduled mainly for the purpose of discussing Korea.

Dulles vowed to keep communism from gaining either on the battlefield or at the conference table, and April 1954 proved indeed a month of decision. The Vietminh were closing the ring around Dienbienphu. French generals called for help. Almost as ominous was the approach of the Geneva Conference, where the presence of Russian, mainland Chinese, and Vietminh representatives was almost certain to result in a compromise of "free-world" territory. Eisenhower tried to explain the danger by telling reporters, "You have a row of dominoes set up, you knock over the first one, and what will happen to the last one is that it will go over very quickly." Dulles met often with Eisenhower and with Admiral Arthur W. Radford, who was chairman of the Joint Chiefs of Staff, Vice President Nixon, and other members of the National Security Council. There is no record that the stillborn policy of massive retaliation against Moscow or Peking was considered. Apparently Dulles and Radford discussed the use of small nuclear bombs against the besiegers of Dienbienphu, but several factors, including the risk of atomizing the French along with their enemies, ruled out the idea. The only alternative was the use of conventional forces, weakened though they were by the massive retaliation policy. Nixon suggested sending in troops, but Dulles and

Radford preferred strikes by carrier aircraft. Eisenhower was wary, wanting more advice and broader support, and Dulles agreed to obtain it.

But intervention in Vietnam received little support outside the National Security Council. Generals Matthew B. Ridgway and James M. Gavin advised that air power would not be effective in guerrilla war and that infantry and tanks would face far greater difficulties in Vietnam than they had in Korea. Hoping for a supportive resolution from Congress, Dulles consulted members of both parties and received a mixed response that happened to include opinions from two future presidents. Senator John F. Kennedy said that the political tangle in Indochina was reason enough for steering clear of the place. Furthermore, "for the United States to intervene unilaterally and to send troops into the most difficult terrain in the world . . . would be far more difficult than . . . Korea." He asked Dulles if Indochina was "absolutely essential" to American interests. The Democratic leader in the Senate, Lyndon B. Johnson, also opposed an intervention that might leave the United States "naked and alone in a hostile world." He cautioned against precipitate policies. "Our friends and allies are frightened and wondering, as we do, where we are headed." Britain played a crucial role in Washington's decision not to intervene in 1954. Much to Dulles's disgust both Prime Minister Winston Churchill and Foreign Secretary Anthony Eden made clear that they wanted nothing to do with the project.

The Geneva Conference opened on April 26 with its assortment of Communist and anti-Communist delegations. Eden said later that the Americans never forgave him his part as an agent of compromise. At first no compromise appeared possible, for the French proved as stubborn as the Vietminh, who were backed by representatives from Moscow and Peking. The French position weakened with surrender of Dienbienphu on May 7 and disintegrated with the fall of the government in Paris on June 12. The new premier, Pierre Mendes-France, had promised to end his country's involvement in Southeast Asia, all the while insisting that France someday would regain its power through substitution of milk for wine as the national beverage. Through a series of private deals with Chinese, Russian, and Vietminh delegates, he produced an armistice; full independence for Vietnam, Laos, and Cambodia; temporary division of Vietnam at the seventeenth parallel with Vietminh sympathizers to be grouped north of the line and Bao Dai's followers in the south; and an internationally supervised election in 1956 naively intended to reunify the country. Dulles had known from the beginning that the victorious Communists would be assigned territory—a reversal rather than the kind of advance called for in his policies. Described as grim and disapproving, he had observed the first few days of the Geneva talks and then returned to Washington. By the time the conference ended on July 21, he was taking pains to dissociate the United States from the results.

While France negotiated itself out of Southeast Asia, the secretary of state prepared an American assumption of freedom's burden there. Determined that no more dominoes should fall, he began to line up nations for membership in a general security system for the region. Six weeks after the end of the Geneva affair, he assembled a conference of his own in Manila with seven other nations—Britain, France, Australia, New Zealand, the Philippines, Pakistan, and Thailand. These governments participated with varying enthusiasm. The British and French, who had no intention of fighting in Asia, attended mainly to soothe Dulles's feelings, which had been ruffled by Geneva. Their disinterest became acute when the secretary added to the SEATO draft a protocol that included South Vietnam, Laos, and Cambodia among the nations to be defended.

Signed on September 8, 1954, SEATO allowed its members to act "at the invitation or with the consent" of any one of the member states in the area (this would include the protocol clients, Laos, Cambodia, and South Vietnam). Action could follow overt aggression or internal subversion, but the only type of action required by the treaty was a certain amount of consultation among the allies. Lack of enthusiasm in some of the governments represented at the Manila conference prevented the kind of binding clauses that had made NATO a formidable alliance; instead SEATO resembled the mutual security pacts of the 1920s. The treaty was anything but meaningless to its sponsor. It provided a legal means, through the invitation clause, whereby any signatory could choose to intervene, unilaterally if need be. SEATO with its loopholes demanded nothing, yet it was possible for any of its members to regard it as imposing a moral responsibility.

With the addition of a few more "allies," Dulles's Cold War scorecard looked better than ever, so long as qualitative analysis could be avoided. Laos and Cambodia were primitive lands, politically unpredictable. South Vietnam seemed more advanced because of its ports and the big city of Saigon, yet it was an unpalatable mix of Ho partisans, anti-Communists with sundry and curious allegiances, dissenting religious sects, gangster armies, government misrule and corruption. The emperor Bao Dai had gone into permanent exile on the Riviera, and Premier Ngo Dinh Diem was calling himself the real ruler in Saigon. Following the signing of SEATO, which had a mutual aid clause, Diem tactfully waited three weeks before applying to the strongest of his new allies for economic assistance. Eisenhower's reply promised an aid program in return for "needed reforms." Diem cooperated in promising reforms, and soon millions of dollars were on their way to Saigon (over three billion by the end of the Eisenhower administration), along with further American promises to support the new leader's regime and train an army for him. These pledges were later viewed as having strengthened the presumed moral commitment that began with SEATO.

Diem manipulated American support to consolidate his rule and in July 1955 announced that South Vietnam would not take part in the "free election" that the Geneva conferees had planned for both Vietnams in 1956. It was a reasonable decision. With the North Vietnamese government reported to be shooting thousands of political opponents, there seemed no chance for an unrigged election north of the seventeenth parallel. South Vietnam went to the polls in October 1955, gave Diem a suspicious 99 percent of the vote, and established him as president of a new Republic of Vietnam.

Smoking from four to five packs of cigarettes each day, the nervous Diem would maintain control over the country for eight turbulent years, a period of declining popularity both for himself and

The War in Vietnam

0   100   200
Miles

CHINA

BURMA

NORTH VIETNAM

Hanoi

Haiphong

Gulf of Tonkin

HAINAN

LAOS

Mekong R.

Ho Chi Minh Trail

Demarcation Line 1954

Danang

THAILAND

Bangkok

CAMBODIA

SOUTH VIETNAM

Mekong R.

Saigon

SOUTH CHINA SEA

MALAYSIA

his American associates. The latter, harried civilians in drip-dry apparel who worked mainly for the State Department's Agency for International Development (AID), had never heard of Polonius and his advice on the dangers of samaritanism. Nor did they recall the subtle techniques of giving that had helped make a success of the Marshall Plan. Foreign aid as it was practiced in the fifties made no distinction between finite and infinite forms of need. Instead of allowing money to work quietly and usefully—if ever it could in hopelessly backward nations—AID officials became Santa

210

Clauses, presiding over dispensation ceremonies in which recipients were expected to show gratitude through political promises. Even more resented, at least by people who lived in poverty, was AID's tendency to provide luxuries for unpopular rulers. Diem and his three brothers each owned more than forty white Palm Beach suits; they possessed more limousines than did Eisenhower, and Diem's sister-in-law, Madame Nhu, was sometimes flown to Paris for shopping sprees. The female relative was just as glamorous as Madame Chiang in her prime, though less diplomatic with statements to American reporters that South Vietnamese liberty could best be preserved through liquidation of dissenters. Her waspish moods were not improved when the State Department equipped the palace with central heating instead of the air-conditioning system she had ordered. (AID officials, most of whom spoke no Vietnamese and little French, often were victimized by interpreters who turned out to be Communists.) A more serious matter was the regime's use of American money, weapons, and police training to close down opposition newspapers and violently dispose of even non-Communist adversaries. The Diems and their successors gravely embarrassed the United States in failing to meet minimal standards expected of an ally that, being non-Communist, was supposed to be democratic.

Between 1955 and 1960 some three hundred American military advisers, mainly veterans of the Korean war, trained a South Vietnamese army to fight a similar kind of conflict. After their training period Diem's soldiers were placed in strong defensive positions just south of the demilitarized zone (DMZ) in which the Geneva hopefuls had encased the seventeenth parallel. The right flank of the front was anchored on the Gulf of Tonkin, but its left was protected only by the border of Laos. Thus the North Vietnamese, in the 1950s as in the 1960s, had no need to repeat the frontal assault tactics of the Korean war. They simply walked into Laos and back into Vietnam once they were below the line, and there they joined southern Communists (Vietcong) in preparations for guerrilla warfare. By 1960 their nocturnal attacks on villages and hit-and-run terrorism in cities had convinced Americans that the Vietnam problem was different from that of Korea. To meet new training needs the strength of the military advisory group was raised to 685, then to over 800 by the end of the Eisenhower presidency. The figures were small and the press had not yet discovered the word *escalation*.

Dulles's career ended in 1959 with an illness that caused his death. It is to his credit that, despite bellicose instincts, he had dropped no bombs and declared no wars. It is probable that he will be best remembered as a major contributor to the catastrophe of the 1960s through his planting and cultivation of a moral commitment that future leaders lacked the wisdom to ignore. In his own time the world feared him as a theologian of diplomacy, threatening international fire and brimstone. With his sense of rectitude he bore no resemblance to Senator Joseph R. McCarthy, yet both men in their different ways symbolized the reaction to communism—self-harming in its impulsiveness—that had overcome a nation admired for leadership in World War II and the tense years immediately following.

When the red scare diminished in the late fifties, it was replaced by immoderate anxieties of another type. How many friends had been lost during the recent intoxication? Did the free world still consider the United States its leader? Poll-taking organizations sent their employees throughout the allied world, asking foreigners what they thought of America. The results, revealed in large headlines, were often disconcerting: "America No Longer Popular in Italy" or "U. S. Popularity Slips Sixteen Points in London." The nation's "prestige rating" became a diplomatic Dow-Jones average, its future prospects analyzed in editorials and by teams of TV newsmen with furrowed brows. University debate teams and government panels argued about ways to improve the "national image," a term of Madison Avenue origin that might suggest that the latest anxiety had all the importance of a deodorant commercial. To crave popularity is to lose it. Besides, rich and powerful nations can never be loved. The most they can hope for is respect, which is unattainable without self-assurance and dignity.

With the popularity crisis at its height in the spring of 1959,

Eisenhower spoke of America's wish to forget angry words of the past, seeking "friendship and goodwill" with all the world, except perhaps Communist China. The most energetic period of his presidency—with Dulles gone, he assumed personal control of foreign policy—began with overtures to the Soviet Union. Khrushchev's tour of the United States in September 1959 marked the beginning of a period of détente known mainly for its brevity; it ended the following May when the U-2 incident became either the reason or the pretext for a new Russian freeze that humiliated the president and his efforts toward better relations. Russo-American antagonism had endured too long for it to be dispelled by slapping Khrushchev on the back.

Meanwhile Eisenhower had been trying to repair the national image through a series of global personal appearance tours. Reporters measured American prestige by estimating the number of foreigners who turned out for the parades. The size of European crowds tended to be disappointing, possibly due to "threats of rain," as television commentators explained. The count was better in Greece, Turkey, and Pakistan, and results in Kabul, the principal urban center of Afghanistan, far exceeded expectations. TV could now report overseas triumphs for the renowned smile and upthrust arms that had helped make Ike so popular in his own country. India's figures topped a million and a half, a stampeding multitude that suffered high casualties. In Brazil, Argentina, Uruguay, and Chile the crowds were large and enthusiastic.

Early June of 1960 found the president in Manila, poised to fly to Japan for another thunderous welcome. It was embarrassing, therefore, when America's most important Far Eastern ally cancelled the invitation at the last moment. Anti-American riots had become uncontrollable, and Premier Nobusuke Kishi could not allow Ike's life to be endangered. It was a comfort to know that the Tokyo demonstrators were from leftist student and worker organizations, but that did not excuse the poor timing of the planned visit, which was to have coincided with the signing of a treaty replacing one that had troubled many Japanese during the 1950s.

The mutual security treaty of 1951, signed during the occupation, had given the United States bases in Japan, control of the

Bonins and Ryukyus, and the right to decide virtually all diplomatic and military issues involving the two allies in relation with other powers. McCarthyism had raised doubts over the quality of American ideals, and Dulles had frightened the Japanese by going to brinks and taking his allies with him. The massive retaliation policy had drawn considerable attention in a country particularly concerned over the effects of nuclear war, and in 1954 Japan saw the possibility that it might be forced to fight again in Southeast Asia and China, this time on Chiang's side. Throughout the uncomfortable decade Tokyo asked Washington for treaty revisions that would give it some voice in mutual policies. In 1957 the United States agreed to withdraw combat troops from Japan, and negotiations for a new treaty began the following year. Russia and mainland China urged the Japanese to drop the alliance, but the Kishi government preferred to keep the American tie—in spite of its implied dangers and even after it became clear that the revised treaty would change nothing in regard to the Bonins and Ryukyus and do little more than broaden Japan's consultative rights. The Diet approved the new pact in the face of the demonstrations that ruined the Eisenhower visit and brought about Kishi's resignation a short time later.

Viewed in perspective, the riots were staged by a small minority, and many Japanese were ashamed of the display; a nationwide election later in the year retained protreaty and pro-American politicians in power. Yet the election result probably represented a lesser-of-the-evils choice more than widespread enthusiasm over being bound so closely to the policies of the eccentric Americans. The alliance survived Japanese fears during the 1950s and the demonstrations of 1960, but the rebuff to Eisenhower proved a dismal chapter in his personal efforts at diplomacy. In the United States the national image was assumed to have taken a turn for the worse, and it became a major issue in the Kennedy-Nixon presidential campaign.

XIII

A Lost
Crusade

WHILE NOTHING IN HISTORY is inevitable, the kind of experience endured in the 1960s had existed within the realm of
possibility since the time of McKinley, when the Far East had first
become an attraction for the more extravagant gestures of American diplomacy. Perhaps the nation could not forever avoid the consequences of overrating its influence and power and belittling difficulties of Asian politics and geography. In spite of the cacophony
of passions it once aroused, the Vietnam involvement as it recedes
far into the past will be remembered mainly as a curiosity. Generations of students, reading books on American history, will encounter thick chapters about a country that reasonably would appear to deserve no more than a paragraph or two. Such chapters
will have to be included, for they will deal with a near totality of
American activity for the better part of a decade, a period that saw
the United States ignore important world interests and domestic
concerns while concentrating upon a relative insignificance. *Imbal-
ance* will be too mild a term to describe a grotesque disproportion
of national interest and national effort.

The Vietnam crusade is associated mainly with the Johnson
presidency (November 1963 to January 1969), but its preparation
was shared by Truman and Acheson, Eisenhower and Dulles, and
the Kennedy administration, which entered office after the Massachusetts senator's victory over Nixon in the election of 1960.
Americans enjoyed a temporary easement of their image crisis
when it became clear, through newspapers and television, that for-

eigners admired the sophisticated style and educational attainments of Kennedy, his family, and some of his associates. It seemed that prestige came looking for those who had no need to seek it. The celebration of "Camelot" would later become a bore—especially to the Kennedy family—but during JFK's presidency it was a positive element in the country's foreign relations.

Self-confidence was the outward mark of the youthful administrators who replaced the tired businessmen of the Eisenhower government. It showed in talk about a New Frontier and "getting the country moving again." It was suggested in the relaxed gaiety of White House parties, sailing off Hyannisport, impromptu games of touch football. It seemed to permeate the views of new cabinet members and advisers, chosen because of proven competence in their fields. Among those who would work in foreign policy were Secretary of State Dean Rusk, a veteran of his department's Far Eastern division, and Secretary of Defense Robert McNamara, a genius in systems analysis and the Ford Motor Company's youngest president. For his White House adviser on national security Kennedy recruited McGeorge Bundy, Harvard's dean of the faculty, and from the faculty of the Massachusetts Institute of Technology came Walt W. Rostow to serve as Bundy's assistant.

The New Frontier's confidence was not in all respects genuine, and this affected its diplomacy. The victory over Nixon had been by the narrowest of margins, and what Democrat could forget how public fury over "no win" policies had led to disaster the last time the party had been in power? Kennedy's inaugural address had stressed his willingness to negotiate along with an intent to stand firm against communism everywhere in the world. Three months later he was shaken by the Bay of Pigs fiasco, a personal humiliation as well as a victory for Cuban communism. Kremlin politics had dictated a tougher Russian policy, and the press noted that Khrushchev's brusque threats were not effectively answered by the young, inexperienced American leader. Kennedy would gain confidence, develop maturity, and by the summer of 1963 display an able diplomacy. But the insecurity of his early months in the White House created a tense overdetermination to show no weakness, even in low-priority cases such as Vietnam.

Kennedy knew that Vietnam was unimportant to American security; he had said so several times while a senator in the 1950s. And it remained relatively unimportant during a presidency that, for all its brevity, experienced more than a normal share of European problems, Russian confrontations, and threats of nuclear war. Distraction, indecision, distaste for showing weakness—for several reasons JFK made no move to end the supposed moral commitment that he had inherited and allowed it to drift toward importance. When he had time to think about the small difficulty, he usually believed that he could resolve it in South Vietnam's favor by taking "one more step." He took that step several times, steadily increasing the American commitment to South Vietnam, the investment of money and prestige. He raised the number of military advisers on the scene from 800 in January 1961 to 15,500 by November 1963.

Nor did the president's advisers see themselves as crusaders. Except for Secretary Rusk, who believed that SEATO represented a moral commitment, the JFK aides had no affection for the Wilson-Dulles tradition of foreign policy guided by high principle. They had read the latest books on realism and were too bright to believe that South Vietnam was a democracy or that it was worth a big American war even if it had been democratic. They saw themselves as hardnosed and practical. Vietnam seemed a case study in power politics, not a crucial problem but one they had been stuck with and had better solve rather than encourage "the other side" by giving it a token of American inability to protect allies. All that was needed was a fresh idea, new input factors for the Pentagon's computer, or the application of a bit more power, carefully measured so that it would be just enough to correct the situation. They would think along such lines with growing desperation, some of them until the winter of 1967–68 when at last it would become evident that Vietnam did not compute.

Kennedy's earliest Southeast Asian worry was Laos, where an American-supported government was losing to the Pathet Lao, an indigenous Communist force backed by neighboring North Vietnam. The president considered sending troops, then decided not to fight in that remote region even though he was nagged by thoughts of showing weakness. The Laotian question was handed over to another Geneva conference, which, after more than a year of deliberation, arranged for a coalition government under Prince Souvanna Phouma. All signatories to the agreement, including the United States and North Vietnam, pledged to respect the neutrality of Laos. This stipulation would be ignored in future years by the CIA's none-too-clandestine operations and in even more dramatic fashion by the North Vietnamese as they used Laotian territory for their main supply routes into South Vietnam. The situation in Cambodia, south of Laos and also contiguous to South Vietnam, was much the same during the 1960s. Cambodian Communists, the Khmer Rouge, were quiescent under the left-leaning neutralist government of Prince Norodom Sihanouk. Neutrality made Cambodia a relatively safe staging area for North Vietnamese penetrations into South Vietnam. Helpless in the face of the Laos-Cambodia problem, many an American commander in the sixties would remember the peninsular war in Korea with something approaching nostalgia.

All the while South Vietnam was heating up. Early in 1961 Russia and China made official their support for "a war of national liberation" south of the seventeenth parallel. Using the Laotian bypass around the DMZ, northerners were reinforcing the Vietcong, now also called the National Liberation Front. Americans in Saigon estimated an average of twenty guerrilla attacks daily and Communist control of 60 percent of South Vietnam in the daytime and upwards of 80 percent after the sun went down. These "people in black pajamas" were elusive with their hit-and-run tactics and infuriating in their refusal to stand up and fight it out, Korea style, with the presumably well-trained armies of Diem.

Challenged, the Washington think tank produced ideas by the dozens, some of them adopted by the president. It was admitted that the war was unconventional and could only be won by "counterinsurgency" tactics. It would be necessary to teach the South Vietnamese how to fight a guerrilla war; therefore a teacher-training facility for Special Forces (Green Berets) was expanded at Fort Bragg. Also desirable was formation of a network of "strategic hamlets,'' surrounded by high fences of poles with pointed tips and reminiscent of army stockades in the American West of the Custer era. Such hamlets, it was hoped, could resist attacks by night as well as by day. Above all, the guerrillas must be deprived of support in the countryside, which meant that the Saigon government must capture the hearts and minds of its peasants through democratic reforms. Diem had grown contemptuous of this persistent plea; he did not need advice, he said, but more money and military aid. Americans were *cochons,* never minding their own business, the irrepressible Madame Nhu confided to a French reporter during one of her junkets in Paris.

Washington officials in growing number were flying to Saigon for firsthand information. Vice President Johnson returned to tell Kennedy that the situation was unpromising but that it was necessary to ''live up to our treaties'' and ''stand by our friends.'' While a ''major effort'' was needed, Johnson believed that American combat involvement was ''not desirable.'' A trip by White House aide Rostow and General Maxwell Taylor produced a ''grave but not hopeless'' analysis—so long as the United States entered the war with a shipment of 10,000 combat troops disguised as flood relief workers. Rusk and McNamara okayed this plan but Kennedy rejected it, preferring to send more noncombatant advisers equipped with helicopters. With thousands of advisers arriving on the scene, it was inevitable that they should be drawn into the fighting—if only to defend themselves when fired upon.

The news seemed better by late 1962. McNamara returned from Saigon, fed the computer again, and announced, ''Every quantitative measurement we have shows we're winning this war.'' ''We are going to win in Vietnam,'' insisted Attorney General Robert F. Kennedy, whose choice of pronouns was criticized in some newspapers. His brother was more cautious at a presidential press conference in December: ''We don't see the end of the tunnel, but I must say I don't think it is darker than it was a year ago, and in some ways lighter.'' In March 1963 Rusk spoke of ''turning an important corner'' and ''gaining the initiative,'' and McNamara soon verified that ''the corner has definitely been turned toward victory in Vietnam.''

Assuming the infallibility of the Defense Department's computer, the mortals who punched its cards were picking up some dubious information. The optimism of early 1963 stemmed partly from Diem's artistry as a confidence man. He had learned how to humor American visitors, lying to them about military prospects and democratic progress. They saw what the man in the white suit wanted them to see, a crack regiment parading in Saigon or his model strategic hamlet. There were hundreds more such regiments and hamlets, he claimed, convincing guests that they were investing in a Far Eastern Rock of Gibraltar. Along motorcade routes crowds cheered as they waved American and South Vietnamese flags, impressive shows of loyalty provided by civil servants under orders from their employer.

Any illusions that Saigon politics was a simple matter of Diem versus communism were destroyed by the riots of mid-1963. When Buddhist monks rebelled, government troops responded with volleys of rifle fire and attacks upon monasteries and pagodas. Some of the monks retaliated by setting fire to themselves in public places, the theatrics of martyrdom touching off demonstrations by Saigonese of assorted classes, religions, and political preferences. Diem filled his jails and "political reeducation camps." The tense condition gave Madame Nhu the opportunity to promulgate laws she had long thought necessary, banning prostitution, handholding, and dancing—a blow to American advisers as well as fun-loving Saigonese. After eight years of sponsoring Diem, Washington was at last ready to admit his liability to the cause.

In August, with the riots at their height, Henry Cabot Lodge arrived in Saigon to replace Ambassador Frederick E. Nolting, Jr., a Diem enthusiast who had provided the State Department with little useful information. Lodge was approached by a group of South Vietnamese army officers who asked what the Americans would do in case of a coup that removed Diem from power. Would the United States continue aid to a government bereft of its present leaders? Lodge sent such queries on to Washington, where they were received with cautious interest. From the State Department Lodge learned that any stable regime would be supported. On October 5, in a message approved by Kennedy, the ambassador was told to "build contacts with possible alternative leadership" through secret methods that could be "fully deniable" in case Diem managed to stay in power. This contact-building was not to include "active covert encouragement to a coup." However inactive the encouragement or subtle the hints from embassy personnel, the plot moved forward. As it neared maturity on October 30, a cable from Bundy reminded Lodge that there must be no "direct intervention" by Americans in a coup, even though it was "in the interest of the U.S. Government that it should succeed." Kennedy, who had expected a bloodless revolution, was shocked by the action of November 1, when South Vietnamese army officers broke into the palace and eventually shot Diem and one of his brothers, Ngo Dinh Nhu, after the two men had escaped through an underground tunnel. Madame Nhu had the good fortune to be on holiday abroad.

In spite of troubles in Saigon, Kennedy's successes during the summer of 1963—the period of his nuclear test ban treaty with Russia, the *Ich bin ein Berliner* speech, and a distinctive address on the need for flexibility in foreign policy—won him international acclaim. The quality of his diplomacy had improved remarkably since shaky 1961, and there were signs of prudent reflection over the Vietnam involvement. JFK told one of his aides, Kenneth O'Donnell, that he intended to withdraw the military advisers but would prefer to wait until after the 1964 election. He was remorseful over the manner of Diem's removal, and to Arthur M. Schlesinger, Jr., he expressed disgust with Vietnam and all that was happening there. It was during this period of rumination that Kennedy kept his speaking engagement in Dallas, after which the question of his future decisions became one of interesting if useless speculation, another of history's might-have-beens.

The blindfolded crusade against communism, begun in the early 1950s, was to continue for a few more years, in its latter stage more pulled by leadership than pushed by public opinion. Who could have expected this from a man whose favorite mottos were

"Come, let us reason together" and "Politics is the art of the possible"? Lyndon B. Johnson understood politics as a system of conflicting parties and interests in which the stubborn idealist, wanting everything, usually won nothing; gains were possible only through reason, compromise, and acceptance of legislation that fell short of one's own concept of perfection. The man who suddenly was president on November 22, 1963, was renowned for subtle political arts demonstrated in the Senate prior to his vice presidency. It had long been assumed that if the persuasive Texan ever occupied the White House he would use his talents and congressional ties to draw forth legislation affecting a variety of domestic ills. "The tragedy of Lyndon Johnson"—a phrase writers began to employ toward the end of his presidency—referred to his preoccupation with a single problem in foreign affairs, a field for which his talents were not best suited. He could not understand that diplomacy is also the art of the possible.

For a little over a year Johnson refused to waste his abilities, and he manipulated congressmen and signed into law a series of domestic programs considered important by his party. Internal matters dominated his 1964 election campaign against Senator Barry Goldwater even though the Republican nominee tried to turn Vietnam into a major issue. The GOP mounted a small-scale version of its effective 1952 campaign, criticizing what it called the indecisive "no win" policy of the Democrats in the Far East. Opinion polls showed that a majority of the public favored sending money, equipment, and advisers to South Vietnam—the old image of Uncle Sam as the benevolent protector of Asians could not die easily—but did not favor direct American involvement in the war. Goldwater's hawkishness was a miscalculation from which Johnson took advantage in speeches that drawled, again and again, that he would never send American boys to fight in Asia.

In remarks of August 2, 1964, the president seemed patient and wise, viewing the Republicans as boisterous children. A few hours later, according to an aide, he was "shaking with fury" over a report that North Vietnamese patrol boats had fired upon the destroyer *Maddox* in the Gulf of Tonkin. The attackers may have assumed that the American vessel was using its radar to guide South

Vietnamese patrol boats in raids against nearby installations. Yet the incident had occurred in international waters, and Johnson chose not to ignore a challenge to maritime rights. He ordered reinforcements for the *Maddox* and a continuance of its mission off the North Vietnamese coast.

Two nights later the commanders of the *Maddox* and *Turner Joy* expected trouble as they cruised the sensitive area. Blips appeared on radar. The response aboard the destroyers was immediate—clear-for-action signals, orders to gun crews, a few rounds fired nervously in the darkness. In later testimony and interviews naval personnel described a confused scene but offered no evidence that the attack had amounted to much more than an incursion of radar screens. Yet in the days just after the incident Americans were allowed to assume that the *Maddox* and *Turner Joy* deserved a place in history alongside the battleships *Maine* and *Arizona*.

At Johnson's request an excited Congress—with only two senators dissenting—passed the Tonkin Gulf Resolution, which gave the President authority

> to take all necessary measures to repel armed attack against the forces of the United States and to prevent further aggression. . . . The United States is . . . prepared, as the President determines, to take all necessary steps, including the use of armed force, to assist any member or protocol state of the Southeast Asia Collective Defense Treaty requesting assistance in defense of its freedom.

Many congressmen would regret the day, August 7, 1964, when they exerted their war-making prerogative in so hasty and unqualified a manner. Some, like Senator J. William Fulbright, would argue that they had been deceived by the administration's description of the Tonkin Gulf action. Seldom would they blame their own careless enthusiasm in having passed a resolution that, along with the SEATO document, provided a strong argument for the legality of future presidential decisions.

LBJ pocketed his blank check and appeared to have forgotten it as the campaign continued. His references to Vietnam were easygoing and patronizing of Goldwater's demands for stronger measures against the Communists. "Some others are eager to enlarge the conflict," Johnson said on August 12. "They call upon us to supply American boys to do the job that Asian boys should do." The theme, repeated in five campaign speeches, contributed to the landslide victory won by the Democrats. Johnson had not consciously deceived the nation; in the autumn of 1964 he did not foresee any significant expansion of the country's role in the war. But he badly underestimated his vulnerability to pressures imposed by American diplomatic traditions or at least his own conception of those traditions.

Throughout 1964 McNamara, General Taylor, and other Kennedy officials who had stayed on to advise Johnson traveled to Saigon and brought back gloomy reports. Diem's elimination had failed to inspire unity and a dedicated war effort for South Vietnam; the rise and fall of seven regimes during 1964 mocked American diplomats in their quest for "viability." Statistics revealed month-by-month increases in Vietcong strength and arrivals of troops from North Vietnam. Johnson continued the Kennedy policy, reluctantly dispatching more money and advisers. The latter stood at 23,000 by the end of 1964, and dozens were being killed or wounded by bicyclists who threw bombs into their Saigon hotels or in mortar raids against their airfields and barracks.

An assault on a barracks at Pleiku on February 7, 1965, killed eight Americans, wounded over a hundred, and destroyed Johnson's patience. Using powers granted him by the Tonkin Gulf Resolution, he brought the United States directly into the war, ordering bombing attacks on North Vietnam and authorizing employment of American troops in combat. The one-more-step policy became a headlong rush of escalations—involving soldiers, equipment, and money—that would continue throughout the Johnson presidency. By June 1965 there were 50,000 American troops in Vietnam, and 180,000 by December; 389,000 by the end of 1966; 480,000 a year later; 550,000 by the end of the Johnsonian era. Over two and a half million American men, most of them draftees, would serve at one time or another in Vietnam, and 56,000 would lose their lives there. Phantom jets, helicopter gunships, and B-52s would dump more tons of explosives on Vietnamese villages and jungles than the United States expended on all fronts during World War II. With exception of the latter war, money costs—$141 billion by the time of Saigon's surrender in 1975—would exceed those of any conflict in American history.

Johnson used principles to explain the war, construing it as a duty imposed upon him by national tradition. He admired those Democratic presidents who had fought America's last three wars and viewed their stands as analogous to his own. Like Wilson, he had defended maritime rights; and his war, like that of 1917, aimed to save democracy. "What is at stake is the cause of freedom," he said early in 1965, "and in that cause America will never be found wanting." In Korea during a critical period of the Cold War, Truman had fought to establish the credibility of American commitments, and LBJ insisted that the point still needed proving. His idol was Franklin D. Roosevelt, who had gone to war to reverse a tide that had threatened to inundate the civilized world; while Johnson seldom referred to dominoes, a Republican metaphor, his speech was full of *Munich, appeasement,* and other terms suggestive of an eternal need to stop aggression long before it reached one's own doorstep. He appeared to have learned all but the most important of history's lessons—that its needs are ever changing. At best his analogies were strained; Vietnam could not measure up to them, and earnest pleas fell on deaf ears.

The United Nations refused to help, as did major partners in SEATO. Far from sympathizing, some Western nations found enjoyment in Gulliver's struggles and in the wit of their own taunts. Insults from Sweden, irrelevant in world affairs for three hundred years, could be ignored. Nor did it matter much what the French were saying. More important were allies that shared some responsibility for world stability. In Germany, Japan, and Britain there was more worry than scorn over a lopsided American diplomacy that seemed to ignore the large concerns of Western civilization. Prestige was sinking faster than it had in the 1950s. Australia and New Zealand offered comfort, sending token forces to Vietnam. Presenting multi-million-dollar invoices for services rendered, Thailand, the Philippines, and South Korea also dispatched small bodies of troops. Washington paid dearly for the cosmetics of mutual security that never disguised the loneliness of the mission and its consequences.

The North Vietnamese remained cold to Johnson's invitations to come and reason together, even when he ordered bombing pauses as inducements. Negotiations seldom occur when both sides believe that they can win. Johnson, Rusk, McNamara, Bundy, and Rostow kept seeing lights at ends of tunnels and corners soon to be turned by new ideas such as "regional pacification" and "search and destroy" missions. Without wanting total war, they applied measured "step-ups," seeking the level of effort that inevitably must force tiny North Vietnam to acknowledge defeat by the world's strongest nation. Hanoi also was confident, counting on support from Russia and China, advantages provided by geography and guerrilla tactics, and its own willingness to fight on indefinitely in probable contrast to the impatient Americans. As the years passed, North Vietnamese demands showed no fundamental change—American withdrawal and acquiescence to Vietcong participation in a coalition government in Saigon. Washington could not accept terms that promised to destroy a regime it had sponsored at great cost since 1954.

Nor could the South Vietnamese be persuaded to behave in a manner that would brighten the meaning of all that was being done for them. No Asian Churchills appeared on the scene. The post-Diem political confusion ended in June 1965 when Nguyen Cao Ky, of the South Vietnamese air force, became premier. Ky seemed an attractive, popular leader, but soon it was clear that his strength and serious dedication left something to be desired. He enjoyed posing for pictures in the goggles and flowing scarf of a Sopwith Camel ace and at conferences belittled the Americans—generals in sweat-stained fatigues and civilians in drip-dries—by appearing in his white dinner jacket, black tie, and red socks. In the summer of 1967 the frivolous Ky gave way to Nguyen Van Thieu, a somber, businesslike president who, with his gray pin-striped suits, affected a style then current in Swiss banking circles. From Diem to Thieu the sartorial variety of Saigon's leaders impressed Americans, but it was difficult to detect other types of change. Diemlike, Thieu pestered Washington for more troops and money, kept promising the democratic reforms that the Americans so badly needed to justify their presence in Vietnam, but remained hostile to what he once called "impudent meddling" in the political affairs of his country.

The many-sided failure of Johnson's persuasive talents included gradual loss of his own political constituency. With every plea that the war was important or was being won, the "credibility gap" widened. At the time LBJ officially entered the war in 1965, polls showed that only 24 percent of the public believed that he was making a mistake. The relentless step-up of that percentage could not begin to suggest the turmoil that swept the country during the peak years of the war. The curious ability of Far Eastern affairs to arouse public emotions had been shown in the past, but the hysteria of the late sixties and early seventies—legions of demonstrators on campuses and streets, buildings burned or bombed, assaults on college deans and military recruiters, heavy-handed police tactics against demonstrators, and the 1970 scene at Kent State University, where four students were killed by undisciplined national guardsmen—was in a class by itself, suggestive of political life in a banana republic. Johnson's Great Society was tearing itself to pieces. At least that was the picture on television, a powerful, clock-dominated medium that had become—to the honest regret of its ablest commentators—the modern example of journalistic oversimplification. On the theory that news is where the action is, TV helped raise the level of excitement by pointing cameras at the most violent of events and quoting the most bizarre of partisans. It had no time to analyze the war's complex issues. That job was left to the New York *Times,* the Washington *Post,* and other papers to which Americans were accustomed to turn for calm objectivity, but even some of these publications seemed in danger of losing reputations for sobriety.

In its largest and loudest arena the Vietnam argument was between flip-side versions of a single national characteristic, the old habit of viewing foreign policy as a morality play. The war was very right or very wrong. Communist atrocities enraged some people; American atrocities enraged others. South Vietnam was democratic and virtuous, or it was undemocratic and evil, its enemy becoming the good guy in a mindless syllogism that could produce North Vietnamese flags and placard pictures of Uncle Ho in antiwar demonstrations. From the far extremes of the debate came superpatriotic slogans vintage 1952 to clash with the equally weary jargon of Marxism—the United States was engaged in a crusade, a holy mission with no substitute for victory, or its mission was one of capitalistic exploitation, imperialistic oppression, and must be ended at once.

Little noticed by TV, those who called themselves realists considered the war. By nature they were not attuned to the noise around them, moralists and sentimentalists chanting demands of one sort or another. They wanted American interests to control decisions on Vietnam, and here they differed, developing a debate among themselves. For one thing they had never been able to agree upon a definition for *realism,* one of those untidy terms that produces several inferences. For some the proper meaning was *Realpolitik,* an unsentimental philosophy of power politics based upon tough stances and no displays of weakness. For others realism meant reason, practicality, verisimilitude, seeing the world not in ideal terms but as it exists; here moralism and sentimentality are feared not necessarily because they can prevent the toughness of *Realpolitik* but because they can obscure reality, distorting the clarity of vision that is necessary to careful study of a diplomatic problem and proper choice of options, among which the unrelenting quality of *Realpolitik* exists as one of several policies to be considered. It was possible, then, for some realists to support the war and others to oppose it.

The prowar realists, called *Realpolitikers* by their critics, were perhaps best represented by the stalwarts of the Kennedy-Johnson advisory staff. Few were interested in the principles that LBJ applied to the war, and they did not view South Vietnam as a bulwark of American security. Most wished that the involvement had never occurred or that it had been ended at some point before the country had poured in enough men, money, and prestige to create a major confrontation and draw the attention of the world. The United States had built its own monster. A small, unnoticed failure no longer was possible. Any failure now must be enormous, instructive to friends and enemies everywhere, and its prevention was an important national interest. Thus it was necessary to hang tough, go on escalating, turn on more power until it could achieve satisfactory results.

Among antiwar realists the most visible were Senator Fulbright, chairman of the Foreign Relations Committee, Lieutenant General James M. Gavin, and the ubiquitous scholar-diplomat George F. Kennan. Their views were known, through writings and testimony before the Fulbright committee, as early as 1966, and later they would be joined by former Undersecretary of State George Ball, Air Force Undersecretary Townsend Hoopes, and others. They could agree with the *Realpolitikers* that the United States had *some* reasons to stand firm in Vietnam, quite a list of them in fact. But it was possible, they said, to compile a different list of American interests that suggested the wisdom of leaving the place—the casualty rate; the financial burden; the risk that further escalation could lead to world war; the ridiculous idea of choosing to fight against the odds, on an enemy's terms in his own backyard; the distraction from more critical areas of policy; the concern of major allies for the quality of American diplomatic judgment; and the threat to public sanity in the United States. Antiwar realists were cost accountants, comparing assets and liabilities. Appalled by the preponderance of red ink over black, they called for liquidation of unsound commitments. Allies such as Germany, Britain, and Japan might be worth a Vietnam-scale investment, but Vietnam was not. They suggested that American policies should become more selective, keeping costs in line with value and reflecting the need not to squander the country's limited wealth, power, and influence. They advised an end to the war, but most of them preferred an orderly withdrawal, if such could be arranged, to the spectacle of a frantic escape.

It is doubtful that the military history of the Vietnam war will ever be portrayed as a series of Valley Forges, Gettysburgs, or Guadalcanals. Heroic episodes—and there were many—do not fit comfortably into descriptions of the nightmare struggle, but the disappearance of pain and repugnance may allow future historians to record that American troops fought well and with remarkable fortitude considering their handicaps. Many of them questioned the meaning of the war and felt nothing but contempt for the regime they were risking their lives to maintain, and those who felt that the battlefield was no place to argue politics knew that their efforts were condemned by large numbers of their own countrymen. Even those unsapped by morale problems felt frustrated by the strategic position in which their government had placed them. Geography, political and physical, was against them, and the fighting was controlled by tactics not of their choosing.

If their record on battle victories was as good as in any previous war, battles and victories seemed to have no lasting meaning in the amorphous context of guerrilla conflict. At the end of January 1968 the Communists began a series of strong attacks, called the Tet offensive, against cities and bases in South Vietnam. The communists were driven back after hard fighting that enabled the Pentagon to announce more victories and favorable ''body counts'' in the continuing mathematics of attrition. Yet such announcements lacked enthusiasm, for the offensive had revealed enemy strength and tenacity wholly at odds with recent computer readouts on such matters. The North Vietnamese and Vietcong seemed capable of carrying on the war indefinitely.

The Tet offensive convinced the Johnsonians, at long last, that the war might be won only at costs that were impossible to pay. The light went out at the end of the tunnel. Rusk declared on March 11 that Vietnam policy was being reexamined ''from A to Z.'' On the last day of that month, in a startling television appearance, the president came close to admitting that he had failed; he stated that he would not run for reelection and was ordering a drastic reduction in the air war in hope of inducing negotiations. Peace talks began on May 13 in Paris, where delegates from the United States, South Vietnam, North Vietnam, and the Vietcong could not agree on the shape of the conference table, marking the beginning of four years of bickering. Violent 1968—with its war casualty reports, assassinations, and confrontations between demonstrators and police—produced presidential nominations for Vice President Hubert H. Humphrey and Richard M. Nixon. Both campaigners promised to end the war honorably, but Humphrey was tarnished by association with Johnson's policies, and his opponent won the election by a narrow margin.

Misfortune in foreign policy had ruined the administration of a leader praised for aptitudes in domestic management. LBJ's successor experienced a contrasting form of tragedy. The manipulative instincts of the Nixon administration proved of some service to the nation in the lawless world of diplomacy. Sadly the same instincts were much in evidence on the domestic scene, where the existence of law encourages behavioral restraints not always possible in international relations. The Watergate affair, with its frightening misuses of power and shabby obfuscations, eventually drove Nixon from the White House in disgrace, leaving some commentators pondering a worrisome pattern in presidential history. Rarely had any one administration provided the country with effective foreign policies along with a high level of honesty and decency in the conduct of internal affairs. In choosing excellence in one area, does the electorate endanger itself in the other?

At the outset of the Nixon presidency, and well into the second term when misfortune struck, everything seemed all right, especially because the new president had enlisted the charismatic Henry A. Kissinger as presidential adviser on national security affairs and then, beginning in September 1973, as secretary of state. Kissinger had seemed an unlikely choice as a presidential adviser, a Harvard professor who had written books on power realities and world balances. His heavy German accent suggested the heritage of Clausewitz, Metternich, and Bismarck. As Dean Acheson had learned, public attitudes toward diplomats had remained fairly consistent since the rise of Jacksonian Democracy, and prospects were dim that a Teutonic Ivy Leaguer, unapologetically professional, could win widespread support. Idiosyncrasy helped as Kissinger cooperated in a public relations campaign that portrayed him "swinging" with a series of sexy actresses. No matter how appealingly festooned, his reputation could not have prospered without achievement. He proved a tireless negotiator in his belief that diplomacy could be manipulated to re-create the flexible balance of power that had not often been practiced in the twentieth-century world. He wanted improved American relations with the Soviet Union and mainland China and looked forward to working on affairs in the troubled Middle East. New policies might confuse allies of long standing, but Kissinger, planning ubiquity, aimed to prevent serious alienations. Could one man juggle so many balls without dropping a few? Time would reveal that Dr. K. could overrate his stamina and agility, but during the first Nixon administration attention was drawn to what appeared a spectacular performance. American diplomacy lost its sense of obsession, emerged from its hiding place in Vietnam, and rediscovered the world. Kissinger exuded professionalism, for once an attractive idea to Americans, who had suffered its absence for too many years.

Administration plans for a large diplomacy underlined the desirability of bringing the United States out of Vietnam with the least damage to its reputation. Victory being impossible, all that remained at issue was the style of defeat. Nixon described the objective as "peace with honor." Kissinger, in a television interview on May 25, 1975, recalled the priorities that had shaped his policy: first was withdrawal, then recovery of American prisoners in North Vietnamese hands; third and least important was survival of the Saigon government. The latter's expendability was implied in the Nixon Doctrine of July 1969, which renounced the national addiction to costly enterprises having little or no connection to the security of the United States. The president declared in 1970: "America cannot—and will not—undertake all the defense of the free nations of the world. We will help where it makes a real difference and is considered in our interest."

Americans were encouraged to expect an early end to the war; few could have suspected that its Nixon phase would last four years. Slowly the administration worked at its top priority, extraction of American troops. From the Johnson maximum of 550,000, the number of soldiers in Vietnam dropped to 480,000 by December 1969, 339,000 by December 1970, 160,000 a year later, and less than 50,000 by July 1972. The reductions, along with a

"Vietnamization" program whereby Thieu's army was to assume a larger share of the fighting, lowered American battle deaths from a weekly average of 300 in 1968 to 26 in 1971 and 4 in the latter half of 1972.

Washington sought to negotiate an end to the fighting that would permit return of the prisoners and a safe departure for the last units to leave the country. Any such agreement, Hanoi insisted, must include establishment of a coalition government in Saigon. Protection of South Vietnam's government was not in itself a major priority in the view of Nixon and Kissinger, but they wished to avoid a kind of agreement that would amount to an overt act of abandonment. At stake was American honor. Administration supporters stressed the importance of the term, all it implied in far-flung diplomatic ramifications. Critics objected to the high costs of honor in a prolonged war or doubted that much of it could be won through some of the military tactics employed by the administration.

The American bargaining position, endangered by declining troop strength, was maintained through new military and diplomatic measures. Nixon's version of air war was heavily punishing and did not ignore the cities of Hanoi and Haiphong in raids called effective or ruthless by partisans at home. Nor did American forces ignore the Cambodian and Laotian sanctuaries, staging areas and supply routes that for years had been used with impunity by the North Vietnamese.

Cambodia's nominal neutrality ended in March 1970 when Prince Sihanouk was deposed in a coup led by the anti-Communist prime minister Lon Nol. Linking its fate to that of South Vietnam, the new Cambodian government launched an attack toward the Communist sanctuaries just inside its eastern border. Quickly the untrained army got itself into trouble. For the purpose of saving the Cambodians and destroying the enemy bases, Nixon in April ordered a combined American–South Vietnamese thrust across the border. He described it as an incursion rather than an invasion—an offensive tactic designed to enhance the safety of the American evacuation. To many Americans it seemed an escalation reminiscent of the Johnson era. On hundreds of campuses there were massive demonstrations, including the tragic affair at Kent State, and

American troops were pulled out of Cambodia perhaps sooner than had been intended. Reports of damages to North Vietnamese bases were inconclusive. News from Cambodia was bad and would remain so. Lon Nol's coup and the American incursion had stirred up the local Communists, the Khmer Rouge, who in short order were closing in on the capital of Phnom Penh. Better results were obtained a year later in Laos, where American air strikes in support of a raid by Saigon's army dislocated North Vietnamese supply routes. The bombing of Cambodian and Laotian targets would continue, Hanoi having lost the advantage of military activity shielded by neutrality.

Along with physical coercion Washington tried diplomacy. Kissinger's approach to China, begun secretly in early 1969, was patiently pursued and resulted in a dramatic Nixon visit to Peking in February 1972. It was also announced that a presidential journey to Moscow would take place in May. These moves improved American relations with both Communist powers and had the effect of playing upon fears and jealousies in the Sino-Soviet rivalry. While seeking détente for its own sake, Nixon and Kissinger were establishing a bargaining position with North Vietnam's most valued friends.

The year 1972 was not a good one for a North Vietnam neglected by friends, pounded from the air, and thus faced with the loss of 1968's dream of ejecting Americans at bayonet's point and becoming the toast of the Communist world. Whatever advice was received from Peking and Moscow, Hanoi was not happy with it. A pleading note appeared in the North Vietnamese army newspaper *Nhan Dan* on March 3: Communists must "never set national interests against the interests of world revolution . . . much less serve their own national selfishness." Hanoi's press and radio became increasingly bitter in remarks about China and Russia. Anxiety also showed in a decision to lay aside patient guerrilla maneuvers and launch a frontal assault across the DMZ. The April offensive scored gains before the northerners were halted by American air strength. Now Nixon ordered the air force to intensify attacks on enemy cities and to lay mine fields in the harbor of Haiphong. Mines represented a threat to supply ships.

Nor did it seem possible for Hanoi to benefit from the 1972 presidential elections. It was a bad year for the Democratic nominee, Senator George McGovern, whose campaign was awkwardly managed and suffered from poor timing in its demands concerning Vietnam. McGovern castigated the war on moral grounds and called for an immediate pullout that would abandon the Thieu government and depend upon Hanoi's "good will" for release of American prisoners. The prisoners issue bothered voters, and McGovern's ideas could not prosper at a time when the incumbent's pressures on North Vietnam at last appeared to be achieving the goal of peace with honor.

The fighting would end on Washington's terms—return of prisoners followed by American departure from a politically unaltered Vietnam. In Paris on October 8, 1972, the Hanoi delegation dropped its long-standing demand that a cease-fire agreement must include arrangements for a coalition government. "Peace is at hand," Kissinger announced prematurely. Thieu was reluctant to sign a document he felt would only postpone the fall of his government, and the North Vietnamese grew stubborn over the agreement's final wording. Kissinger could afford to be just as stubborn. Having assessed McGovern's chances from public opinion polls, the administration felt no need to present the country with a preelection peace. The Paris talks stalled and the war continued through an election day that brought overwhelming defeat for McGovern. There were ferocious B-52 raids on Hanoi and Haiphong in December, the "Christmas bombing" that the administration claimed was useful in prompting resumption of the Paris negotiations. The agreement was signed on January 27, 1973, ending America's longest war.

The agreement of 1973 ending the war proved a mixed victory, although time was necessary to show this result. Kissinger's first two priorities soon were achieved. The last American contingents departed quietly from Vietnam, marching rather than running. Meanwhile the prisoners returned, in a dignified manner. Concerning his third goal, preservation of South Vietnam, from the beginning there was some doubt. The agreement kept President Thieu in power, his government free of Vietcong participation. It also allowed North Vietnamese troops to remain in the south, in good position to resume the war if they so desired. Such action would be illegal, according to the agreement, and the cease-fire would be policed—casually, as it turned out—by international teams of observers.

With the world puzzling over the meanings and implications of the agreement, its very obscurity was welcome to Americans who remembered 1968 and their fear that the war would end with a catastrophic clarity of definition. By early 1973 they were not even sure that they had suffered defeat. If so, it had been beautifully disguised. A few spoke of victory or at the very worst a tie. The meaning of the American involvement—not to mention Kissinger's agreement—was expected to improve with each passing year of existence for the Saigon government.

Unhappily South Vietnam was eminently forgettable in a Washington distracted by Watergate, Nixon's resignation, his replacement by Gerald R. Ford, concerns over oil and recession, and the emergence of a Congress demanding a stronger voice in foreign policy and emotionally unequipped to approve requests for more aid to Thieu. The Saigon regime would last only two more years. Thieu himself seems to have sensed this result, and resisted as best he could. He annoyed the negotiators of the 1973 accord by refusing to condone any settlement allowing North Vietnamese forces to remain in his country. He pointed out later that he had signed the agreement only after Washington assured him that "all necessary aid" would be provided in event his enemies renewed the war. But everything had proceeded to fall apart. Issues that might have arisen over the amount, nature, and legitimacy of the promissory note to Saigon disappeared with the administration that signed it. Full-scale war returned to South Vietnam early in 1975. The Communists resumed the march toward Saigon, and the city's defenders fled in panic.

In the spring of 1975 three Indochinese dominoes fell in a two-week period. After Lon Nol's tearful exit from Cambodia, Phnom Penh surrendered to the Khmer Rouge on April 17, 1975. The change-over in Laos with its coalition government was quiet, almost unnoticed, accomplished through a few cabinet adjustments.

And in South Vietnam Thieu said goodbye to the Saigonese and left by jet on April 21. Former premier Ky joined tens of thousands of refugees bound for the United States. Helicopters hoisted out the last of American embassy and AID personnel on April 29. Following South Vietnam's surrender, Communist troops entered the capital on May Day.

The sad denouement, so quickly following the agreement of 1973, mocked the Nixon-Kissinger phase of the war, that long and expensive effort to gain peace with honor. There were desultory complaints that the agreement had been shabby or fraudulent, containing hopeful phrases meant to obscure an inevitable fate for the Saigon government. But the "loss of Vietnam," unlike the "loss of China," produced no furious hunt for scapegoats. For no political advantage could be found in a humiliation prepared by twenty years of bipartisan contributions. Nor were most Americans inclined to question the means, fair or foul, through which their ordeal had ended. They welcomed President Ford's advice to "forget Vietnam."

XIV

End

of a Chapter

W HEN SAIGON SURRENDERED, President Ford announced the "end of a chapter" in American-Far Eastern relations, thus drawing attention to the whole story with its mixture of melodrama, romance, farce, and tragedy. It was possible to hope that post-Vietnam Americans would settle for less excitement in future installments. Policies of the 1970s toward Far Eastern countries other than Vietnam clearly were moderating, if not entirely from choice. Relations with China improved, but there was little chance that the ill-advised romance of the past with mainland China would recur. The relationship with Japan managed to survive new tests that strained it. And the loss of SEATO's three protocol nations meant liquidation of Dulles's most foolish investment. In the jaded post-Vietnam period it was possible that other commitments would be examined with less sentiment and more figuring of their latest assessed value to American interests.

Small nations shaken by their protector's performance in Vietnam likewise were assessing their own alliances with the United States. Leaders' statements at the time of Saigon's fall showed respect for the "good intentions" of Ford and Kissinger but believed that public opinion in the United States was swinging toward isolationism. Not many Asians thought that Americans would enter another Asian civil war, at least not for many years to come. South Koreans and Taiwanese expressed alarm, the Filipino president discounted the value of American friendship, and leaders in Thailand had reason to publicize their contemptuous rejection of further association with the United States.

The Thai decision helped prompt discussion of a new defensive perimeter in the Far East. Thailand had been a full SEATO partner, sending a small contingent of troops to fight in Vietnam and providing the Americans with air bases throughout the war. Suddenly, in April 1975, neighboring Cambodia and Laos were Communist states. Seeking to buy good relations with these neighbors, Thailand brusquely told Americans to leave the country. But Washington was less than pained in contemplating the end of its last commitment on the Southeast Asian mainland. It appeared as if the Americans would depart Thailand with little if any hesitation.

It did seem that after the fall of Saigon the United States would continue to protect the Philippines. The perimeter line now ran *under* the Southeast Asian mainland, then curved north to protect the Philippines, though doubts were expressed that Filipinos deserved protection. American ideological vanity had suffered blow after blow in the thirty years since World War II, when it had been assumed that nations emerging from colonialism would choose democracy over assorted totalitarian options. Failure of the American political example was painfully underlined in 1972 when the Filipinos, of all people, calmly accepted cancellation of their civil liberties. After instituting martial law, President Ferdinand Marcos explained that democracy was too weak a system to cope with the volatile politics of his country. When South Vietnam fell, Marcos joined the Thais in a denunciation of American alliances. Washington was surprised, having expected that the Filipino president could understand the geographical difference between his country and Thailand. At any rate, naval defense of the islands probably would continue, whether the Filipinos deserved it or wanted it.

After May Day 1975 the line extended north between Taiwan and mainland China. There was no mention of Quemoy and Matsu. The claim that Taiwan was eternally at war with the Peking government was still being used to justify martial law on the island, but Chiang Kai-shek had been applying it less vigorously and the effects of autocracy had been softened by success in foreign trade and an economic boom that raised living standards. At age eighty-seven Chiang died in April 1975. There was a small burial ceremony, but the state funeral was postponed in hope that some-day it could be held on the mainland. Rule in Taiwan passed to the generalissimo's elder son, Premier Chiang Ching-kuo. There was fear that Washington would drop the alliance for the sake of closer ties with Peking.

The post-Vietnam line passed west of Japan, of course, then traversed the thirty-eighth parallel in defense of a last mainland commitment. In South Korea as in South Vietnam, American pleas for democratic reforms had been ignored. Under President Rhee's successor, President Park Chung-Hee, the cause of consti-tutional rule lost so much ground that Ford's visit to Seoul in November 1974 became a showpiece of intra-alliance embarrass-ment; photographers watched Park edge close to his visitor and the latter edge away. Yet Ford reaffirmed alliance pledges, mainly because Japan was still very much interested in keeping the nearby peninsula out of North Korean control. The American abandon-ment of South Vietnam shook Seoul, where two million residents participated in a proalliance celebration on the day after Saigon's surrender. A nervous Park asked the United States to honor its defense commitment and "bravely meet" any act of aggression by North Korea.

While American diplomats of the 1970s tried to weed their com-mitment system, they also worked toward a relationship with Peking. Washington had known dangerously little of dynamic Chinese changes in the years following establishment of the Peo-ple's Republic in 1949, years when the Communist theories of 1949 were translated into political, social, and economic realities. There had, of course, been many problems. The world's largest omelette cost millions of lives. Dissension and inefficiency re-mained. Results of the industrial Five Year Plan disappointed Mao's government, and the commune system seemed to be failing to meet food production goals. More than revolutionary ardor was needed to construct and operate a modern nation. Especially per-plexing to the regime were the Chinese intellectuals, as all experts were called, who had created a dilemma. China needed brainwork in the form of planners, managers, scientists, and technicians. Some such persons were found or trained, improving the systems in which they specialized and rising to important positions in government, industry, and the universities. But they were poorly equipped, through the quality of their minds, for ideological enthusiasm. At first, in the early sixties, they were mildly criticized for distractionism and privatism, which meant that their professional concentration left too little time for Marxist memorizations. More serious charges followed—of impure thoughts, Soviet revisionism, capitalist reversionism through elitist habits, White Terrorism, and treason to the people.

The great Proletarian Cultural Revolution, an effort to remove impurities is said to have begun on September 3, 1965, when Lin Piao—second only to Mao and never suspecting that he would one day be purged—called for a purge of all revisionist elements. Mao's wife Chiang Ching demanded death for those who were "left in form but right in essence," and Mao himself contributed a book of *Thoughts*—Chinese Marxist ideals explained in elementary form—in the hope that its widespread distribution might cleanse the country of "political confusionism." The little books with red plastic covers, held aloft by thousands of hands at great Peking rallies, symbolized the Cultural Revolution. But the ultra-left faction of the CCP had needed more than books in its program. Excited teenagers were welcomed into a semimilitary Red Guard, which became prominent in eradication of individual intellectuals and in the factional warfare that broke out in the provinces. Uncounted numbers of Chinese died before the orgy ended in 1968. By the late sixties Peking was playing down revolutionary ideals for the sake of practical approaches to internal and external problems. The Cultural Revolution proved a desperate attempt to forestall a Soviet style of postrevolutionary evolution, in which a puritan society gradually accepts compromise, preserving its existence by adjusting to realities. The Cultural Revolution ended either because it had accomplished its purpose, as Mao insisted, or because it was too self-rending, or because it reached a state of ideological catharsis.

All the while the growth of China's military power, in spite of civil upheavals, gravely worried its foreign rivals. Territorial quarrels with India had led to border wars in 1962 and 1965 in which the Chinese were victorious in establishing their claims. More important, the Sino-Russian split of 1959 turned into a vicious propaganda conflict; there were frontier clashes throughout the sixties, including a regiment-level battle at the Ussuri River in March 1969. Fear arose of a final showdown that could touch off world war. The Chinese exploded a nuclear device at Lop Nor in 1964 and within a few years were testing hydrogen weapons and missiles. With Peking in an early stage of nuclear development, the idea of a preemptive attack must have occurred to Moscow.

The Lop Nor tests bothered Americans because they were signals of proliferation and because of the assumption that Peking would not be impressed by the logic that had brought stalemate to the Russo-American arms race—Americans were concerned about the Chinese government's unpredictability, political zeal, and seeming disinterest in the lives of its own people.

Peking's main military concern was the northern border, but it also had to look south to Vietnam. During the 1960s there was never much fear that the United States would break into North Vietnam and race to the Chinese border, as it had in Korea in 1950. But prestige was at stake. The capitalist enemy was operating within China's proclaimed sphere of influence, and Peking won the approval of revolutionaries everywhere with its aid to North Vietnam. Rivalry with Russia for world Communist leadership was also an important reason for Chinese aid to Hanoi, even during the most debilitating years of the Cultural Revolution.

Was there nonetheless some possibility of better ties between the Chinese and American peoples? The idea surely occurred to Peking because of the menace of Russian power along the northern border. The end of the Cultural Revolution, its ideals temporarily spent, permitted the CCP's Central Committee in 1968 to make a practical diplomatic decision, a resort to realism that would have caused heads to roll a year or so earlier. In spite of the Vietnam war, Russian-American tensions had eased since the critical period of the early sixties, a fact noted by the Central Committee and translated into apprehension that those two powers might combine against China. Also, at a time when the country was exhausted from the Cultural Revolution, Russia was raising its military strength on the northern border.

Chou En-lai, a moderate whose diplomatic talents had preserved him during the purification period, was allowed to seek improved relations with the United States, and Nixon and Kissinger responded for several reasons. In the animosity of the past twenty years there had always been the threat of war between the United States and China, and the American people did not want a war. The frozen flow of information, normally provided through exchanges of diplomats, travelers, and spies, had been adjudged more harmful to an "open" society than to one that was closed. Kissinger wanted to apply his balancing techniques to the dangerous Chinese-Russian confrontation. There was the hope that deals with Peking could cut some roots of North Vietnamese stamina. And at the beginning of the 1970s the situation of the American president was right; Nixon, the first president since Hoover who could never be accused of leftist sympathies, could talk with Peking without hurting himself politically.

Chou and Kissinger communicated secretly and cautiously. Vietnam hurt the effort but the Ussuri River battle helped it. By early 1971 Washington was signaling that it would no longer oppose mainland China's admission to the United Nations. Its new "two-China policy" proposed representation for both Peking and Taipei in the General Assembly. On October 25, 1971, a General Assembly dominated by small Asian and African nations voted enthusiastically to admit mainland China. It also voted to eject Taiwan. On the surface the latter move seemed an American defeat, and there was bitter talk in Washington. But Kissinger moved on, more easily now. Within several months he was flying to Peking for last-minute arrangements of the détente's formal celebration.

Nixon spent late February of 1972 in Peking, Hangchow, and Shanghai, eight days of banquets, table-tennis exhibitions, tours of the Great Wall and charming temple gardens, and tiresome revolutionary pageantry—"the best ballet I've ever seen," the president carefully told his hosts. With Chou and Mao he talked of Vietnam, trade, cultural exchanges, and normalization of relations.

The presidential journey—followed by another to Moscow—proved popular in the United States, viewed with relief and with little of the passion that had so often accompanied directional changes in Asian-American relations. The information flow attending the visit portrayed modern China imperfectly and yet more clearly than at any time since 1949. Peking was a city of bicycles; the ricksha, a class symbol, had long since disappeared. There were not so many dogs and flies as in Chiang's time. Streets were clean, no longer full of disorderly crowds, ragged beggars, and hollow-cheeked children. Some journalists were delighted to find a China untormented by starvation and disunity. Others wrote of the price of unity, of recent massacres, of full stomachs and blank minds, and—with suitable references to Orwell and Solzhenitsyn—of the drab uniformity of every aspect of Chinese life. As ever, travelers saw what they wanted to see, and the mixture of opinions helped Americans to accept the new relationship without overexcitement.

The results of the détente were as mixed as the journalists' opinions of China. The Chinese were not noticeably joyful over détente in the years after its arrangement. It appreciated the musk-ox Nixon had sent in return for the gift of a panda. There were exchanges of orchestras, dance groups, and athletes. China's touring Ping-Pong players allowed Americans to win some of the matches, but in May 1975 an undiplomatic American track team swept all events and held a drunken celebration. Attempts to normalize relations resulted in an exchange of permanent diplomatic missions, but there was little chance that these could be raised to embassy level so long as the United States kept an ambassador in Taiwan. Peking could not agree that there were two Chinas and made known its resentment of American-Taiwanese relations, which included an alliance. The chiefs of the Peking mission, David K. Bruce followed by George Bush, often received chilly treatment. The Chinese continued to boast of accomplishments at Lop Nor and of a future industrial growth powered by the oil they would get from the coastal shelf and the region once known as Manchuria. (What if Japan had known of this oil in the 1930s?) Unable to control the growth of a population that had passed the eight hundred million mark, Peking called itself the champion of all overpopulated nations at a time when food was becoming a critical diplomatic issue. Taunting Americans on their self-proclaimed humanitarianism, CCP spokesmen demanded that the United States share its resources on an equal basis with less favored areas of the world; nor were American scientists to engage in the "counterrevolutionary" activity of teaching troubled societies how to regulate population growth.

Would the regime in Peking become more friendly with Americans? In 1975–1976 there were conflicting reports that aging moderates had strengthened their hold on the government or that younger extremists were preparing to seize power. Observers speculated tirelessly. As Chinese communism grew older, would it continue to compromise, revise, and go the way of the Soviet Union? Or was a new Cultural Revolution in preparation, another round of ideological self-assertion that would refreeze relations with the United States? How much did China need its imports of American wheat and corn?

For the American government, one purpose of improved relations with China and Russia had been to play an adjusting role in their dispute. The Soviets had increased their border forces to sixty divisions, over a million men, and deep air raid shelters were being excavated in major Chinese cities. Hopefully, the Americans would be cautious of interfering in Sino-Russian squabbles. Hopefully, after some seventy years of hot and cold policies, the United States was moderating its China position to one of noncommittal but useful diplomacy, refreshingly tentative, devoid of thrills, and ever prepared to avoid entrapment in any cataclysms of the Chinese future.

America's Asian policies of the sixties badly needed a silver lining, and Japan usually supplied it. That busy exporting nation had no time for diplomatic troubles. Economically, the decade was the best in Japanese history, and anything associated with good times—the Liberal Democratic party, Premier Eisaku Sato (in power from 1964 to 1972), close ties with the United States—was regarded with approval. Japan was more patient than most allies during the Vietnam war. While Sato opposed storage of nuclear weapons at American bases in Japan, he continued to endorse Japanese-American friendship. The alliance thrived in a sort of natural state, based upon mutuality of political attitudes and diplomatic needs. Washington drew comfort from having at least one strong ally in the Far East. The alliance freed Tokyo from heavy military budgets and the need to face obnoxious decisions on development of its own nuclear weapons.

Everything had seemed to work well with the postwar Japanese economy. Government programs helped reduce the birthrate, cutting import needs as well as social costs, while populations soared in other Asian countries. Armament costs were low, through preference and a money-saving alliance with the United States, helping the country absorb trade deficits in the 1950s and early 1960s. High tariffs were out of style in the post-1945 world; conditions favored efficient nations in the competition for markets. Japanese efficiency had never been questioned, and during the occupation the American government had decided not to thwart that efficiency by destroying the business combines and encouraging a strong system of labor unions. Japanese industry had taken it from there, using monopolies, mergers, diversification, organizational innovation, computerization, and any other technique that could increase the flow of cheaper and better products into the world market.

In the post-1945 years factory workers threw few monkey wrenches into the machinery of national progress. Their wages were low by Occidental standards, but they enjoyed their fringe benefits, which included free vacations at company-owned resorts. Loyalty to employers was an ancient tradition, and workers also felt themselves part of a national enterprise. Western labor publications sneered at "Japan, Inc.," describing an old-fashioned system in which workers were too backward to understand that labor and management were natural enemies. Some Japanese writers also criticized the paternalistic system, but the working majority would have agreed with a poster that appeared in a Mitsui subsidiary at the time of the 1960 riots: "It is foolish to sink one's own boat." Japanese employees were anything but backward; the literacy rate among them was exceptionally high. They were not unaware of the high wages obtained through labor's long struggle in Europe and the United States, but they also read about American workers losing their jobs in the 1960s as payroll costs forced some companies out of business and others to transfer manufacturing functions to areas of the world where labor was not so demanding.

Cooperation—no matter what it implied to Western labor leaders—helped produce Japan's "economic miracle," its "polluted paradise" of the sixties. In the great east coast cities forests of television antennas rose in the tawny haze, and little houses were cluttered with appliances. Per capita income reached European averages and promised to match Europe's best examples. Total trade increased by 16 percent annually, about twice the growth rate for all world trade. Sales figures climbed the graph, approaching the import burden, then carrying it, then crossing the line in 1967 when the government announced a balance-of-payments surplus, a figure that reached $2 billion by 1970. The real annual growth rate climbed to 12 percent by 1970, over twice the Western average. Some economists say that gross national product is the proper measure of wealth and capacity for power. If so, Japan became the third leading nation, passing West Germany in 1968; according to GNP predictions Russia would be overtaken in the late 1970s and the United States by the end of the century.

Startling statistical projections may not have exaggerated what the Japanese could accomplish under optimum conditions, but they ignored the fact that the country's future was not entirely in its own capable hands. The economy, far more than that of most nations, was geared to international trade and therefore vulnerable to forces beyond control. Tokyo's economic seismograph in the early seventies recorded tremors, at first distant then rippling toward Japan. Government and business leaders could only cross their fingers and hope that there would be continued stability in world currencies and price levels, that other governments would indefinitely honor the competitive spirit by refusing to protect their own industries, and that foreign consumers would continue to enjoy prosperity and purchasing power.

It is an interesting fact that a major threat against the Japanese economy first arose from—of all places—the United States in the early 1970s, well before the oil crisis in 1973 signaled a turndown in the general international economy. American shoppers had been attracted by the discount prices of Japanese textiles, electronics merchandise, cameras, cars, motorbikes, plastic items, and other goods. Soon price was not the only attraction. "Made in Japan" lost its ancient meaning as many products bearing that label proved superior to those manufactured by highly paid American labor. By 1970 the United States, taking over 30 percent of Japan's exports, had become the latter's best customer. Inevitably American businessmen and labor leaders called for consumer boycotts and pressed the government for tariffs or quotas. The influx continued as Japan became a major contributor—in spite of sizable purchases from the United States—to American trade deficits and factory layoffs. Washington faced a paradox. How could it protect its own economy without damaging that of a valued ally?

Nixon launched a "defense of the dollar" program in August 1971, asking Americans to buy domestic products and imposing surcharges on critical imports. Tokyo's stock market plunged. To this setback was added fear that the surcharges might inspire protectionism in other nations. A surcharge on textiles was lifted only after Japan—in addition to Taiwan, South Korea, and Hong Kong—agreed to "voluntary restraints" in export of cloth products to the United States. More importantly Japan was forced to raise the value of the *yen* in relation to other currencies, whereupon the American government dropped all surcharges. Currency revaluation increased the price of Japanese products, and the effect was immediately felt in foreign markets.

Tokyo newspapers spoke of the "twin shocks" of late 1971, one economic and the other brought by the Nixon-Kissinger overture to China. The American jugglers had dropped something, forgetting to consult with or even advise the Japanese government before announcing a China policy that could change the meaning of Far Eastern history. The Japanese were sensitive to being forgotten, for they had long felt that Washington took their loyalty too much for granted. A few months after Nixon's Peking visit Japanese leaders followed suit, opening diplomatic relations with mainland China for the first time in forty years. They also broke with Taiwan, outdoing the Americans in shifting policy. Tokyo looked forward to new markets in China, but memory of Washington's faux pas still rankled.

Japanese-American relations reached a postwar low, but there were ameliorative factors. Following Japan's adept management of the Winter Olympic Games at Sapporo in February 1972, Nixon's comment that the games were "the most successful and beautiful" ever held was widely quoted. More important was the return of Okinawa to Japanese sovereignty, a promise that became a reality in May 1972 and meant that the future of American bases on the island would be determined by Tokyo.

Fears of increasing trade difficulties were not easily soothed. The continuing bearish trend of Japan, Inc., could not be blamed on protectionist experiments in Washington so much as on disruptions throughout the international market. The Middle Eastern war of 1973 resulted in oil embargos and then a fivefold rise in the price of this commodity, frightening a nation that had to import all of its oil.

Inflation, another international experience, represented a double threat; Japanese consumer prices rose at a per annum rate of 24 percent in 1974. In countries concerned with their own recessions, journalistic analysis had time to pity Japan, described as a remarkable machine but without inner resources to draw upon if the machine broke down. It was freely predicted that recession would quickly become depression, wrecking the financial system and bringing devastating unemployment. A labor publication in Detroit smugly described the prospect: the revalued *yen* in a world of consumer resistance, storage yards full of Datsuns and Toyotas, empty holds in ships leaving Japan, and TV sets repossessed from "millions of little houses." Other editors worried about Japanese democracy. In the early 1970s they had pondered GNP projections, fearing that growing power might lead to arrogance and a return to militarism. The concern of the mid-seventies was over democracy's historic vulnerability to hard times. Japan's postwar political system, it was said, lacked strong roots and was yet to be tested by adversity.

Reassurance was the purpose of Ford's visit to Japan, the first by any American president, in November 1974. There were no public ceremonies, due more to lack of interest than to security. Leftists dropped plans for an antialliance demonstration; nor were police lines tested by cheering multitudes, although the government arrayed a few dozen Old Glory wavers within Ford's field of vision. The president had a knack for humanizing mistakes that disarmed hosts. For a formal dinner he chose the wrong tie, and his trousers were six inches too short as he stood beside Emperor Hirohito at a photography session. The Japanese did their best. Never mind, an official confided, the emperor's trousers were too long. Ford and Kissinger offered the expected reassurances on trade, oil diplomacy, Korean policy, and the issue of nuclear weapons aboard United States warships at anchor in Japan. Afterward Japanese leaders spoke well of Ford's earnest manner, but they found the secretary of state "rude" and "insensitive" to the problems that Kissinger may have considered of low priority in comparison to others on his nonstop troubleshooting itinerary. Japan ought to make some trouble for the United States, a Tokyo columnist suggested. "Then we will cease to be a blind spot in Dr. Kissinger's world-view."

The recession hurt Japan, but Western predictions of catastrophe failed to materialize. The bad effects of a shrinking market were eased by Japanese ability to win a larger share of it, appealing to Americans and Europeans increasingly forced to consider the price and utility of their purchases. Japan's performance continued to be the envy of Britons, who had long lost their industrial efficiency, and of Americans, who were losing it.

Nonetheless the Japanese were disturbed by events of the seventies, which brought an end to the stable market of the past decades and foreshadowed a future of oil shortages, rising costs for food and raw materials, and perhaps a return of full-scale foreign protectionism, the sort that had so damaged the Japanese economy in the late 1920s. Even if Tokyo and Washington could avoid bilateral trade clashes, which was by no means certain, Japan's desperation for oil and other commodities might lead it down paths of policy strange and perhaps abhorrent to the American government. The Third World was beckoning Japanese diplomats, who surveyed it with more attention to mineral deposits than to politics.

End of a Chapter

All of the economic disturbances necessarily affected the American alliance. In discussing the alliance's future there were those in Tokyo who said that diverging interests had become more important than mutual interests—that in event of another Sino-American crisis Japanese decisions would be, at the least, less predictable than in the past. The sturdy alliance with Japan, nearly a quarter-century old at the time of the Ford-Kissinger courtesy call, was perhaps the best thing that had ever happened to the Asian diplomacy of the United States. Through it two strong nations had contributed to their own security and to world stability. But by the mid-seventies it was evident that the relationship might not survive further careless handling by Washington, or a further buffeting by international economics, that it had entered an era requiring great patience and skill and, perhaps, luck.

Thoughts about future chapters of American-Far Eastern relations permit little hope that it is the Far East that will do the changing. Except perhaps for quaintness, Asia has lost none of those qualities that used to appeal to a challenge-seeking people. In China and the small nations the cause of democracy fares no better than in the days of the Manchus and Western imperialism. Villainy persists, as do helplessness and distress. Population growth threatens to produce human misery on a scale unknown in the past, and its story will be portrayed by television cameras rather than by obscure missionary tracts. Oriental attitudes, though no longer called inscrutable, can still perplex and frustrate. Asia will not lose its capacity for creating problems that cry out for solving.

Less predictable than Asian troubles will be America's response to them. It is possible that the eccentric tradition will continue. The dullish diplomacy of the middle 1970s may represent exhaustion more than a dawn of reason, the midpoint of a pendulum's swing from overinvolvement toward another period of isolation. Reminders of the 1920s are present. Those congressmen most disgusted by Vietnam insist upon diplomatic and budgetary restraints that sometimes seem to ignore the needs of American security. Such terms as *national security* and *national interest* are called old-fashioned in seminars of TV journalists, those articulate but often inexperienced sources for most of the public's news and opinions. Assuming the nation can survive an isolationist reprise, how many years will pass before it can rest sufficiently, repent its truancy, and come charging back too eager to reassert its power, political influence, and humanitarian reputation?

An optimist might believe that disillusionment is the mother of maturity, the post-Vietnam era is a coming of age, and the calm of the seventies does not mean that Americans are tired of diplomacy but turning away from adolescent ups and downs, impossible dreams, and tantrums of self-loathing. It is possible to hope that the public, press, and Congress will confront national problems with confidence, self-discipline, and a sense of proportion; with increased ability, as Reinhold Niebuhr once suggested, to know the difference between changes that are possible and those that are not. Realism and cynicism are not synonymous; it is not an unhealthy society that learns to adjust to life in a less than perfect world.

Given a reasonable degree of public patience, diplomats might improve their ability to make sense of that tiresome necessity called the national interest. If readers of future chapters of American–Far Eastern history were deprived of traditional cliffhanging thrills, this sort of loss would be acceptable. People could live with it.

READING SUGGESTIONS

The necessarily selective lists that follow will reflect the present writer's tastes in judging the importance of books or the enjoyment they may afford readers. (In a few cases a work will be included simply because it is a source of material used in a chapter.) Regrettably some excellent books on American–Far Eastern relations must be omitted, and there will be the temptation to add "and many others" after every bibliographical grouping.

General works that are valuable to the study of many if not all of the time periods are mentioned first and seldom referred to after later chapters.

I. EARLY STEREOTYPES

A. Whitney Griswold's *The Far Eastern Policy of the United States* (New York, 1938) retains its "most reliable" reputation for the span 1898–1938; it is best in the early period. Meribeth E. Cameron et al., *China, Japan and the Powers* (New York, 1960), offers good detail without interpretation, and the interpretation of experts is available in John K. Fairbank, *The United States and China,* 3rd ed. (Cambridge, Mass., 1971), and Edwin O. Reischauer, *The United States and Japan,* 3rd ed. (Cambridge, Mass., 1965). An excellent overview of America's Asian policies can be found in Robert H. Ferrell's compilation of documents bearing on American diplomacy, 3 vols. (New York, 1968, 1971, 1975), and Foster Rhea Dulles in *America's Rise to World Power, 1898–1954* (New York, 1955) is Asia-oriented.

George F. Kennan's *American Diplomacy: 1900–1950* (Chicago,

1951) contains a well-known realism versus idealism discussion, and the same issue is well served in Robert E. Osgood, *Ideals and Self-Interest in America's Foreign Relations* (Chicago, 1953), and Norman A. Graebner, ed., *Ideas and Diplomacy* (New York, 1964), a collection of documents and essays by the editor. Among general works stressing economics as the driving force of American diplomacy, perhaps the most representative are William A. Williams, *The Tragedy of American Diplomacy* (New York, 1959), and Lloyd C. Gardner, Walter LaFeber, and Thomas J. McCormick, *Creation of the American Empire* (Chicago, 1973).

An interesting selection of short biographies from Benjamin Franklin to Henry A. Kissinger appears in Frank Merli and Theodore A. Wilson, eds., *Makers of American Dilomacy,* 2 vols. (New York, 1974). For longer accounts of diplomats consult the multi-volume standard work edited by Samuel F. Bemis and Robert H. Ferrell, *The American Secretaries of State and their Diplomacy.* For a period-by-period study of historiographical issues in Asian-American relations there is Ernest R. May and James C. Thomson, Jr., eds., *American–East Asian Relations: A Survey* (Cambridge, Mass., 1972).

Informal elements in diplomacy—call them impressions, images, national attitudes—are sometimes as important in the creation of history as battles and treaties. Changing American views of China and India are examined in Harold R. Isaacs, *Images of Asia* (New York, 1972), a later edition of *Scratches on our Minds,* the author's metaphor for stereotyped opinions. Akira Iriye's *Across the Pacific: An Inner History of American–East Asian Relations* (New York, 1967) is an intriguing study, and other books that emphasize "feelings" are Robert S. Schwantes, *Americans and Japanese: A Century of Cultural Relations* (New York, 1955); William L. Neumann, *America Encounters Japan: From Perry to MacArthur* (Baltimore, 1963); Paul H. Clyde and Burton F. Beers, *The Far East: A History of the Western Impact and the Eastern Response, 1830–1965* (Englewood Cliffs, N.J., 1966); and Ralph E. Weber, ed., *As Others See Us* (New York, 1972). The latter is a collection of newspaper accounts, some from Asian journals dating back to Cushing and Perry.

Readings more specifically related to the nineteenth century, the subject of this first chapter, include two venerable works of interest nowadays mainly for anecdote: Tyler Dennett, *Americans in Eastern Asia* (New York, 1922), and Payson J. Treat, *Diplomatic Relations between the United States and Japan, 1853–1895* (Palo Alto, Calif., 1932). On early trade relations see Samuel E. Morison, *The Maritime History of Massachusetts* (Boston, 1961); John K. Fairbank, *Trade and Diplomacy*

2 5 4

on the China Coast: The Opening of the Treaty Ports, 1842–1854 (Cambridge, Mass., 1953), and G. C. Allen and A. G. Donnithorne, *Western Enterprise in Far Eastern Economic Development, China and Japan* (London, 1954).

Key works on Chinese-American subjects include Kenneth S. Latourette, *A History of Christian Missions in China* (New York, 1929); Stuart C. Miller, *The Unwelcome Immigrant: The American Image of the Chinese, 1785–1882* (Berkeley, Calif., 1969); and Mary C. Wright, *The Last Stand of Chinese Conservatism* (Palo Alto, Calif., 1957). A colorful account of Americans in the Taiping Rebellion appears in Lawrence Hanson and Elizabeth Hanson, *Chinese Gordon* (New York, 1954).

Possibly the best Japanese treatment of the Perry period is Kiyoshi Tabohashi's *History of Modern Japanese Relations with Foreign Countries* (Tokyo, 1943). More accessible is Arthur Walworth's *Black Ships off Japan* (New York, 1952). Some information appearing in this chapter was supplied by the thorough research of John D. Kazar, "The United States Navy and Scientific Exploration, 1837–1860" (Ph.D. dissertation, University of Massachusetts, 1973), and tidbits on Perry's scientists come from the newspapers *China Mail* (Hong Kong), April 6, 1854; *North China Herald* (Shanghai), Nov. 11, 1854; and the *Times* (London), June 1, 1854. Oliver Statler's *The Shimoda Story* (New York, 1969) is an engaging account of Townsend Harris's adventures, and the history of Japanese-American affairs in the Meiji period is well represented by Foster Rhea Dulles, *Yankees and Samurai: America's Role in the Emergence of Modern Japan* (New York, 1965), and Marius B. Jansen, ed., *Changing Japanese Attitudes toward Modernization* (Princeton, N.J., 1965).

II. STEPPING STONES TO ASIA

Hilary Conroy's *The Japanese Seizure of Korea, 1868–1910* (Philadelphia, 1961) contains a diplomatic-military account of the Sino-Japanese War. The first full treatment of American diplomatic, naval, and public activities in that war appears in Jeffrey Dorwart's *The Pigtail War: The American Response to the Sino-Japanese War of 1894–1895*, scheduled for publication in 1975 by the University of Massachusetts Press, Amherst. For lease-taking see the reading notes at the end of the next chapter.

Among historians who deal with the complexity of the "spirit of the nineties," with its war and empire, are Ernest R. May, *Imperial Democ-*

racy: The Emergence of America as a Great Power (New York, 1961) and *American Imperialism* (New York, 1968); David Healy, *U.S. Expansionism: The Imperialist Urge in the 1890s* (Madison, Wis., 1970); Ralph H. Gabriel, *The Course of American Democratic Thought* (New York, 1961); and Foster Rhea Dulles, *The Imperial Years* (New York, 1956). The variety of causes also is collected in Robert L. Beisner, *Twelve Against Empire: The Anti-Imperialists, 1898–1900* (New York, 1968), and in the lively old standard account by Walter Millis, *The Martial Spirit* (Boston, 1931). The anecdotes of exuberation fill Margaret Leech's *In the Days of McKinley* (New York, 1959) and Frank Freidel's *The Splendid Little War* (Boston, 1958). Modern authors have not done justice to the postwar jubilees and their thunderous boasting; for such samples contemporary works are best, for example, Robert I. Fulton and Thomas C. Trueblood, eds., *Patriotic Eloquence Relating to the Spanish-American War and its Issues* (New York, 1903).

Other writers have examined particular themes. The moralistic urge comes through in Frederick Merk, *Manifest Destiny and Mission in American History* (New York, 1963). Richard Hofstadter, *Social Darwinism in American Thought: 1860–1915* (Philadelphia, 1944), contains diplomatic material. Mahan's Darwinist ideas, best shown in the magazine articles he wrote, are studied in William E. Livezey, *Mahan on Sea Power* (Norman, Okla., 1947). For naval expansion not necessarily stressing Darwinism see Walter R. Herrick, *The American Naval Revolution* (Baton Rouge, La., 1966), and W. R. Braisted, *The United States Navy in the Pacific, 1897–1909* (Austin, Texas, 1958). Aggressiveness through insecurity is the theme of Hofstadter's "Cuba, the Philippines, and Manifest Destiny," an essay published most recently in that historian's *The Paranoid Style in American Politics and Other Essays* (New York, 1967). It might be interesting to read the Hofstadter article along with Erich Fromm's analysis of democratic stresses, *Escape from Freedom* (New York, 1941). For a debate on economic influence—how much and how soon—contrast Julius W. Pratt, *Expansionists of 1898* (Baltimore, 1936), with Walter LaFeber, *The New Empire, An Interpretation of American Expansion, 1860–1898* (Ithaca, N.Y., 1963). Seconding LaFeber's belief in the dominance of economic motives are Thomas McCormick, *China Market* (Chicago, 1967); Marilyn B. Young, *The Rhetoric of Empire* (Cambridge, Mass., 1968); and William A. Williams, *The Roots of the Modern American Empire* (New York, 1969).

American writers have shown little interest in their country's war against the Filipino rebels, though the subject is sometimes included in more general works such as Joseph R. Hayden's *The Philippines: A Study in National Development* (New York, 1942). Leon Wolff's *Little Brown Brother* (London, 1960) offers a colorful story of the war without providing the documentation necessary in a monographic treatment. Some documents, heavy on atrocities, are presented by Henry F. Graff, ed., *American Imperialism and the Philippine Insurrection* (Boston, 1969).

III. A DOOR TO COMMITMENT

The diplomacy of the open door notes, while not in itself the subject of a book, receives detailed attention in many of the general works listed earlier. A. Whitney Griswold's *The Far Eastern Policy of the United States* is superior on the writing and sending of the two notes, which is also a subject in Alfred L. P. Dennis, *Adventures in American Diplomacy, 1896–1906* (New York, 1928). The policy-principle connection is vividly described in Kennan's *American Diplomacy* and the economics in Williams's *Tragedy of American Diplomacy* and McCormick's *China Market*. Where open door negotiators are concerned, the best biography is Paul A. Varg, *Open Door Diplomat: The Life of W. W. Rockhill* (Urbana, Ill., 1952). For two view of Hay consult the admiring William R. Thayer, *The Life and Letters of John Hay* (2 vols., Boston, 1915), and the rueful Tyler Dennett, *John Hay: From Poetry to Politics* (New York, 1933). The image-oriented books listed earlier contain public attitudes on the open door and China, as do Paul A. Varg, *The Making of a Myth: The United States and China, 1897–1912* (East Lansing, Mich., 1968), and Robert F. McClellan, Jr., *The Heathen Chinee: A Study of American Attitudes Toward China, 1890–1905* (Columbus, Ohio, 1970).

Customs in the court at Peking are described by one who lived there, Daniele Varé, in *The Last Empress* (Garden City, N.Y., 1938). Recent studies of the Boxer Rebellion include C. C. Tan, *The Boxer Catastrophe* (New York, 1955); Victor Purcell, *The Boxer Uprising: A Background Study* (Cambridge, England, 1963); John Schrecker, *Imperialism and Chinese Nationalism* (Cambridge, Mass., 1971); and John S. Kelly, *A Forgotten Conference: The Negotiations at Peking, 1900–1901* (Geneva, 1962).

IV. A PERIOD OF RESTRAINT

The study of this period has been dominated by biography, as might be expected. Early accounts of Roosevelt's life bore such titles as *Great-*

Heart, a contribution by Daniel Henderson in 1919. One relatively early work still deserving mention on merit, mainly one of anecdotal color, is Henry Pringle's *Theodore Roosevelt* (New York, 1931). Biographers have not moved toward consensus, and modern opinions of TR seem increasingly argumentative, among them John M. Blum, *The Republican Roosevelt* (Cambridge, Mass., 1961); William H. Harbaugh, *Power and Responsibility: The Life and Times of Theodore Roosevelt* (New York, 1961); George Mowry, *The Era of Theodore Roosevelt* (New York, 1958); and G. Wallace Chessman, *Theodore Roosevelt* (Boston, 1969). One of the most notable documentary collections concerning any historical figure is Elting E. Morison, ed., *The Letters of Theodore Roosevelt,* 8 vols. (Cambridge, Mass., 1951–54). Other biographies include Richard W. Leopold, *Elihu Root and the Conservative Tradition* (Boston, 1954); John A. Garraty, *Henry Cabot Lodge* (New York, 1953); and the works on John Hay mentioned earlier.

A disapproving view of TR's preferences among Far Eastern nations can be found in Howard K. Beale, *Theodore Roosevelt and the Rise of America to World Power* (Baltimore, 1956). Roosevelt's Asian policies are more acceptable to Charles Neu, *An Uncertain Friendship: Theodore Roosevelt and Japan, 1906–1909* (Cambridge, Mass., 1967), and Raymond Esthus, *Theodore Roosevelt and Japan* (Seattle, 1966).

On specific phases consult John A. White, *The Diplomacy of the Russo-Japanese War* (Princeton, N.J., 1964), which concentrates on the records of the belligerent powers, and Thomas A. Bailey, *Roosevelt and the Russo-Japanese War* (New York, 1925); Eugene Trani, *The Treaty of Portsmouth: An Adventure in American Diplomacy* (Lexington, Ky., 1969), an important work that employs sources from all the governments involved; Roger Daniels, *The Politics of Prejudice: The Anti-Japanese Movement in California* (Berkeley, Calif., 1962); Thomas A. Bailey, *Theodore Roosevelt and the Japanese-American Crisis* (Palo Alto, Calif., 1934); and Robert A. Hart, *The Great White Fleet: Its Voyage Around the World, 1907–1909* (Boston, 1965). Attention is called to some excellent readings on this period that are contained in the more general books listed earlier.

V . '' F O O L S   R U S H   I N . . . ''

The Taft-Wilson period has, for different reasons, appalled revisionist schools of both the 1950s and the 1960s. For the former see Kennan's

Reading Suggestions

American Diplomacy, Osgood's *Ideals and Self-Interest in American Foreign Relations,* and John M. Blum's *Woodrow Wilson and the Politics of Morality* (Boston, 1956). For the latter see Williams's *Tragedy of American Diplomacy;* Jerry Israel, *Progressivism and the Open Door: America and China, 1905–1921* (Pittsburgh, 1971); and N. Gordon Levin, Jr., *Woodrow Wilson and World Politics* (New York, 1968).

Important new works include Akira Iriye, *Pacific Estrangement: Japanese and American Expansionism, 1897–1911* (Cambridge, Mass., 1973), which contains Japanese attitudes on Taft's policies; Walter V. Scholes and Marie V. Scholes, *The Foreign Policies of the Taft Administration* (Columbia, Mo., 1970); Robert H. Wiebe, *The Search for Order, 1877–1920* (New York, 1967); and Julius W. Pratt, *Challenge and Rejection, 1900–1921* (New York, 1967).

Also interesting on the Taft period—Scott Nearing and Joseph Freeman, *Dollar Diplomacy: A Study in American Imperialism* (New York, 1926); Charles S. Campbell, Jr., *Special Business Interests and the Open Door Policy* (New Haven, 1951); Charles Vevier, *The United States and China, 1906–1913* (New Brunswick, N.J., 1955); George E. Mowry, *The Era of Theodore Roosevelt, 1900–1912* (New York, 1958); and F. R. Dulles's *America's Rise to World Power.*

On Wilson and Asia—Li Tien-yi, *Woodrow Wilson's China Policy, 1913–1917* (New York, 1952); Russell H. Fifield, *Woodrow Wilson and the Far East: The Diplomacy of the Shantung Question* (New York, 1952); Roy Watson Curry, *Woodrow Wilson and Far Eastern Policy, 1913–1921* (New York, 1957); Burton F. Beers, *Vain Endeavor: Robert Lansing's Attempt to End the American-Japanese Rivalry* (Durham, N.C., 1962); and Betty Miller Unterberger, *America's Siberian Expedition, 1918–1920* (Durham, N.C., 1956). On the Paris conference, a much treated subject, it has proved difficult to surpass Sir Harold Nicolson, *Peace-making* (Boston, 1933), and Thomas A. Bailey, *Woodrow Wilson and the Lost Peace* (New York, 1944). Japanese government policies of an expansionist era may be examined in Kikujiro Ishii's *Diplomatic Commentaries* (Baltimore, 1936).

The standard biographies are Henry F. Pringle, *The Life and Times of William Howard Taft,* 2 vols. (New York, 1939); Herbert F. Wright, "Philander C. Knox," in *The American Secretaries of State and Their Diplomacy* series; and Herbert D. Croly's sympathetic view of *Willard Straight* (New York, 1924). Wilson's numerous biographies include John A. Garraty's excellent short work, *Woodrow Wilson* (New York, 1956); Arthur Walworth's *Woodrow Wilson,* 2nd ed. (Boston, 1965); and the impressive *Wilson,* Arthur S. Link's multi-volume, unfinished study published at Princeton beginning in 1947. Too much Wilson is hard to take; the reader may prefer Link's single volume on *Wilson the Diplomatist: A Look at His Major Foreign Policies* (Baltimore, 1957).

VI. . . . AND OUT

The degree of sardonic comment varies in modern books looking back at the idealistic isolationism of the twenties: Selig Adler's *The Isolationist Impulse* (New York, 1957) and his *The Uncertain Giant: 1921–1941* (New York, 1965); Allan Nevins, *The United States in a Chaotic World: 1918–1933* (New Haven, 1950); G. C. Reinhardt and W. R. Kintner, *The Haphazard Years* (New York, 1960); Pierre Renouvin, *War and Aftermath, 1914–1929,* English ed. (New York, 1968); Byron Dexter, *The Years of Opportunity: The League of Nations, 1920–1926* (New York, 1967), in which the illusions created by the League are seen as having been dangerous; and L. Ethan Ellis, *Republican Foreign Policy, 1921–1933* (New Brunswick, N.J., 1968). For defense of idealism see the new study by Charles Chatfield, Jr., *For Peace and Justice: Pacifism in America, 1914–1941* (Knoxville, Tenn., 1971) as well as dozens of books written during the twenties, thirties, and forties (during the latter decade interest in the UN produced a reprise of the old faith).

For the Washington Conference see Thomas H. Buckley, *The United States and the Washington Conference, 1921–1922* (Knoxville, Tenn., 1970); J. Chalmers Vinson, *The Parchment Peace* (Athens, Ga., 1956); and Merze Tate, *The United States and Armaments* (Cambridge, Mass., 1948). Of several excellent biographies of Charles Evans Hughes, most detailed is Merlo J. Pusey, *Charles Evans Hughes,* 2 vols. (New York, 1951). Naval implications of the conference can be found in Harold Sprout and Margaret Sprout, *Toward a New Order of Sea Power,* 2nd ed. (Princeton, N.J., 1943); George T. Davis, *A Navy Second to None* (New York, 1940); and Gerald E. Wheeler, *Prelude to Pearl Harbor: The United States Navy and the Far East, 1921–1931* (Columbia, Mo., 1963). Masanori Ito is the authority on Japanese naval plans in the twenties, but his translated work, *The End of the Imperial Japanese Navy* (New York, 1962), only briefly touches on the period.

The overall Japan-in-Asia picture is portrayed by Akira Iriye, *After Imperialism: The Search for a New Order in the Far East, 1921–1931* (Cambridge, Mass., 1965). Best on the Exclusion Act and its background

is John Higham's *Strangers in the Land: Patterns of American Nativism,
1860–1925* (New Brunswick, N.J., 1955). For Chinese-American relations in the period there is Dorothy Borg, *America and the Chinese Revolution, 1925–1928*, 2nd ed. (New York, 1968), and two colorfully styled
biographies of recent years contain anecdotes of Americans in China during the time of Chiang's rise to power: Barbara W. Tuchman, *Stilwell
and the American Experience in China, 1911–45* (New York, 1971), and
W. A. Swanberg, *Luce and His Empire* (New York, 1972).

United States diplomacy in the late twenties and early thirties has its
authority in Robert H. Ferrell—*Peace in Their Time: The Origins of the
Kellogg-Briand Pact* (New York, 1952); *American Diplomacy in the
Great Depression: The Hoover-Stimson Foreign Policy, 1929–1933* (New
Haven, 1957); and the latter's expanded version, *Frank B. Kellogg and
Henry L. Stimson* (New York, 1962), a volume in the Bemis-Ferrell
series, *The American Secretaries of State and Their Diplomacy*. Other
highly regarded biographies are L. Ethan Ellis, *Frank B. Kellogg and
American Foreign Relations: 1925–1929* (New Brunswick, N.J., 1961),
and Elting E. Morison, *Turmoil and Tradition: A Study of the Life and
Times of Henry L. Stimson* (Boston, 1960). Biographical treatment of
Harding, Coolidge, and Hoover has at last reached a stage of fairness and
objectivity, but there was not enough diplomacy in their careers—in itself
a comment on the age—to justify listings here.

VII. TILT

Most of the general works on isolationism listed after the last chapter
cover the 1930s as well as the 1920s, and studies of the Hoover adminis-
tration carry into the early thirties. For isolation thirties-style there are
John E. Wiltz, *From Isolation to War: 1931–1941* (New York, 1968);
W. L. Langer and S. E. Gleason, *The Challenge to Isolation:
1937–1940* (New York, 1952); Allan Nevins, *The New Deal and World
Affairs: 1933–1945* (New Haven, 1950); Manfred Jonas, *Isolationism in
America, 1935–1941* (Ithaca, N.Y., 1966); Wayne S. Cole, *America
First: The Battle Against Intervention, 1940–1941* (Madison, Wis.,
1953); and two studies by Robert A. Divine, *The Illusion of Neutrality*
(Chicago, 1962) and *The Reluctant Belligerent: American Entry into
World War II* (New York, 1965).

An important new look at Japanese naval planning in the 1930s is
provided by Stephen E. Pelz, *Race to Pearl Harbor: The Failure of the*

Second London Naval Conference and the Onset of World War II (Cambridge, Mass., 1974). Also see works on navies and disarmament treaties listed after the last chapter.

For the volcanic scene in Japan see Delmar M. Brown, *Nationalism in Japan* (Berkeley, Calif., 1955); Y. C. Maxon, *Control of Japanese Foreign Policy: A Study of Civil-Military Rivalry, 1930–1945* (Berkeley, Calif., 1957); and James B. Crowley, *Japan's Quest for Autonomy: National Security and Foreign Policy, 1930–1938* (Princeton, N.J., 1966), and for the importance of Manchuria to Japan see Ogata Sadako, *Defiance in Manchuria: The Making of Japanese Foreign Policy, 1931–1932* (Berkeley, Calif., 1964). Feelings of army officers and vivid assassination scenes appear in Robert J. C. Butow, *Tojo and the Coming of the War* (Princeton, N.J., 1961), and John Toland, *The Rising Sun: The Decline and Fall of the Japanese Empire, 1936–1945* (New York, 1970).

Dorothy Borg, *The United States and the Far Eastern Crisis, 1933–1938* (Cambridge, Mass., 1964), presents FDR's passive view of Chinese woes; other Sino-American interaction, passive or otherwise, is the subject of James C. Thomson, Jr., *While China Faced West* (Cambridge, Mass., 1969); Arthur N. Young, *China and the Helping Hand, 1937–1945* (Cambridge, Mass., 1963); H. S. Quigley, *Far Eastern War, 1937–1941* (Boston, 1942); and Manny Koginos, *The Panay Incident, Prelude to War* (West Lafayette, Ind., 1967). The "feeling" of Americans toward China comes through in such already mentioned works as Isaacs's *Images,* Iriye's *Across the Pacific,* Fairbank's *United States and China,* Swanberg's *Luce,* and Tuchman's *Stilwell;* a reading of such Pearl Buck novels as *The Good Earth* and *Dragon Seed* might add to understanding of this subject.

Among the best memoirs are Henry L. Stimson and McGeorge Bundy, *On Active Service* (New York, 1948); Joseph C. Grew, *Ten Years in Japan* (New York, 1944) and *Turbulent Era,* 2 vols. (New York, 1952); Shigenori Togo, *The Cause of Japan* (New York, 1956); and Shigeru Yoshida, *The Yoshida Memoirs: The Story of Japan in Crisis* (Boston, 1962). Cordell Hull's *Memoirs,* 2 vols., naturally (New York, 1948), are important for an understanding of the man more than history.

Biographies include Julius W. Pratt, *Cordell Hull,* 2 vols., (New York, 1964) in *The American Secretaries of State* series, and Waldo H. Heinrichs, *American Ambassador: Joseph C. Grew and the Development of the United States Diplomatic Tradition* (Boston, 1966). Of the widely admired multi-volume treatments of FDR by Frank Freidel and Arthur M.

Schlesinger, Jr., only Schlesinger's third volume, *The Politics of Up-heaval* (Boston, 1960), has reached a date relative to 1930s diplomacy. Other excellent studies are James M. Burns, *Roosevelt: The Lion and the Fox* (New York, 1956), and Robert E. Sherwood, *Roosevelt and Hopkins* (New York, 1948). For documents of 1933–38 consult Edgar B. Nixon, *Franklin D. Roosevelt and Foreign Affairs*, 3 vols. (Cambridge, Mass., 1969).

VIII. HARD LINES

Aforementioned general works on American-Japanese relations contain many a valuable chapter on the critical two years 1940 and 1941, years also included in many books listed in connection with the 1930s, e.g., Nevins, Divine, Wiltz, Heinrichs, Pelz, Butow, Toland, Togo, Yoshida, Grew. Specific studies of 1940–41 usually contribute, mildly or otherwise, to the many arguments: was FDR a model of candor; if not, was he justified by necessity; what were his aims; to what lengths would he go to achieve them; were Japanese aims justified by vital interests; if not, where lay blame?

Roosevelt's "guilty foreknowledge" of the attack can be pondered in the outdated George Morgenstern, *Pearl Harbor, The Story of the Secret War* (New York, 1947), and Robert A. Theobald, *The Final Secret of Pearl Harbor* (New York, 1954). The unprepared naval commander in Hawaii, Admiral Husband E. Kimmel, placed blame on Washington in *Admiral Kimmel's Story* (Chicago, 1955). Charging FDR with wanting and planning war—but not necessarily knowing beforehand of the Pearl Harbor raid—are Charles Tansill, *Back Door to War: The Roosevelt Policies, 1937–1941* (Chicago, 1952), and Charles A. Beard, *President Roosevelt and the Coming of War, 1941* (New Haven, 1948). An example of calmer, more mature criticism of Roosevelt's diplomacy is Paul W. Schroeder, *The Axis Alliance and Japanese-American Relations, 1941* (Ithaca, N.Y., 1958), stating that Washington overreacted to Japanese policies. Revisionism, 1960s style, is represented by Lloyd C. Gardner, *Economic Aspects of New Deal Diplomacy* (Madison, Wis., 1964).

Some of Roosevelt's early champions, distressed by the virulence of charges against him, defended his morality more than his sense of realism. For a sampling see Basil Rauch, *Roosevelt: From Munich to Pearl Harbor* (New York, 1950), and Walter Millis, *This is Pearl!* (New York, 1947). FDR's best defense—which can accept trickery and toughness in the service of national security—has been established by William L. Langer and S. Everett Gleason, *The Undeclared War: 1940–1941* (New York, 1953); Herbert Feis, *The Road to Pearl Harbor* (Princeton, N.J., 1950); Robert A. Divine, *Roosevelt and World War II* (Baltimore, 1969); and James M. Burns, *Roosevelt: The Soldier of Freedom* (New York, 1970). A valuable piece of research by Roberta Wohlstetter, *Pearl Harbor: Warning and Decision* (Palo Alto, Calif., 1962), had the effect of dismissing the old Pearl Harbor "plot" theories by offering a reasonable explanation of how Washington, even with MAGIC, remained ignorant of the direction of the attack. Akira Iriye's impressive *Across the Pacific* deals with much more than FDR's diplomacy yet enhances the meaning of that diplomacy with the view that it was not based on interest in China but on global concerns implied by the Tripartite Pact and the Japanese move toward East Indian resources.

Japanese expansion finds advocates in Tansill and Beard and with qualification in Schroeder and William L. Neumann, *America Encounters Japan,* mentioned earlier. A balanced work, finding fault on both sides, is David Lu, *From the Marco Polo Bridge to Pearl Harbor: Japan's Entry into World War II* (New York, 1961). Assuming the presence of at least some aggressive tendencies in Japan, numerous authors have blamed the army, among them Butow in *Tojo* and Richard Storry in *Japan's New Order in East Asia: Its Rise and Fall, 1938–1945* (London, 1954). Having the same effect is an interesting biography by John D. Potter, *Yamamoto* (New York, 1965). Pelz's *Race to Pearl Harbor* will inspire more historians to examine the role of the Imperial Japanese Navy. David Bergamini, *Japan's Imperial Conspiracy* (New York, 1971), tries to prove Hirohito's responsibility, while other books concentrate on the industrial *zaibatsu,* nationalist societies, or nationalism in general.

IX. VIOLENT REDRESSMENT

In the front rank of histories dealing with general wartime diplomacy are Gaddis Smith, *American Diplomacy During the Second World War: 1941–1945* (New York, 1965), and John L. Snell, *Illusion and Necessity: The Diplomacy of Global War, 1939–1945* (Boston, 1963).

Dependable sources for the naval war in the Pacific are Samuel Eliot Morison, *History of United States Naval Operations in World War II,* 15 vols. (Boston, 1947–62) and the same author's one-volume study, *The Two-Ocean War* (Boston, 1963); E. B. Potter and Chester W. Nimitz, eds., *The Great Sea War* (Englewood Cliffs, N.J., 1960); Louis Morton, *Strategy and Command: The First Two Years* (Washington, 1962); and Masanori Ito, *The End of the Imperial Japanese Navy,* English trans. (New York, 1962). Several pages of bibliography would be needed to list even the best of the hundreds of memoirs and books about battles and other aspects of the great adventure; the present writer can mention only a few random examples that he has found instructive and/or entertaining: Butow's *Tojo* and Potter's *Yamamoto;* John Toland, *But Not in Shame* (New York, 1961), an account of Japan's victory streak in early 1942, and the same author's *The Rising Sun,* listed earlier. Also M. Fuchida and M. Okumiya, *Midway, The Battle that Doomed Japan* (Annapolis, 1955); M. Okumiya and J. Horikoshi, *Zero* (New York, 1956); Saburo Sakai, *Samurai* (New York, 1957); Ernest J. King and Walter M. Whitehill, *Fleet Admiral King* (London, 1953); Robert Sherrod, *Tarawa* (New York, 1944); Richard Tregaskis, *Guadalcanal Diary* (New York, 1943); Stan Smith, *The Battle of Savo* (New York, 1962); and C. Vann Woodward, *The Battle for Leyte Gulf* (New York, 1947).

Studies of the war's end: Robert J. C. Butow, *Japan's Decision to Surrender* (Palo Alto, Calif., 1954); Toshikazu Kase, *Journey to the "Missouri"* (New Haven, 1950); L. Giovannitti and Fred Freed, *The Decision to Drop the Bomb* (New York, 1965); and Herbert Feis, *The Atomic Bomb and the End of World War II,* rev. ed. (Princeton, N.J., 1967). The assertion that Russia, not Japan, was on Truman's mind at the time of the atomic bomb decision appears in Gar Alperovitz, *Atomic Diplomacy: Hiroshima and Potsdam* (New York, 1965).

The China issue includes works that, while not enthusiastic about Chiang Kai-shek, understand his interests and the oversimplified nature of American policy; see Herbert Feis, *The China Tangle: The American Effort in China from Pearl Harbor to the Marshall Mission* (Princeton, N.J., 1953), and Charles F. Romanus and Riley Sunderland, *Stilwell's Mission to China* (Washington, 1953) and *Stilwell's Command Problems* (Washington, 1956). Another dubious view of Stilwell's diplomacy appears in a chapter in Jonathan Spence, *To Change China: Western Advisers in China, 1620–1960* (Boston, 1969). Swanberg's *Luce* describes the magazine publisher's view that Chiang could do nothing wrong, while two of Luce's reporters in wartime China, Theodore H. White and Annalee Jacoby, failed to agree with the boss and with colorful fury exposed Nationalist shortcomings in *Thunder Out of China* (New York, 1946). White also edited *The Stilwell Papers* (New York, 1948). A modern defense of Vinegar Joe is Barbara W. Tuchman's *Stilwell and the Ameri-*

can Experience in China, 1911–1945 (New York, 1970). See listings after the next chapter for books that include the postwar phase of the China controversy.

X . THE NEW BALANCE

Among many general studies of the post–World War II period are Dexter Perkins, *The Diplomacy of a New Age: Major Issues in U.S. Policy Since 1945* (Bloomington, Ind., 1967); Norman A. Graebner, *Cold War Diplomacy: American Foreign Policy, 1945–1960* (Princeton, N.J., 1962); John W. Spanier, *American Foreign Policy Since World War II*, 5th ed. (New York, 1973); Denna F. Fleming, *The Cold War and its Origins: 1917–1960*, 2 vols. (New York, 1961); and Walter LaFeber, *America, Russia, and the Cold War: 1945–1966* (New York, 1967). These samplings offer a scan of the so-called nationalist-realist-radical controversy on the Cold War. For Cold War wrangling as it disrupted American life in the late 1940s and early 1950s, see H. Bradford Westerfield, *Foreign Policy and Party Politics: Pearl Harbor to Korea* (New Haven, 1955); Herbert Agar, *The Price of Power: America Since 1945* (Chicago, 1957); and especially the colorful work, still a standard, Eric F. Goldman, *The Crucial Decade and After* (New York, 1960). Robert H. Ferrell, ed., *America in a Divided World, 1945–1972* (New York, 1975), presents pertinent documents of the age.

The previous chapter's listings, for example Feis's *China Tangle*, provide background for the post-1945 phase of the civil war that ended in 1949. The charge that America "lost" China is at its most persuasive in Tang Tsou, *America's Failure in China, 1941–1950*, 2 vols. (Chicago, 1963). More concerned with conspiracy in Washington is Anthony Kubek, *How the Far East Was Lost* (Chicago, 1963). Acheson's reasonable view that the United States could not have altered the course of the revolution comes through in books by and about officials of the period: Harry S Truman, *Memoirs*, 2 vols. (Garden City, N.Y., 1955–56); Robert H. Ferrell, *George C. Marshall* (New York, 1966), in *The American Secretaries of State* series; P. S. R. Payne, *The Marshall Story* (New York, 1951); John Leighton Stuart, *Fifty Years in China* (New York, 1954), an account by the American ambassador to Chiang's government from 1946 to 1952; George F. Kennan, *Memoirs: 1925–1950* (Boston, 1967); and Dean Acheson, *Sketches from Life of Men I Have Known* (New York, 1961) and his *Present at the Creation* (New York, 1969).

Again, Fairbank's *United States and China* is valuable for this period. For a military view see John Melby, *The Mandate of Heaven: A Record of Civil War—China, 1945–1949* (Toronto, 1968).

On the occupation of Japan: E. J. Lewe Van Aduard, *Japan: From Surrender to Peace* (New York, 1954); Frederick S. Dunn, *Peace-Making and the Settlement with Japan* (Princeton, N.J., 1963); Richard H. Minear's excellent study of *Victors' Justice: The Tokyo War Crimes Trial* (Princeton, N.J., 1971); an account by the Japanese premier during the occupation period, Shigeru Yoshida, *The Yoshida Memoirs: The Story of Japan in Crisis* (Boston, 1962); and newspaperman Kazuo Kawai's *Japan's American Interlude* (Chicago, 1960). MacArthur's Japanese interlude appears in his *Reminiscences* (New York, 1964); C. A. Willoughby and J. Chamberlain, *MacArthur: 1941–1951* (New York, 1954); and Courtney Whitney, *MacArthur, His Rendezvous with History* (New York, 1956). These, including the memoir, incline toward hero worship. Less awed is John Gunther, *The Riddle of MacArthur* (New York, 1951). Books on the Korean phase of the general's career will be listed after the next chapter.

XI. DRAWING A LINE

Representative of a current British interest in analyzing the decline and fall of twentieth-century empires are Sir Anthony Eden, *Full Circle* (London, 1960), and Edward Grierson, *The Imperial Dream* (London, 1972). The best surveys of the American imperial experience are Garel A. Grunder and William E. Livezey, *The Philippines and the United States* (Norman, Okla., 1951), and Theodore Friend, *Between Two Empires: The Ordeal of the Philippines, 1929–1946* (New Haven, 1965).

For general events of the Korean war see Goldman's *Crucial Decade;* David Rees, *Korea: The Limited War* (London, 1964); Martin Lichterman, *To the Yalu and Back* (Tuscaloosa, Ala., 1963); and Robert E. Osgood, *Limited War: The Challenge to American Strategy* (Chicago, 1957). On the fighting: S. L. A. Marshall, *The River and the Gauntlet* (New York, 1953), and memoirs of two American commanders—Mark W. Clark, *From the Danube to the Yalu* (New York, 1954), and Matthew B. Ridgway, *The Korean War* (Garden City, N.Y., 1967).

Aspects of the war appear in Max Beloff, *Soviet Policy in the Far East,1944–1951* (London, 1953); Allen S. Whiting, *China Crosses the Yalu: The Decision to Enter the Korean War* (New York, 1960); L. M.

Goodrich, *Korea: A Study of United States Policy in the United Nations* (New York, 1956); and William H. Vatcher, Jr., *Panmunjom: The Story of the Korean Military Armistice Negotiations* (New York, 1958). Glenn D. Paige, *The Korean Decision* (New York, 1968), concerns Truman's decision to intervene; for a view that the decision was brought about by internal political pressures see Gregory Henderson, *Korea: The Politics of the Vortex* (Cambridge, Mass., 1968).

For the Truman-MacArthur confrontation: Truman's *Memoirs* and the books praising MacArthur mentioned after Chapter X. Heavy-handed criticism of the general appears in Richard H. Rovere and Arthur M. Schlesinger, Jr., *The MacArthur Controversy and American Foreign Policy* (New York, 1965). Readers seeking calmer treatments may consult John W. Spanier, *The Truman-MacArthur Controversy and the Korean War* (Cambridge, Mass., 1959), and Trumbull Higgins, *Korea and the Fall of MacArthur* (New York, 1960). And the issue is prominent in Walter Millis, *Arms and the State: Civil-Military Elements in National Policy* (New York, 1958).

A sharp turn in foreign policy was one of the results of internal unrest in the early fifties; differing approaches to the crisis include Joseph R. McCarthy, *America's Retreat from Victory: The Story of George Catlett Marshall* (New York, 1951)—the senator always stressed Marshall's middle name; Richard H. Rovere, *Senator Joe McCarthy* (Cleveland, 1960), an attempt to understand the investigator's inner motives; Earl Latham, *The Communist Controversy in Washington: From the New Deal to McCarthy* (Cambridge, Mass., 1966); Robert Griffith, *The Politics of Fear: Joseph R. McCarthy and the Senate* (Lexington, Ky., 1970); Daniel Bell, ed., *The Radical Right* (New York, 1963); and H. B. Westerfield, *Foreign Policy and Party Politics: Pearl Harbor to Korea* (New Haven, 1955).

XII. POSITIVE THINKING

Eisenhower's somewhat tedious account of the 1950s appears in *Mandate for Change* (New York, 1963) and *Waging Peace* (New York, 1964). For the more urgent Dulles style see his *War or Peace* (New York, 1950) and Andrew H. Berding's collection of the secretary's writings, *Dulles on Diplomacy* (Princeton, N.J. 1965). White House "insiders" had mixed opinions, ranging from the sarcasm of Emmet J. Hughes, *The Ordeal of Power* (New York, 1963), to the praise of Arthur Larson, *Eisenhower: The President Nobody Knew* (New York, 1968), and Richard M. Nixon, *Six Crises* (Garden City, N.Y., 1962). Robert J. Donovan, *Eisenhower: The Inside Story* (New York, 1956), offers much on Far East policy. An excellent biography by Louis L. Gerson, *John Foster Dulles* (New York, 1967), in *The American Secretaries of State* series, is concerned with facts more than ideas. Dulles's abilities are admired in Michael Guhin, *John Foster Dulles: A Statesman and His Times* (New York, 1972), and criticized in Herbert S. Parmet, *Eisenhower and the American Crusades* (New York, 1972); Marquis Childs, *Eisenhower: Captive Hero* (New York, 1958); and Richard Rovere, *Affairs of State: The Eisenhower Years* (New York, 1956). High-ranking military officers had no affection for the Dulles strategies: Maxwell D. Taylor, *The Uncertain Trumpet* (New York, 1959), and Matthew B. Ridgway, *Soldier: The Memoirs of Matthew Ridgway* (New York, 1956). For the "Cold War mentality" genre of criticism (which certainly applies to Dulles), see Walter LaFeber, *America, Russia, and the Cold War, 1945–1966* (New York, 1967), and Ronald Steel, *Pax Americana* (New York, 1967). A most important actor in the stressful 1950s is the subject of Gabriel A. Almond's *The American People and Foreign Policy* (New York, 1960).

For topics related to China in the 1950s: A. Doak Barnett, *Communist China and Asia* (New York, 1960), is detailed, balanced, and includes much on American policies. Equally good on the first five years of Maoism is Richard L. Walker, *China Under Communism* (New Haven, 1955). Accounts by travelers during the early period of communism include Derk Bodde, *Peking Diary: A Year of Revolution* (New York, 1950); Frank Moraes, *Report on Mao's China* (New York, 1953); and Robert Guillain, *600 Million Chinese* (New York, 1957). Best on its subject is Donald S. Zagoria, *The Sino-Soviet Conflict* (New York, 1962); also Klaus Mehnert, *Peking and Moscow* (New York, 1964), and David J. Dallin, *Soviet Foreign Policy After Stalin* (Philadelphia, 1961). For Dulles-Chiang policies see Neil Jacoby, *U.S. Aid to Taiwan* (New York, 1966), and Tang Tsou, *Embroilment over Quemoy* (Salt Lake City, Utah, 1959). The rubber army appears in A. J. Liebling, *The Press* (New York, 1961).

On Japan in the 1950s: R. Scalapino and J. Mosumi, *Parties and Politics in Postwar Japan* (Berkeley, Calif., 1962); James Cary, *Japan Today: Reluctant Ally* (New York, 1962); and George Packard, *Protest in Tokyo: The Security Treaty Crisis of 1960* (Princeton, N.J., 1966). In *Japan's Economic Recovery* (London, 1958), G. C. Allen provides an early look at a subject that would have increasing meaning to Japanese-American relations.

Another reminder of the value of general works mentioned earlier, among them Fairbank's *China* and Reischauer's *Japan.* Concerned over the excessive use of military pressure and aid programs in Asia by the mid-fifties, Edwin O Reischauer wrote *Wanted: An Asian Policy* (New York, 1955), which suggests that democratic ideology would have a better chance through relaxation of American do-or-die attitudes toward the Far East. Such prorealist, antimoralist writers as Hans Morgenthau, Robert E. Osgood, George F. Kennan, and others have important things to say about the 1950s. Dulles's old-time-religion approach to an increasingly interdenominational world—perhaps his greatest failing—finds stimulating interpretation in Edmund Stillman and William Pfaff, *The New Politics: America and the End of the Postwar World* (New York, 1961). Also on this subject are Laurence W. Martin, ed., *Neutralism and Non-Alignment* (New York, 1962), and Eugene Staley, *The Future of Underdeveloped Countries* (New York, 1954). Unlimited American foreign aid is defended with statistics in Lloyd D. Black, *The Strategy of Foreign Aid* (Princeton, N.J., 1968), and with little more than sentimentality in Barbara Ward, *The Rich Nations and the Poor Nations* (New York, 1962). Herbert Feis, *Foreign Aid and Foreign Policy* (New York, 1964), believes that post–Marshall Plan aid programs have been marked by bungled methods, lack of connection to American interests, and an enormous sympathy that does not include American taxpayers.

For Vietnam in the 1950s consult the bibliography for Chapter XIII.

XIII. A LOST CRUSADE

The origins and early phases of the war can be studied in Joseph Buttinger, *Vietnam: A Dragon Embattled,* 2 vols. (New York, 1967); Hans J. Morgenthau, *Vietnam and the United States* (Washington, 1965); and a short book by Arthur M. Schlesinger, Jr., *The Bitter Heritage* (Boston, 1967). The most objective overall treatment of events to 1970 is Chester L. Cooper, *The Lost Crusade* (New York, 1970).

Military action is presented in Richard Rovere, *Waist Deep in the Big Muddy* (Boston, 1968), an example of frustration felt during the Johnson period, and Don Oberdorfer, *Tet! The Story of a Battle and its Historic Aftermath* (New York, 1971). For grimness see Frances Fitzgerald, *Fire in the Lake: The Vietnamese and the Americans in Vietnam* (New York, 1972). The North Vietnamese general Vo Nguyen Giap describes guerrilla strategy in *People's War, People's Army* (New York, 1967), and *Big Victory, Great Task* (New York, 1968).

Lyndon B. Johnson, *The Vantage Point* (New York, 1971), is a self-justification; other prowar arguments are Frank N. Trager, *Why Vietnam?* (New York, 1967), and Chester A. Bain, *Vietnam: The Roots of Conflict* (Englewood Cliffs, N.J., 1967). The Kennedy-Johnson advisers and their brand of realism come under attack by David Halberstam, *The Best and the Brightest* (New York, 1972). Antiwar realism, critical of idealistic overconfidence, produced such books as J. William Fulbright, *The Arrogance of Power* (New York, 1967); Theodore Draper, *Abuse of Power* (New York, 1967); Schlesinger's *Bitter Heritage;* George Ball, *The Discipline of Power* (Boston, 1968); and Townsend Hoopes, *The Limits of Intervention* (New York, 1969). George F. Kennan's view of the Vietnam war is best explained by Marvin Kalb in "The Vital Interests of Mr. Kennan," *New York Times Magazine* (March 27, 1966). The view that the mission was prompted by economic interests is represented by Noam Chomsky, *At War with Asia* (New York, 1970); Howard Zinn, *Vietnam: The Logic of Withdrawal* (Boston, 1967); and Gabriel Kolko, *The Roots of American Foreign Policy* (Boston, 1969). An assortment of arguments appears in Richard M. Pfeffer, ed., *No More Vietnams?* (New York, 1968). For a subject of much argument see *The Pentagon Papers,* as published by the *New York Times* (New York, 1971), one of several collections of these documents.

The standard Kennedy biographies are Arthur M. Schlesinger, Jr., *A Thousand Days* (New York, 1965), and Theodore C. Sorensen, *Kennedy* (New York, 1965). For material on Ngo Dinh Diem see Denis Warner, *The Last Confucian* (Baltimore, 1964). Other significant works are Eric F. Goldman, *The Tragedy of Lyndon Johnson* (New York, 1969); Hugh Sidey, *A Very Personal Presidency* (New York, 1968), an examination of the LBJ personality; Stephen R. Graubard, *Kissinger, Portrait of a Mind* (New York, 1973); and Marvin Kalb and Bernard Kalb, *Kissinger* (Boston, 1974). A reasonably dispassionate biography of Nixon is certain to appear with the passing of time. Meanwhile he is prominent in Theodore H. White, *The Making of the President, 1972* (New York, 1973), a perceptive description of men and forces at work in the nation during the war's last year.

XIV. END OF A CHAPTER

Paul Y. Hammond, *Cold War and Détente* (New York, 1975), includes American–East Asian affairs. For the sixties see Edwin O. Reis-

INDEX

275